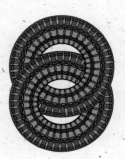

CAROLYN
KIZER

CAROLYN
KIZER

Perspectives
on Her Life
and Work

EDITED BY

Annie Finch

Johanna Keller

&

Candace McClelland

CavanKerry ◊ Press LTD.

FORT LEE, NEW JERSEY

Library of Congress Cataloging-in-Publication Data

Carolyn Kizer : perspectives on her life & work / edited by Annie Finch, Johanna Keller
& Candace McClelland.

    p. cm.

   Includes bibliographical references and index.

   ISBN 0-9678856-5-5

   1. Kizer, Carolyn. 2. Poets, American--20th century--Biography. 3. Women and
literature--United States--History--20th century. I. Finch, Annie, 1956- II. Keller,
Johanna. III. McClelland, Candace. IV. Kizer, Carolyn.

PS3521.19 Z74 2001
811'.54--dc21
[B]

                                             00-052359

Cover photograph: Thomas Victor

Cover design: Charles Casey Martin

Interior design: Greta D. Sibley & Associates

FIRST EDITION

For Carolyn Kizer
In her 75th year
With gratitude
And love

Contents

Preface   xi

Acknowledgments   xiii

MAXINE KUMIN
 Introduction   1

Essays, Articles and Reviews

HENRY TAYLOR
 Passwords at the Boundary:
  Carolyn Kizer's Poetry   7

CAROL MUSKE
 Postscript: Carolyn Kizer, Superkid   23

ALFRED CORN
 The Impact of Character on Character   29

TERRY EHRET
 "Semele Recycled":
  A Sacred Tale of Regeneration   41

JACK FOLEY
 "In Hell with Virg and Dan," Review of
  Harping On by Carolyn Kizer   49

RUTH SALVAGGIO
 Kizer's Politics: Poetry and Feminism   55

MARGARET RABB & JACKSON WHEELER
 Kizer's Commandments: Dicta for Student Writers   71

ROBERT PHILLIPS
Larger Than Life:
Mythology and Carolyn Kizer   75

ANNIE FINCH
Carolyn Kizer and the Chain of Women   85

FRED CHAPPELL
A Swift Education   93

JUDITH JOHNSON
Re/Membering the Goddess:
Carolyn Kizer and the Poetics of Generosity   97

KIM VAETH
The House of Madame K.   127

DOMINIC CHEUNG
Carolyn Kizer and Her Chinese Imitations   133

HAYDEN CARRUTH
Afterword   143

Poems for Carolyn

MARIE PONSOT
Inviting Carolyn Kizer   147

ROBERT CREELEY
Bub and Sis   149

KELLY CHERRY
On Some Qualities in Her Self and Poetry   151

LUCILLE CLIFTON
Sisters   153

TERRY STOKES
Because You Are Always There   155

C.L. RAWLINS
Drifting in Montana   157

CAROL MUSKE
Haiku   159

AGHA SHAHID ALI
I Dream It Is Afternoon When I Return to Delhi   160

ANNIE FINCH
A Carol for Carolyn   163

MAXINE KUMIN
Pantoum, with Swan   164

Interviews

MICHELLE BOISSEAU
Intensity and Effect: An Interview with
Carolyn Kizer (1997)   169

WILLIAM HOLLAND
An Interview with Carolyn Kizer (1967)   181

BARBARA THOMPSON
Carolyn Kizer: The Art of Poetry (2000)   195

Bibliography   213
Contributors' Notes   215
About the Editors   221
Index   223

Preface

THIS BOOK was born during a writers' conference in the spring of 1997, during which I found myself in an all-too-familiar conversation with another poet: a conversation on the theme of how glad we were that Carolyn Kizer existed. I had been an admirer and appreciator of Kizer's since first hearing her read in San Francisco to introduce several Chinese poets. That day I was young and intimidated by her very presence, but she addressed me with such respect and affection that it was hard to forget her. Years later, her warm and supportive response to my poetry during hard and lean times had earned my perpetual gratitude. So it was that I finally found myself blurting, "you know, somebody should edit a book in her honor . . .".

Though everyone to whom I made this remark in the subsequent months and years agreed with me passionately, it worked out as it so often does when one ventures such a thought: "somebody" would have to be me, at least in the beginning. Eventually I was lucky to be able to take on the good-humored, invaluable help of my talented and well-organized former student Candace McClelland. And ultimately I was able to turn the project over to the inspired guidance of fellow poet Johanna Keller, who shepherded the book brilliantly into its current shape and into print.

Three seems a fittingly exuberant number of editors with which to celebrate Kizer's multifaceted influence and impact. We soon discovered the extent of Carolyn's support of younger poets, especially women. As the book progressed we also discovered the depth of her influence and uniqueness. The contributors to this collection respond to numerous aspects of Carolyn Kizer's gift: her humor, her mythological scope, her political awareness, her satirical wit, her feminism, her craft, her lyricism, her role in shaping literary institutions, her charisma. And yet they are always attuned to the strength, courage, and generosity that manifest themselves in all facets of Kizer's work.

As this volume goes to press, Carolyn Kizer's complete poems, entitled *Cool, Calm, & Collected*, has just been published by Copper Canyon Press; the existence of this volume of Kizer's collected poems should only increase the understanding of her poetry's importance. Ours is not the first book about Carolyn Kizer and undoubtedly it will not be the last. We owe a great debt to David Rigsbee, who edited a volume in honor of Carolyn's 60th birthday in which several of these pieces were previously published.

We are grateful to the contributors for their insights, enthusiasm, and resourcefulness. Many thanks to Molly Peacock for her creativity and support. At CavanKerry Press, we offer our gratitude to Joan Cusack Handler, for her courage and unique artistic vision, and to Florenz Greenberg for her unflagging optimism and able coordination of so many details. Charles Casey Martin and Greta D. Sibley contributed their artistry to the design of this book. And finally, our thanks to Pat Jalbert Levine for production work of the highest professional standard.

Annie Finch
Cincinnati, Ohio
February 2001

Acknowledgments

Every effort has been made to trace the ownership of copyedited material and to secure the necessary permission to reprint the selections in this book. In the event of questions about the use of any material, the editors and publisher, while expressing regret for any inadvertent error, will be happy to make the correction in future printings. Thanks are due to the following for permission to reprint the material listed below:

Agha Shahid Ali. "I Dream It Is Afternoon When I Return To Delhi," copyright 1987. Originally published in *The Half-Inch Himalayas* (Wesleyan University Press, 1987). Reprinted by permission of the author.

Michelle Boisseau. "Intensity and Effect: An Interview with Carolyn Kizer," copyright 1997 by Michelle Boisseau. Transcript of a March 3, 1997 radio interview aired on KCUR radio on "New Letters on the Air," a National Public Radio program produced by Angela Elam. A version of this interview, edited by Robert Stewart, appeared in *New Letters*, vol. 64, no. 3, 1998. Published by permission of the interviewer/author.

Hayden Carruth. "Afterword," copyright 1990 by Hayden Carruth. Originally published as "Foreword" in *An Answering Music: On the Poetry of Carolyn Kizer*, edited by David Rigsbee (Ford-Brown & Co., Boston, 1990). Reprinted by permission of the author.

Dominic Cheung. "Carolyn Kizer and Her Chinese Imitations," copyright 1978 by Dominic Cheung. Originally published in *The New Asia Bulletin*, 1978, and subsequently in *An Answering Music: On the Poetry of Carolyn Kizer*, edited by David Rigsbee (Ford-Brown & Co., Boston, 1990). Reprinted by permission of the author.

Fred Chappell. "A Swift Education," copyright 2000 by Fred Chappell. Published here, for the first time, by permission of the author.

Kelly Cherry. "On Some Qualities in Her Self and Poetry," copyright 2000 by Kelly Cherry. Published here, for the first time, by permission of the author.

Lucille Clifton. "Sisters," copyright 2000 by Lucille Clifton. Published here, for the first time, by permission of the author.

Robert Phillips. "Larger Than Life: Mythology and Carolyn Kizer," copyright 2000 by Robert Phillips. Published here, for the first time, by permission of the author.

Marie Ponsot. "Inviting Carolyn Kizer," copyright 2000 by Marie Ponsot. Published here, for the first time, by permission of the author.

Margaret Rabb. "Kizer's Commandments: Dicta for Student Writers," copyright 2000 by Margaret Rabb and Jackson Wheeler. Published here, for the first time, by permission of the authors.

C.L. Rawlins. "Drifting in Montana," copyright 1998 by C. L. Rawlins. Originally published in *In Gravity National Park* (University of Nevada Press, 1998). Reprinted by permission of the author.

Ruth Salvaggio. "Kizer's Politics: Poetry and Feminism," copyright 1990 by Ruth Salvaggio. Originally published in *An Answering Music: On the Poetry of Carolyn Kizer*, edited by David Rigsbee (Ford-Brown & Co., Boston, 1990). Reprinted by permission of the author.

Terry Stokes. "Because You Are Always There," copyright 2000 by Terry Stokes. Published here, for the first time, by permission of the author.

Henry Taylor. "Passwords at the Boundary: Carolyn Kizer's Poetry," copyright 1997 by Henry Taylor. Originally published in *The Hollins Critic*, volume XXXIV, No. 3, June 1997. Reprinted by permission of the author.

Barbara Thompson. "Carolyn Kizer: The Art of Poetry," copyright 2000 by Barbara Thompson. Originally published in *The Paris Review*, No. 154, Spring 2000. Reprinted by permission of the author and the editors of *The Paris Review*.

Kim Vaeth. "The House of Madame K.," copyright 2000 by Kim Vaeth. Published here, for the first time, by permission of the author.

Jackson Wheeler. "Kizer's Commandments: Dicta for Student Writers," copyright 2000 by Margaret Rabb and Jackson Wheeler. Published here, for the first time, by permission of the authors.

CAROLYN
KIZER

Introduction

WHEN I FIRST read that Carolyn was descended from a Dutch Mennonite minister who settled in Germantown, Pennsylvania, in 1690, I was beguiled. For I was born and raised in Germantown, child of another distinctive culture, descended on my father's side from the shtetls of Eastern Europe, and on my mother's, from a youth fleeing conscription in Metternich's army in 1848.

Carolyn, who grew up in Spokane, Washington, recites her girlhood address: two-oh-two Coeur d'Alene (pronounced by locals Cord Elaine). I can still recite mine: one-fifty-two Carpenter Lane. Both roll on the tongue in comparable scansions. Both of us were enchanted with the eccentricities of our old and roomy childhood homes, their corridors and closets, their back staircases originally designed for servants. I, at least, was convinced bears lurked there, under the steps. Carolyn, whose imagination was very likely more fecund than mine, confesses that her house continues to haunt her dreams.

We were born in the same year, Carolyn an only and late child, I the fourth and only girl in my family. Her ancestors are named and numbered; mine, buried and forgotten in their haste to reach the New World. Carolyn's parents revelled in the precocity and imagination of their prodigy. She was the spoiled darling, the young tyrant, an early reader and memorizer, playwright and poet at age eight. I too was an omnivorous reader and dreadful precocious poet. Would we have liked each other back then? Probably not.

Both of us attended the local public schools, blessed with impoverished but dedicated spinster teachers who loved us. And why not? We were early readers, attentive and eager for more. Both of us noticed the One Good Dress Miss Blomberg or Miss Odell wore three days a week, the Other Good Dress on Tuesdays and Thursdays. Teachers who married immediately lost their jobs; this was the Depression. Carolyn's school drew in equal proportions from middleclass homes, the nearby army post, and a slum area of Spokane. The principal of my elementary school boasted that her population contained no "Negroes"; any who applied were shunted to the adjoining, poorer district. East and West, Carolyn and I learned all the words and melodies of Stephen Foster's romantic spirituals in our once-a-week music class and neither of us has forgotten the racist lyrics about Old Black Joe, Carry Me Back to Ole Virginny, or Massa's in de Cole Cole Ground. Carolyn had a fine singing voice; I was notably deficient in that area.

In 1959, emboldened by acceptances in *The New Orleans Poetry Journal* and *Audience*, I sent poems to a new publication founded by a then-unknown-to-me editor. The magazine was *Poetry Northwest*, the editor, Carolyn Kizer; the poem she accepted was a sestina. Our first books came out in the same year, 1961.

Destiny didn't actually bring us together until a few years later, in Washington, D.C. Carolyn, the first director of the Literature Program of the newly founded National Endowment for the Arts, had invited a clutch of poets to read from their work. I remember being escorted that afternoon by someone else to the Library of Congress auditorium so that the audio engineer could take a voice level. That evening was to be my first experience on so imposing a stage. To add to my terror, a Junoesque woman in a large, stylish hat was overseeing the procedure from the last row of the theater.

That was Carolyn. She took me home with her, assuaged my anxiety with a bowl of matzo ball soup (canned, I hasten to add), and thence our friendship began.

All sorts of interesting people gathered in Carolyn's livingroom in Georgetown, among them, Ajaz Ahmed, the Bengali poet, and John L'Heureux, a former priest who turned first to poetry and then to fiction. Carolyn's three quite spectacular children came and went, very much at home in the melange, much as I now imagine Carolyn herself had been, among the assorted lawyers, politicians and literati of her girlhood.

But it wasn't until 1986 that we began to exchange worksheets of our poems. I was in California visiting a daughter; Carolyn was scheduled to read from her new book, *The Nearness of You*, at the renowned Black Oak Books in Berkeley. We entered arm in arm, singing from that hit song of our college days, "It's not the pale moon that excites me, / that thrills and delights me / Oh no. It's just the nearness of you." Later, over cocktails, we found ourselves lamenting the loss of a fellow poet-critic; in my case, Anne Sexton, twelve years dead, and in Carolyn's, Stanley Kunitz, who was no longer up to the weekly or monthly exchanges. There was, we agreed, no mercy to be shown. From then on, poems crossed the continent to be scribbled on, rearranged, or in rare instances, simply applauded. We're still at it, I am happy to say. One of the poems I could simply applaud is "Parents' Pantoum," to be found in *Harping On*. It is quite simply perfect.

At the bottom of a worksheet of mine that opens: "The world is awash in unwanted dogs," Carolyn has written: "My dove, you're asking *me* if this is too polemical? I *love* it when you get down and deal with the dirty world." And in reply to a copy of "The Oration," I wrote: "I love this. I am always troubled by incipient rhymes that then get dropped but I know we have differing opinions here." Often, on the poems themselves, words are crossed out, synonyms suggested, stanza orders are rearranged, better endings are plucked from the middle of the text and held up for scrutiny.

Letters, too, travel from California to New Hampshire and back at irregular intervals. Carolyn's, sometimes typed but frequently in longhand, tidy and readable; mine initially on the IBM Selectric I still treasure, then on my Mac word processor. No computers for Carolyn! No e-mail! She would have none of that glib, facile, rat-tat-tat exchange. When there were decisions to be made, we communicated by phone, which was somewhat limiting, given the three-hour time difference.

Each of us was chosen to join the Board of Chancellors of The Academy of American Poets in the same year, 1995. I think we both had reservations from the outset about entering what was clearly The Establishment; these were enhanced when James Merrill's death created an opening on the board and candidates to fill the position were to be nominated by the chancellors. We two, without prior consultation, proposed Lucille Clifton. She did not make the cut; we were outvoted by a sizeable majority. The following year, there was once again an opportunity to lobby for Lucille to fill a vacancy and once again a white male poet was elected instead.

The decision to resign was arrived at independently over the winter of '98–'99, but once made, we agreed that our renunciations needed to count for something. It was Carolyn who took hold, phoning *The New York Times* to inquire if our situation was newsworthy. The rest is history. Today, the Academy of American Poets boasts a multicultural Board of Chancellors. The terms of office are reasonable, and the entire organization has acquired a benign sparkle.

This book celebrates a remarkable woman, a witty, generous, lyrical, philosophical poet, often angry, never resigned. Testimonials from former students, old friends, colleagues and editors are worthy, to be sure, but the voice of the poet herself is what matters. Carolyn Kizer was a feminist before the word came into vogue. Her famous poem "Pro Femina" legitimized a new generation of women writers' attention to the undisclosed facts of their lives, but "Pro Femina" is merely the curtain raiser. The work of the last fifteen years has grown more political, more worldly, while at the same time preserving the candor and tenderness that illuminate such poems as "Gerda" and "Pearl," in which she writes from the point of view of the child she was, taking refuge in the third person in order to deliver these passionate elegies.

Cheek by jowl are poems about the Alaskan oil spill; the Gulf War; a stunning disquisition on Franco's regime; a deeply moving and tightly knit retrospective about Einstein, Pearl Harbor, Heisenberg, and Hiroshima titled "Twelve O'Clock," in which Kizer seeks to contrast the belief in an orderly universe with the theory of a random, disorderly one. Interspersed among these poems of conviction are less immediately topical ones alight with blinding flashes of satire and sharp humor. One of the best of these arose from a translation of Canto XVII of *The Inferno* she had been asked to undertake by Ecco Press. Hers was deemed irreverent and unsuitable for inclusion in their text, but it is a delight.

Carolyn's mind has the broad range of a predator, the vocabulary of a lexicographer, and the rich lyricism of those song writers of the forties whom we both adore. Remembering the ways in which our lives intersected has been gratifying. It is even more gratifying to introduce her to you now in these pages.

Essays,
Articles
and
Reviews

HENRY TAYLOR

Passwords at the Boundary:
Carolyn Kizer's Poetry

AT THE OUTSET, a disclaimer (or perhaps a claimer): my acquaintance with Carolyn Kizer began in the fall of 1965, when, in a car George Garrett had rented, I was her chauffeur through part of a reading tour in Virginia and North Carolina. Astonishment, hilarity, profound sympathy, minor legendry, and abiding friendship have been among the results of that journey. So there is a respectable school of criticism which would hold that my opinions of Kizer's work, however thoroughly acquired, are not for publication. Friendship, however, is a primary stimulus and a central theme in Kizer's poems, and it moves me to take another long close look at them.

Kizer's collection *Harping On* (1996) contains twenty-nine poems; this is her seventh collection, and, with the obvious exception of her first book, it is the third to consist entirely of poems not previously collected. Kizer makes her poems with unusual care and technical brilliance, and has rarely revised the poems she has reprinted. But she also brings great care to the making of her books, and there have been several opportunities to place an older poem in a fresh setting. This strikes a fresh note in a new book, or gives an older poem a chance to do something it had not previously done. It is a reminder that there is great fluidity in the relation between a poem and its readers, and that its readers eventually include its author.

In *Harping On*, however, the retrospective urge is in many of the poems themselves. Recollections of people who figured in her childhood (a nursemaid in "Gerda") and in her young womanhood (Einstein in "Twelve O'Clock") appear among joyously wistful and sometimes elegiac evocations of friendship. There are plenty of other kinds of poems here, too, from the domestic humor of "Mud Soup" to the publicly prophetic stance of "The Valley of the Fallen" or "Suppressing the Evidence." By now the voice in most of these poems is strong and immediately recognizable; with an almost wisecracking ease, Kizer's poetry moves among line-lengths and meters ranging from the various and nonexistent to the regular and strict, in a style suggestive of conversation— albeit immensely sophisticated and compassionate. No other writer of my experience could be so immediately apparent as is Kizer in her remark about Dante, in a note to her irreverent version of *Inferno* XVII: "I just don't care for Dante's obsessions with shit and revenge."

Indeed, "In Hell with Virg and Dan" is both amazingly faithful and surprisingly personal; it was too much for the editors of the Ecco Press project for which it was written, but its energetically ambivalent stance toward the original is of a piece with Kizer's way of inviting the literary community into her work, and of reminding us that community is what it is—or ought to be. Others represented in this book by epigraph, dedication, and echo include Valéry, Longfellow, Pope, Tu Fu, Li Po, Maxine Kumin, and Muriel Rukeyser; writers merely mentioned here and there are more numerous.

"Fin-de-Siècle Blues," for example, which closes the collection, hovers tensely between elegy and rant, in vigorously conversational yet wittily mournful diction. It opens with a recollection of youthful doubt that evil exists, followed by a litany of the century's ills. The third and final section begins,

> Now to personalize and trivialize the topic,
> as writers, what are we to do?
> We gag on scandal, our lives are gossip fodder.
> In our marginal way, we are becoming stars.
> Never mind the work. Who cares for that?
> Did the man who reinvented the sonnet
> urinate in his bed one night when drunk?
> Did our great fat nature poet
> throw up in his hat?
> Forget the revolution they created
> with their raw confessional poetry;

it's the suicides of two women
which fascinate,
not their way of working
but their way of death.

According to a note at the back of the book, the poets referred to in this passage are John Berryman, Theodore Roethke, Anne Sexton, and Sylvia Plath. The next stanza makes clear that the scandalous episodes in their lives amounted to less than their periods and acts of responsibility. We are all in this together, the poem says, and some of us make poems about it.

In a more purely humorous vein, Kizer even brings Longfellow into the book. "Mud Soup," an account of making lentil soup according to a Craig Claiborne recipe, is cast in trochaic tetrameter, the meter of *Hiawatha*:

Dice the pork and chop the celery,
Chop the onions, chop the carrots,
Chop the tender index finger.
Put the kettle on the burner,
Drop the lentils into kettle:
Two quarts water, two cups lentils,
Afternoon is wearing on.

The pure fun of this does not keep it from making a point that Kizer has touched upon before, namely, that the challenge of a writer's life is maintaining a balance between duty to the daily life of the household, and duty to the art. This poem ends with the discovery that the soup is no good— "Tastes like mud, the finished product"—and gets thrown away:

Say to hell with ham bone, lentils,
New York Times's recipe.
Purchase Campbell's. Just add water.
Concentrate on poetry:
By the shores of Gitche Gumee
You can bet the banks were muddy,
Not like Isle of Innisfree.

The decision to give domestic and literary ambitions their rightful emphases appears also in a section of Kizer's second book, *Knock Upon*

Silence (1965); it is entitled "from 'Pro Femina'," the preposition indicating that the three numbered parts are to be taken as fragments of something larger. The first line of each part is like a chapter heading or topic sentence. First, "From Sappho to myself, consider the fate of women." Second, "I take as my theme 'The Independent Woman'. . . ." Third, "I will speak about women of letters, for I'm in the racket." The stance is directly polemical and satirical. The meter is difficult to establish definitively, but tends toward a five-stress line with plenty of variation in the number of unstressed syllables; the effect is to evoke classical Roman meters, where the dactylic hexameter had a theoretical syllabic range from twelve to eighteen. In a little more than a hundred of these capacious lines, Kizer lays out the situation of women in a way that became clearer to a great many more people only a few years later.

When lyric is the predominant poetic mode, it is tough to produce a verse essay; Kizer manages it by delicately controlling her tone, compounded of piercing intelligence, graceful allusiveness, a tendency to wisecrack, and a depth of compassion that provides some of the most satisfying surprises available in recent poetry. In the second section, there is first a nod toward equal need for being taken care of:

> But we need dependency, cosseting and well-treatment.
> So do men sometimes. Why don't they admit it?
> We will be cows for a while, because babies howl for us,
> Be kittens or bitches, who want to eat grass now and then
> For the sake of our health. But the role of pastoral heroine
> Is not permanent, Jack. We want to get back to the meeting.

In the third section, after excoriating women who "try to be ugly by aping the ways of the men," she ends the poem by striking a chord composed of optimism and amusement, tempered in the sadness from which the poem would have us awaken:

> But we're emerging from all that, more or less,
> Except for some lady-like laggards and Quarterly priestesses
> Who flog men for fun, and kick women to maim competition.
> Now, if we struggle abnormally, we may seem almost normal;
> If we submerge our self-pity in disciplined industry;
> If we stand up and be hated, and swear not to sleep with editors;

If we regard ourselves formally, respecting our true limitations
Without making an unseemly show of trying to unfreeze
     our assets;
Keeping our heads and our pride while remaining unmarried;
And if wedded, kill guilt in its tracks when we stack up
     the dishes
And defect to the typewriter. And if mothers, believe in the luck of
     our children,
Whom we forbid to devour us, whom we shall not devour,
And the luck of our husbands and lovers, who keep free women.

"We may seem almost normal": the subtlety with which this observation is almost thrown away is an element of the immensely resourceful craft that has characterized Kizer's work since it first began to appear. "From 'Pro Femina'" was a few years in advance of the great burst of feminist writing in the late 1960s; like most of Kizer's writing about the situation of women, it acknowledges more of the situation's complexities than were confronted in many of the era's oversimplifying polemics.

Kizer's first book, *The Ungrateful Garden* (1961), contains "Hera, Hung from the Sky," which describes the aftermath of a rebellion that takes some of its force from the Greek myths of Zeus and Hera, and some from the rebellion of Lucifer. The first strophe ends with these lines:

I pitted my feminine weight
Against God, his terrible throne.
From the great dome of despair,
I groan, I swing, I swing
In unconstellated air.

The poem captures the exuberance of the revolt, the energy of being "mad, but beautifully mad," the grief of loss and defeat. At the same time, its end-stopped trimeters and repetitions acknowledge the voice of Theodore Roethke, whose words on the back cover of *The Ungrateful Garden* have about them a whiff of the "condescending praise" that had enraged Hera: "Miss Kizer is one of the livelier literary females on the scene: knowledgeable, witty, never boring—willing to take chances with unusual material. . . . There is energy, verve, intelligence in her work." It is a remark to treasure, and to chuckle over; wherever Roethke's blind spots may have been, he had a rare gift for inspiring younger poets to bear down on the craft. James Wright was one of Kizer's classmates under Roethke's tutelage, and tells in an interview about the master's approach. The kind of thing he regularly did is exemplified by his having sent the students out to the library, with instructions to return to the next class with twenty examples of iambic trimeter with the caesura after the first syllable. Years later, Kizer addressed Wright on two widely spaced occasions; the two poems now appear side by side at the end of *The Nearness of You*, her collection of poems for and about men (1986). Like many another pair or small group of her related poems, these two give us separate moments in two rapidly changing lives. They demonstrate the unpredictable ways in which poetic genius can settle upon troubled spirits, and they show us a durable friendship in its early days and in the last hours of Wright's life. Courageous grace in the presence of a dying friend may come easier than courageous grace in the presence of one's own death, but saying what is beautiful in such circumstances is never easy.

One of Kizer's finest poems on this or any theme appears in *The Ungrateful Garden*; "The Great Blue Heron" is a rare convergence of power and delicacy. This poem, too, is written in three-stress lines unpredictably rhymed, but Roethke's voice is not audible in them. Dedicated to the memory of the poet's mother, the poem begins with a recollection of seeing a heron on the shore,

> Superimposed on a poster
> Of summer by the strand
> Of a long-decayed resort,
> Poised in the dusty light
> Some fifteen summers ago;
> I wondered, an empty child,
> "Heron, whose ghost are you?"

The child runs to the house for her mother, and brings her out to where the heron had stood, but he is gone. Yet her mother locates him in the sky, and recognizes him in a way that the child, comparing the wings in flight to their earlier folded stillness, cannot forget:

> Could they be those ashen things,
> So grounded, unwieldy, ragged,
> A pair of broken arms

That were not made for flight?
In the middle of my loss
I realized she knew:
My mother knew what he was.

The final strophe brings the speaker to the present, and to recognition of the heron's prophecy:

O great blue heron, now
That the summer house has burned
So many rockets ago,
So many smokes and fires
And beach-lights and water-glow
Reflecting pin-wheel and flare:
The old logs hauled away,
The pines and driftwood cleared
From that bare strip of shore
Where dozens of children play;
Now there is only you
Heavy upon my eye.
Why have you followed me here,
Heavy and far away?
You have stood there patiently
For fifteen summers and snows,
Denser than my repose,
Bleaker than any dream,
Waiting upon the day
When, like gray smoke, a vapor
Floating into the sky,
A handful of paper ashes,
My mother would drift away.

By the last few lines, when internal rhymes (flare/bare; eye/my/sky; day/gray; vapor/paper) are almost as plentiful as end-rhymes, the texture of the verse is so effortlessly complex that the three occurrences of *away* seem quite unobtrusive. The merging of rhyme, meter, and syntax in the final sentence is flawless.

Though "The Great Blue Heron" alone does not immediately reveal an indebtedness to Chinese and Japanese models, poems in its company suggest that Kizer could visualize those wings against the sky as such images are sometimes rendered in Asian landscape painting, the context stripped to the point that even mountains can seem weightless. Though Kizer pays homage simultaneously to Japanese models and to Roethke in a few poems in *The Ungrateful Garden*, it is *Knock Upon Silence* in which her exploration of Asian poetry is most energetic and thorough. Like many Western poets who have made versions of Chinese and Japanese poems, Kizer came to them by way of Arthur Waley's translations. Unlike many of her contemporaries, however, Kizer has the technical prowess to make convincing rhymed imitations and translations, though she does not do this in all instances.

The first section of the book is called "Chinese Imitations," and according to a note at the back, the first three of its seven poems are in the manner of Po-Chü-I. "Amusing Our Daughters," dedicated to Robert Creeley, is one of the best of these; it combines treatment of the ordinary with a slightly extraordinary diction, so that each image or moment is intensified. The narrative situation of the poem is that the speaker and her family descend as guests on the home of Robert Creeley, and as the second evening grows later,

> Nothing occurs, though we are aware you have three daughters
> Who last year had four. But even death becomes part of our ease:
> Poems, parenthood, sorrow, all we have learned
> From these, of tenderness, holds us together
> In the center of life, entertaining daughters
> By firelight, with cake and songs.
>
> You, my brother, are a good and violent drinker,
> Good at reciting short-line or long-line poems.
> In time we will lose all our daughters, you and I,
> Be temperate, venerable, content to stay in one place,
> Sending our messages over the mountains and waters.

"But even death becomes part of our ease": this surprisingly quiet statement is followed by lines whose low-key directness seems almost impossible. But the sound carries them; dense without being packed, the echoes come close to having a texture of their own: *parenthood, tenderness, together, center, entertaining*, then *temperate, venerable, content*; it is rewarding to take such a course over *mountains* and *waters*.

Kizer's most extended work in Asian-inspired modes is "A Month in Summer," whose form, she tells us, is derived from that of Issa's *The Year of My Life*, in the translation of Nobuyuki Yuasa. The narrative of its thirty sections ("First Day" through "Thirtieth Day") recounts the last month of a love affair, but the effectiveness of the piece is in the details, and in the importance it gives to the transforming power of poetry. The form suggests that of a journal, alternating long lines and haiku. The long lines often have the sound of prose, though only the entry for the eighth day has a justified right margin.

"First Day" introduces two ways of writing haiku, one in three lines and one in four, both liberated from the precise seventeen-syllable requirement. The long lines are flat and direct, and the references to love in the poems are glancing:

> I have come to prefer the four-line form which Nobuyuki
> Yuasa has used in translating Issa because, as he says,
> it comes closer to approximating the natural rhythm of
> English speech:
>
> > Let down the curtain!
> > Hamlet dies each night
> > But is always revived.
> > Love, too, requires genius.

"Fifth Day" hovers between prose and the short forms; the lines are noticeably *ended*, but the diction is casual; the energy arises in part from the almost thoroughly suppressed humor in the tone:

> I listen to myself being deliberately annoying,
> deliberately irritating. I know so well, now,
> what he hates; I can so easily provoke it.
> It is a kind of furious attempt to rouse us both
> from the inert boredom with which we regard our
> life together. I'd like to sting him into madness,
> as if I were one of the Erinyes. I don't believe
> he is capable of understanding why I behave this way.

There you have them, I sometimes think, looking at this passage: seventy-three words that perfectly describe, but do not solve, one of the essential mysteries about the ways men and women work on each other. Though there are passages elsewhere in this poem that specify differences between men and women, and though this one is careful to assign behaviors and emotions to one or the other of the principals, even invoking the Furies, it is easy to imagine this situation with the genders reversed. The last sentence lays down the final barrier: it does not matter what his capabilities of understanding might be, as long as the speaker believes what she believes.

In the entries for the last ten days, the agony of separation, the fear of being alone, "the terror of loss," are all dealt with directly, and the poem takes many handsome risks with self-indulgence or melodrama. But on the twenty-ninth day the matter is regarded with Olympian humor. The entry opens with a reference to "playing the Telemann concerto over and over"; it was introduced in "Third Day," and now, almost symmetrically, it verges on being the music this couple might have called "our song"—a banal notion, as the speaker is aware:

Now

I am reduced to wondering whether we are listening
to the same record at the same time of night.

    The music I play
    This summer and fall:
    Will I hear it at sixty
    And be ready to die?

Perhaps at the extremes of happiness or unhappiness,
one should take care that only inferior works of art
will be contaminated by nostalgia. And, after all, it
is well known that a cheap popular song can arouse
through its associations a more violent reaction than
the greatest composition.

"Thirtieth Day" ends with three very short paragraphs, the last a pair of sentences from Donald Keene's translation of Bashō's *The Unreal Dwelling*:

Nothing remains.

And the worst, unimaginable until now: it is as if
nothing had ever been.

"Is that what is meant by dwelling in unreality? And here
too I end my words."

The question in that last quotation is ambiguous, since "that" may refer
to the whole episode, or to the immediately foregoing statement. Either way,
it is a brilliant strategy to end with a quotation from Basho, to bring the
poem back to the ground from which it started, and to put the non-literary
material in its place. To be sure, it is a place of importance; but it is through
the poem that it arrives there. The point is emphasized in the placement of
"from 'Pro Femina'" immediately following "A Month in Summer."

KIZER'S THIRD book, *Midnight Was My Cry: New and Selected Poems*,
appeared in 1971. It adds sixteen new poems to a curiously one-sided
selection from the earlier two books. *The Ungrateful Garden* is reprinted
almost entire, one of its thirty-seven poems having been left behind.
Knock Upon Silence, however, is represented by only eight poems, and
among the omitted are "A Month in Summer" and "from 'Pro Femina'."
Several of the new poems are overtly polemical, so the absence of these
two important pieces might have been a matter of space, a page-limit
imposed by a commercial publisher. More remotely, Kizer may have
leaned away from those poems for a while in the late 1960s, when more
angrily polemical poetry was in fashion; several of the new poems in this
book are directly concerned with civil rights protests, Viet Nam, and the
assassination of Robert Kennedy.

Often in Kizer's work, of course, the public and the private concerns
intersect and transcend polemic. In "Streets of Pearl and Gold," one of the
new poems, the speaker recalls a youthful session posing as Venus for a
painter, in a studio condemned to demolition, and then moves into a
description of New York's chaotic teeming toward destruction; there is a
recollection of the city's weird ascent/descent from having been "a pas-
toral Dutch village," followed by a section in which "the Bridge" looms
over a wino sleeping in a tray from which the Fulton vendors have been
selling fish.

The fourth of the poem's five sections dwells on the cityscape and its
condemned buildings, the meditation giving rise to warlike images:

Bits of the old town lean on the August air,
Wait blindly for the X of the builder-killers,
Their multitudinous eyes taped out.

Racks of white crosses fenestrate the night,
Before the two hairs cross in the last bomb-sight.

And who are we, for whom our country cares?
America makes crosses of us all.
Each artist in his fortress: boiling oil
A weapon still. Seething across his canvases, a fury
Flung over white, ripped out: the X in paint.

The final section urges the artist to "observe the world with desperate affection," so that recorded loss might be a kind of gain:

So stamp your canvas with the X of loss,
Art mutilated, stained with abuse and rage.
But mark it also as the cross of love
Who hold this woman-flesh, touch it alive,
As I try to keep us, here upon the page.

There are passages in this poem which may have seemed less preachy in the mid-1960s than they do now; but even at her most direct, Kizer maintains electrifying tension, and finds a way to speak, almost at the same time, of anger and of love.

IN 1984, thirteen years after the publication of *Midnight Was My Cry*, Kizer published two books. One was *Mermaids in the Basement: Poems for Women*, and the other was *Yin: New Poems*. The first selected poems from previous books (including four from *Yin*), and included half a dozen new poems. Even *Yin* contains a couple of previously collected poems; "The Copulating Gods" and "The Dying Goddess" both appeared first in *Midnight Was My Cry*.

These two books are superb achievements of somewhat different kinds. *Yin* is perhaps the most diverse of Kizer's individual collections, including all kinds of open and closed forms, and a brief meditation in prose. It received the Pulitzer Prize for 1985. *Mermaids in the Basement* is a judicious selection, carefully arranged. It is so thorough and well-rounded a collection that at first nothing appears to be missing: it gives a momentary and entirely erroneous impression that Kizer has written only poems for and about women. (This impression is quite thoroughly dispelled not only by a moment's reflection, but also by *The Nearness of You*, published two years later.)

After a group of poems called "Mothers and Daughters," which includes "The Great Blue Heron," there is a group of five poems gathered under the title "Female Friends." Two of these are addressed to a friend of many years; "For Jan, in Bar Maria," first collected in *Knock Upon Silence* among the poems in the style of Po Chü-I, recalls a couple of escapades from a long friendship; the present of the poem is in Ischia:

> Remember, fifteen years ago, in our twin pinafores
> We danced on the boards of the ferry dock at Mukilteo
> Mad as yearling mares in the full moon?
> Here in the morning moonlight we climbed on a workman's cart
> And three young men, shouting and laughing, dragged it up
> through the streets of the village.
> It is said we have shocked the people of Forio.
> They call us Janna and Carolina, those two mad *straniere*.

"For Jan as the End Draws Near" is the first of two or three poems of Kizer's that take up, with brilliance and courage, the difficult subject of long friendship. A note at the back identifies Jan Thompson as "my oldest friend, for whom I write a poem once a decade." This one begins with a recollection of their having imagined, when they were young, how they would be old together, "picking peas in California":

> To us it meant a hellish kind of heaven,
> a kind that unbelievers could believe in;
> a warm land, where we could be
> companionable crones
>
> in our little shack, a stinking stove,
> a basin of warm water for cracked feet,
> each other's hands to stroke
> our twisted spines. . . .

The slant rhyme between the ends of the stanzas is one of several this poem executes with unobtrusive deftness. Earlier, the same device rhymes *any* with *than we* and *most* with *coast*. The distance between the rhymes is slightly offset by the symmetry of their locations, but it is a quiet effect all the same; it moves at last through *were* and *here* to the poem's deeply affecting ending:

Well, we were a pair of feckless girls!
Depression children, idealists and dreamers
as our parents and grandparents were.

Of the two of us, you had the darker view.
As it turns out, it wasn't dark enough.

Now the sun shines bright in California
as I shell peas for supper.
Our old-crone fantasies have moved much closer
to an obscure isle in Greece
though we well know that there's no hiding place
down here.

Meanwhile, we've had nearly forty years
to crack our dismal jokes and love each other.
This was our providence, this was our wisdom.
The present is this poem, O my dear.

The vision of aging self-sufficiency, of living off the land, turns in another direction in a poem that appears in both of these books. "Fanny" is presented as a new poem, a separate item in *Yin*, but in *Mermaids in the Basement* it becomes the fourth section of "Pro Femina," now titled without the excerpting preposition. The narrator of this quite substantial poem—loose blank verse, thirty-three stanzas of seven lines each—is Fanny Osbourne Stevenson, the American woman who went with Robert Louis Stevenson to Samoa and nurtured him there for about seven years, until his death of a stroke in 1894; the poem is in the form of entries in her journal.

The poem recounts a nearly obsessive frenzy of planting and harvesting; it is a necessity for the soul as well as for the body, apparently. The journal entries refer occasionally to themselves and their diminishing frequency as various crises press in. A weird calm pervades the final stanzas of the poem, as Samoa erupts into war, families receive the severed heads of their relatives, and Stevenson suffers his cerebral hemorrhage and dies:

I will leave here as soon as I can, and never return,
Except to be buried beside him. I will live like a gipsy
In my wild, ragged clothes, until I am old, old.
I will have pretty gardens wherever I am,

But never breadfruit, custard apples, grenadilla, cacao,
Pineapple, ylang-ylang, citron, mango, cacao,
Never again succumb to the fever of planting.

The earlier three sections of "Pro Femina" are filled with concrete images, but they are presented as exemplary or general, rather than specific. It is a deeply persuasive move, backward in time to a life of pioneering independence, in a world too accustomed to dependence to understand what Fanny was doing.

Two items in *Yin* are especially direct in their approaches to questions of dependence in relationships; they are spectacularly different in mode and tone, but they establish their places in this book. One is the five-page memoir, "A Muse," which recounts the ways in which the poet's mother doted on her, and the inescapable fact of the poet's calling: "I wrote the poems for her. I still do." The other poem is "Afternoon Happiness," a fine poem which complains about the difficulty of writing a happy poem, compared to the ease of writing out of misery:

No, love, the heavy poem will have to come
From *temps perdu*, fertile with pain, or perhaps
Detonated by terrors far beyond this place
Where the world rends itself, and its tainted waters
Rise in the east to erode our safety here.
Much as I wanted to gather a lifetime thrift
And craft, my cunning skills tied in a knot for you,
There is only this useless happiness as gift.

The second of these poems opens *The Nearness of You*, and the first has its companion piece in a memoir about the poet's father, the distinguished jurist Benjamin Kizer. It is a portrait of a brilliant man who learned gradually, along with his daughter, how to be less remote from her. If she writes the poems for her mother, it may well be that she reads them aloud for him.

The joy of persistence, the discovery that today is here after all, is a subject that calls for extraordinary tact, a sharp ear for the minor chords that just sufficiently dampen the cheer. Kizer's alertness to such stimuli is not excelled in recent poetry of my experience; in her world, the lovely and the dreadful are always going on, often together, as in "An American Beauty," the magnificent elegy for Ann London in *Harping On*. It celebrates a life of considerable difficulty, in which moving on from apparent error was a recurring motif, along with bravery of both mind and heart.

Finally, a poem not quite elegiac, "Poem for Your Birthday," addresses an old friend about the present, in a manner not unlike that of "For Jan as the End Draws Near." This friend gives Kizer an occasion to recall, as she has a few other times, that her early life was unusually blessed:

> Let us reflect a while on us, my dear:
> Born fortunate, two creatures petted and well-fed
> With milk and vitamins, thus our good teeth and skin;
> Curled hair and handmade clothes and patent slippers,
> This side of the moat from the desperate unemployed.

The occasion is one of the decadic milestones, and gives rise to reminiscence of triumph, trial, loss, and gain, and to reflection on the range of importances a friendship can engage. The end of the poem is as strong a case as I have seen for faith in the human enterprise:

> Truly to relish trivia in flower,
> Woman-talk of recipes and clothes,
> One must be aware of that high discourse
> On art and life we could deal with if we chose.
>
> "The flow of soul," as Pope extravagantly called it,
> Unstopped, though years of parting intervene,
> Though illness, duties, children interrupt,
> We know we'll go on talking till the end
>
> Or after, when we still reach out in thought,
> Or waking, sense the living person near.
> The password at the boundary is *Friend*.

That faith stands out strongly in a great many of Carolyn Kizer's poems. It is a body of work that says, over and over, that the life led, the friendships made, are more than can ever be said about them, even though the saying is the only way to get that right.

CAROL MUSKE

Postscript:
Carolyn Kizer, Superkid

REVIEWING children's books not long ago in *The New York Times Book Review*, Carolyn Kizer quoted a favorite childhood "poem," a nonsense ditty by Gertrude Stein:

> Be cool inside the mule
> Be cool inside the mule

She described walking along and saying the lines over and over to herself, having no other awareness of the rhyme than its aural pleasures, the incantatory sound of the words themselves. The words are indeed lulling, but the diction is subversive of "sense"—it is the mantra of a child who is very aware of conventional rhythms, but (like the literary renegade who wrote the words) supremely disinterested in imposing convention on thought.

Gertrude Stein, master of this lovely sedition process, stayed in touch with the child's desire to hang on to a language not preempted by logic. Children love rhyme, but love of rhyme merely indicates a delight in repetition; it does not presume a conventionally organized sensibility. Nonsense rhymes delight in their overthrow of syntactical hierarchies, even natural sequence—up is down and left is right, pigs fly and it is cool inside the mule.

I'd like to take a look at a poem by the grownup Carolyn Kizer written in the sensibility, if not the voice, of the child (ergo the poet)—all-observing, anarchical, word-intoxicated. The poem is "The Intruder," recently collected

23

in *Mermaids in the Basement*, and it begins with a long litany of unorthodox delights:

> Dove-note, bone marrow, deer dung,
> Frog's belly distended with finny young,
> Leaf-mould wilderness, harebell, toadstool,
> Odd small snakes roving through the leaves, . . .

Beyond its echo of *Macbeth*'s three witches, brewing up trouble, it has the feel of Vergilian hexameters, long ten or eleven syllable lines; it feels Sapphic, with its heavy trochaic and dactylic accents. The result is a poem which is the structural opposite of Stein's—quirky irregular, authoritative rhythms combined with a nearly courtroom logic. At first the irregular rhythms seem to underscore an offbeat maternal love, but further study yields a suggestion of underlying contradiction: the mother's much-vaunted unconventionality is shown up for what it in fact is. The poem is finally one of real and chilling epiphany, the remains of a dead bat on the floor and the corpse of her mother's hypocritical "pity."

> Wild and natural!—flashed out her instinctive love, and quick, she
> Picked up the fluttering, bleeding bat the cat laid at her feet,
> And held the little horror to the mirror, where
> He gazed on himself, and shrieked like an old screen door far off.

The mother holding the wounded bat makes a bold, oddly coquettish figure ("Depended from her pinched thumb, each wing. . . .") and her murmured words, "It's rather sweet," clinch the self-regarding sentimentality of her gesture. It is only when the mother sees the lice, "pallid, yellow / nested within the wing-pits" that the tone alters significantly. The reader can hear the mocking echo of the poem's beginning, the Diana-like striding-through-the-forest litany in "pallid, yellow / nested within the wing-pits" and the denouement comes as "the thing dropped from her hands" to be devoured by the unselfconscious cat. The mother, left standing by the puddle of dark blood on the floor, stands now in a harsher light, recognized by her child as victim of her own "tender, wounding passion" for a "whole wild, lost, betrayed and secret life."

The child's loyalties never desert the mother. They rather alter with sudden enlightenment, perceiving the enemy: "benevolence, alien / as our clumsy traps"—and the reader feels the wild daughter chafing in that same snare of love and vanity. The mother still appears attractive, if now slightly ludicrous—we watch her as she sweeps to the kitchen,

> Turning on the tap,
> She washed and washed the pity from her hands.

The terrible word "pity" burns like acid on the mother's hands. Again, in a *Macbeth* echo, the stained hands are held up as dramatic symbols. The irregular meters have rolled over and transformed, like the child's consciousness of the mother, into a more conventional stance. Indeed, the mother is "put in her place" by the return to straightforward iambic pentameter.

She is not wild, after all; she is completely civilized, a mother appreciative of the pathos of nature, though she is finally caught red-handed feeling pity, that most condescending of virtues.

> She washed and washed the pity from her hands.

The daughter, however, *is* wild. Her sympathies are forever among the dens and burrows, "whose denizens can turn upon the world / with spitting tongue, an odor, talon, claw." She has thought much further than the mother, even at a tender age, into natural "politics," and the wounded bat and the cat make sense to her in a way that is innate, in the same way the joyous anarchic "cool inside the mule" makes sense. The daughter is a poet and not one afflicted by the pathetic fallacy. Her respect for the mysteries and contradictions of nature, of people and language is already in place. It is clear that in this mind, nothing can be imposed willfully on the world from above—the world must be lived in at all levels, without care for "sting or soil."

It is this sensibility, represented here as a child's, that I find most typical of Carolyn Kizer's world view. "Cool inside the mule" and this refusal to look away from the bleeding bat signal a kind of tonic imagination always riveted in the actual. As she says in "Pro Femina" (about women):

> As we forgive Strindberg and Nietzsche, we forgive all those
> Who cannot forget us. We are hyenas. Yes, we admit it.

Or:

> What pomegranate raised you from the dead,
> Springing, full-grown, from your own head, Athena!

There is a childlike delight in the natural outrageousness and a "sagesse" that is close to primitive wisdom—and finally, an all-embracing love of the world frankly and unapologetically without pity.

CODA—Prague, 1999

Many years later—and half a world away from California (where both Carolyn and I live) she and I were among the writers "featured" at the Summer Seminars Program that takes place in Prague every July, sponsored by Charles University and the University of New Orleans.

It would not be an exaggeration to say that Carolyn was the matriarchal ruler of the conference. Powerful, outspoken, witty (incapable of containing her lethal sense of humor), she limped about on an arthritic ankle (soon to be bionically re-made in surgery), bristling with energy and irony—trailed by students and friends, her distinguished architect-husband John Woodbridge unable to slow her down.

At an evening reading in a tiny Prague theater, where two well-known male poets preened, she grew obviously restless. Then a young woman, one of the conference attendees, rose to her feet to ask a question during the Q and A period after the reading. She wanted to know which "poets who are women" these two guys most admired. There was a silence which grew into a much longer silence. Then slowly, a name or two was uttered uncertainly. A Bishop, a Dickinson. It was very clear that not only was the question unexpected—it was embarrassing. "Poets who were women" were not at the top of their literary Rolodex. One mentioned Muriel Rukeyser and the other shook his head dismissively. There was more silence. At last, one of them looked up and had the presence of mind to mention Carolyn. "Took you long enough," she barked, making it clear exactly how much this kind of acknowledgment was worth.

Carolyn Kizer is not a man-hater, not at all dogmatic—but her sense of justice is legendary. And funny. ("We *are* hyenas. Yes, we admit it." —"Pro Femina") Her resignation as Chancellor of the Academy of American Poets (along with Maxine Kumin) ripped the facade of "open-ness" and fair representation from that establishment's smiling face—and gave rise to the new diverse Board that has been assembled since her departure.

Not many would care to take on such a juggernaut—in conversation or political debate. But Carolyn Kizer is a friend of both men and women—student of Theodore Roethke, champion of the NEA as well as editor of *Poetry Northwest*, translator of Chinese and French, Pulitzer Prize winner, late night restaurant raconteur, travelling Ambassador to China, the former Yugoslavia and ports all over the world. Her politics and sense of fair play flow naturally in her poetry and her public and private life. In her poems, her voice always carries the authority of clarity and the somewhat anarchical sense of humor ("Spring forth, full-grown from your own head, Athena!"). That characterizes a Wild Woman who also knows how to settle down and solve a problem. Put her at the top of your literary Rolodex under "Super Kid," under "Eternal"—there's not going to be another Carolyn Kizer soon.

ALFRED CORN

The Impact of Character
on Character

AMONG POSSIBLE MODELS for the poet's life, consider two. First, Dickinson's solitary existence spent at a writing desk in an upstairs bedroom in Amherst, the valves of her attention closed like stone; her unmarried state, her lack of interest in travel; her writerly anonymity, rejoiced in because, instead of croaking all day to an admiring bog, she could explore the inward universe of language. Second, Octavio Paz, leaving Mexico as a young man to travel in Spain and France, forming associations with progressive poets that he meets; wide and intense erotic experience, a first marriage and then a second lasting one; eventual appointment to serve as Mexico's ambassador to India; resignation from that post in response to violent government repression of a student protest; a return to Mexico to found one of Latin America's leading literary journals, with the inevitable result that he was called on to make frequent public appearances and comment on the state of Mexican letters and politics.

Carolyn Kizer's life as a poet resembles Paz's more than Dickinson's. She has traveled widely, to Europe, of course, but also to China and Pakistan, as a United States cultural ambassador; formed associations with dozens of contemporary poets and visual artists, edited a poetry magazine, directed the Literature Program for the NEA, married twice, and brought up three children; served as a Chancellor for the Academy of American Poets but then (along with Maxine Kumin) resigned in order to call attention to the failure of the Academy ever to name an African-American to serve in the same capacity. Part of the record of this wide spectrum of experience appears in her poems.

She probably wouldn't have been drawn to an active public life if her childhood experiences had been restricted to a narrower ambit. Kizer's memoir of those years (collected in *Proses*) describes a progressive upper-middle-class household, whose doors were open to many international visitors and notables, including the poet Vachel Lindsay. At an early age she took her place at the dinner table with guests and participated in discussions of current topics. No one meeting Carolyn Kizer fails to notice her social ease and self-possession, traits not common among the Hamletish brood of poets. Skills acquired when she was a child have only been amplified in the fulfillment of public duties discharged during adulthood. Those skills include saying what she actually thinks, even when her statements aren't designed to make her listeners comfortable. It's clear that the reticence, forbearance, and self-abnegation traditionally regarded as appropriate for women hold no interest for her. She is aware of but not deterred by the risks incurred when a woman speaks with authority—one of the reasons why we find insights in her poems not found elsewhere.

Given that she has led her life so much in company, among family, friends, and professional associates, it naturally follows that Kizer has written more than a few poems that depict other people, a practice that sets her somewhat apart from her contemporaries. Where there is character portrayal, narrative, however brief and elliptical, must operate. Although lyric, often in "experimental" form, has been the dominant mode for poetry during the twentieth century, a few poets have maintained a narrative tradition whose origins in the West are as old as Homer. That tradition includes Virgil, Dante, Chaucer, Shakespeare, Dryden, Pope, Wordsworth, Byron, Keats, Tennyson, Elizabeth Barrett Browning, Robert Browning, Hardy, E.A. Robinson, and Robert Penn Warren, a roster that should justify any contemporary poet's decision to compose narratives. Carolyn Kizer doesn't write epic or novel-length poems, though a few of her poetic sequences move into the ten-page range. Narrative and plot play a role in her work, roughly as they do in short stories—which means that these verse narratives often describe and develop characters who interact with the poems' speaker. Like her early mentor Theodore Roethke, Kizer is mainly an autobiographical poet, and my sense is that characters in her work are modeled on actual persons, with an adherence to fact closer than is normal for prose fiction. Some of these characters are portraits of people that can be found in literary reference books. As such, they belong to what we might call Kizer's verse memoirs.

In this essay I won't be considering love poems or elegies. Although they obviously involve representation of other people, poems in those genres, more than the character of the beloved or the deceased, take as their subject the author's own mind. This doesn't mean that an elegy like "The Death of the Public Servant" (which appeared in *The Ungrateful Garden* and again in *The Nearness of You*) or a love poem like "The Copulating Gods" (from *Yin*) fails to describe the person it is addressed to; but physical description and psychological analysis take second place in poems like these. Meanwhile, in the more objective character poems, we sense that the author wants to compose a fable, tell a story (however concise), and to make a verse portrait of the nature and actions of another person. Inevitably Kizer's own feelings come into the portrayal, otherwise she wouldn't have been spurred to write the poems. Yet the first goal of these poems is to represent another person, a psychology not her own; in order to achieve it, Kizer has had to apprentice herself to the novelists and short story writers.

If you turn the book upside down and look closely at the painting used for the cover of *The Nearness of You*, you will see a stylized, foreshortened portrait of Flaubert. Choosing that particular work for the book cover amounts to a kind of homage. In her *Paris Review* interview (see p. 195 in this volume), Kizer comments that she has been influenced by Flaubert, saying, "I would put Flaubert first, not only the novels, but the incomparable letters he wrote to George Sand." [Thompson, *The Paris Review*, Spring 2000] Though she has drafted several short stories, only one has been published ("A Slight Mechanical Failure," collected in Howard Moss's *The Poet's Story*). Meanwhile, she has taken reams of notes for a projected novel without ever getting to the point of writing it. Instead, she has produced a series of poems that deal with the character and destiny of people she has known, and they are among the very best things she has written.

The longest and most detailed is the poem "Gerda" (*Harping On*), which describes the Swedish-American nanny who looked after Kizer until age eight. The text of a traditional Swedish child's prayer opens the poem, prefiguring the odd, hagiographical glow that surrounds this portrait of a woman who appears to have been unusually devoted, going beyond routine domestic tasks with affectionate extras like knitting sweaters for her young charge and sewing her a quilt. Kizer begins her narrative at a moment of crisis: Gerda trudging down the front walk with packed bags as she departs from the Kizer household. The grief-stricken eight-year-old (referred to throughout "Gerda" as "the child") cries *"Gerda, don't leave!"*, her "stony mother" explaining that the decision is irrevocable. Gerda has asked to have her salary raised from twenty-five to thirty-five dollars a month and been refused. Elsewhere in her writings Kizer has provided praising portraits of her parents, but, in "Gerda," some darker touches are added:

Thirty years on, her father will remark,
Your mother was jealous
So we let her go. Of course I could have raised her wages,
Gerda ran the house! The child's throat fills with bile
As, casually, he continues: *I always let your mother*
Decide these matters. Smug, he often used that phrase
As if the abdication of his parenthood
Had been a sacrifice. What did he know
Of the child's needs or passions?

For a moment we imagine that it's jealousy concerning the child's father, but Gerda's "gray bob" and steel-rimmed spectacles work against that interpretation. Instead, the mother has become jealous of the love the child feels for her nanny and seized on the excuse of the requested pay hike to dispose of her rival. The poem never terms this decision a "betrayal," and yet the above passage establishes it as one, in word choices such as "Smug" and "abdication of parenthood" and the searing final question. Even at age thirty-eight, the narrator can say her throat "fills with bile" at this revelation, which has the power to make her revert to the earlier, vulnerable identity and again become "the child."

Kizer's narrative method in this poem is to juxtapose several time-frames in an astute montage. Near the conclusion she recounts a tragi-comic moment in young adulthood when, during a train trip taken at age eighteen, she uses a brief layover in Minneapolis as a chance to try to re-establish contact with her lost nanny. The plan, nursed for ten years, utterly fails when she discovers that the local directory lists column after column filled with the name "Gerda Johnson." After several futile telephone calls, she must give up and resume her journey; she will never find Gerda again, a certainty she accedes to but cannot really accept. The poem's final lines shift to a second-person address, the author late in life again referring to herself as "the child" and calling for her lost caretaker:

Now from another life she summons you
Out of the earth or ether, wherever you are,
Gerda, come back, to nurse your desolate child.

If that is true, then we can begin to understand why the poet has developed so many friendships, friendships intense enough, crucial enough, to require the memorializing that poetry can offer. This passage implies that the early trauma of Gerda's loss has never been entirely healed. In all these relationships, Kizer hopes to rediscover some equivalent to that selfless devotion and, if only in fragments, to retrieve it. The poem's direct address leads us to feel as readers that we, too, are being scanned for solacing remnants of the nurse's kindly nature. To refuse that appeal is to risk seeming (or being) coldhearted.

Kizer's volume *The Nearness of You* borrows a Hoagy Carmichael song title to remind us, with amused irony, that the second-person pronoun is a shortcut to an intimate tone and stance toward the character being presented. In fact, that book contains many affectionate I-to-you poems that develop portraits of writers like Robert Creeley, Ruthven Todd, and James Wright. Equally affectionate are poems spoken directly to women friends who are not artists, for example, "An American Beauty," from *Harping On*. In a few instances her feelings of solidarity with a woman friend is so strong that Kizer dispenses with either "I" or "you" and writes the whole poem in the first-person plural. The most cheerful instances are the poems "For Jan, in Bar Maria" and "For Jan as the End Draws Near" (in *Mermaids in the Basement*). Along with the magisterial "Pro Femina," Kizer's poems to her women friends, the elegy for her mother ("The Great Blue Heron"), and the poems to her daughter ("For My Daughter" and "The Blessing") constitute her most important contribution to that growing body of work written by women in affirmation of women. *Mermaids in the Basement* went so far as to subtitle itself *Poems for Women*, which, in my opinion, is a gallant but mistaken assertion about the probable readership for the book. Even apart from its achievements in language, imagery and form, the book has a content that will engage male readers of poetry, too—leaving out those indifferent to the experience of the gender that makes up more than half the world's population.

"Pro Femina," by the way, holds the distinction of containing the only poem Kizer has written in the voice of a historical personage—Fanny Osbourne Stevenson, wife to the author of *Treasure Island*. (On the other hand, Kizer has written a number of poems appropriating personae from Greek mythology, in particular, "Hera, Hung from the Sky," "Persephone Pauses," and "Semele Recycled," plus a few first-person monologues like "Exodus," spoken by unnamed characters she has invented.) Originally written as an independent poem and published in *Yin*, "Fanny" was annexed to "Pro Femina" when that poem appeared again in *Mermaids in the Basement*. In the recent chapbook republication (BkMk Press, 2000) "Pro Femina" has now added yet another poem, "The Erotic Philosophers," which, who knows, may eventually prove *not* to be the poem's last section. Kizer's publishing history involves selective inclusion of some of her early poems as later volumes appeared, and so purposeful is this practice that we can regard her oeuvre as a twentieth-century counterpart to *Leaves of Grass*: fluid, open to the production and qualification of meanings lent to it in the process of recycling and expansion. The author's preface to this new edition of "Pro Femina" explains the inclusion of "Fanny" as follows:

> "Fanny Stevenson, in my mind, stood for generations of women who selflessly served men—fathers, sons, and lovers—until their loss enabled these women to blossom as artists themselves. Before their liberation [from] their willing servitude, they found other ways of expressing themselves. In Fanny's case it was the outdoors in Samoa, digging in the earth, planting." (p. vi.)

Whatever the origins and scope of the poem, however its meaning is altered by inclusion in the larger work, "Fanny" fully succeeds as the verse rendering of a brilliant, high-spirited character from the history of literature, whose work would be less often read today if Kizer hadn't called attention to her in this characterized monologue.

Although a number of her poems celebrate poet friends, others—among the most compelling Kizer has written—present the writer's profession in a harsh and even terrifying light. Early instances include "To a Visiting Poet in a College Dormitory" and "Promising Author" (both in *The*

Nearness of You). The latter poem may or may not be a poem of failed love. Some of the details imply a brief love-affair between the narrator and the "promising author," with his "witty, gap-toothed face / Half-ruined in a dozen shore-leave brawls, / And the straw hair and softening gut / Of a beat-up scarecrow out of Oz." The thirty-five lines of the poem sketch out a kind of rake's progress for this straw-man of letters. He marries a rich woman, whose cushy patronage, however, quickly sours and dries up with predictable results.

> You became glib as any Grub Street hack,
> Then demanded help
> To write the novel you never would write:
> As I turned you from the door
> You cursed me, and I cursed you back.

Nothing sentimental in this portrait of a con-artist, this "you" briefly near and dear and then despised and repudiated, who "wept for mercy as you died." What gives the poem more force than it would otherwise have is Kizer's awareness that no bond is ever formed without affecting both parties involved, this, even if the association has to be terminated. In the *Paris Review* interview she said:

> Well, I think if there's a major theme in my work, once we get past the love and loss of the early days, it is the impact of character upon character, how people rub against one another and alter one another. A poem of mine called "Twelve O'Clock," which was published in *The Paris Review*, was based on that principle of Heisenberg's that you can't look at a subatomic particle without altering it. Equally you cannot meet someone for a moment, or even cast eyes on someone in the street, without changing. That is my subject.

In "Promising Author" part of the alteration—part of the *damage*— appears in the phrase "and I cursed you back." Negative qualities in the would-be writer have stirred up a current of venom in the narrator, who can't have failed to acknowledge the harm active in those feelings and those words, both to the addressee and to herself. When we speak violently to someone else, we also absorb the impact of that violence. Although the straw man portrayed in the poem wept for mercy at his death, no mercy was forthcoming, as the poem itself demonstrates. Penance for hard-heart-edness in this poem takes the unusual form of self-disclosure without apology or special pleading: "He did that, and I said this, words I know to be wrong but will not conceal." A troubling feature of contemporary American poetry is the self-congratulatory tone it often takes, probably a perversion of the ringing opening line of *Song of Myself*: "I celebrate myself and sing myself." How many thousands of poems published have pitted a noble and brilliant "I" against an evil "they" or "he" or "she" or "you." Kizer knows that life isn't that simple.

Self-inculpations can be unconscious, too, as they are in the poem "To an Unknown Poet" (from *TNOY*). Because the poem is written in the first-person singular, with no name assigned to the speaker, we at first read it as autobiographical. Like Carolyn Kizer, the monologuist has extended herself to penniless aspiring artists; like Kizer, she has received a literary award from the American Academy and Institute of Arts and Letters. Finally, though, the equation is imperfect, and what we have instead is an ironic rendering of the consciousness of an "unreliable narrator," not fully aware of the implications of what she says. The poem begins, "I haven't the heart to say / you are not welcome here," and concludes with a description of the annual awards ceremony of the Academy and Institute of Arts and Letters, where, at a continent's distance from the insolvent poet and his untidy children, the speaker and her artistic associates "eat and drink and congratulate each other / in this bastion of culture." Like a good novelist, Kizer renders this character as a mixture of good and bad qualities, not as a plaster saint or as a garishly painted villainess. The poem's speaker is too honest to deny that the settled habits of middle age make houseguests like the poet and his flock of unruly children unbear-able. And yet she puts herself out for him, attending a reading that no one else attends, and according him a respect otherwise withheld from him. Though she accepts a literary award from the Academy, she regis-ters the implicit smugness of the proceedings in lines recalling her indi-gent poet, a contemporary counterpart of Rimbaud, "while we eat and drink and congratulate each other / in this bastion of culture."

"Bastion of culture" is an especially damning phrase, by implication pointing the finger at those who hold shares in the corporate academy, whose very existence is posited on the inclusion of some and the exclusion of others deemed, for whatever reason, unsuitable. We might also pause to reflect on another irony at work here: Although Kizer herself has received an award like the one her speaker has been tapped for, she was not invited to become an Academy member. Just as the poem's speaker has closed her doors to the "Unknown Poet," Kizer was perhaps led to reflect that Academy doors have in turn been closed to her, even though her dossier (which includes a Pulitzer Prize) contains sufficient justification for membership when compared to that of many current Academy members. The poem asks us, then, to hold in mind two different instances of inequity. One has to do with a poet who, though deserving, doesn't earn enough money to support his family, and another who has enough income to serve briefly as his patron, though she doesn't have the forbearance or means to house him and his family permanently. She, on the other hand, is accorded only partial recognition by a cultural institution whose primary function is to honor excellence in the arts. Life isn't fair partly because people aren't fair, or not always. It's a problem without a solution, as matters stand; but irremediable woe, as Frost reminded us, is one of poetry's oldest preoccupations.

I turn to one of Kizer's most recent poems, titled "Eleutheria," published in *Shenandoah* (Summer 1999) and included in *Cool, Calm, & Collected* (Copper Canyon Press, 2001). The poem tells us that the title means "freedom" and that it was the name of the wife of a poet whose own name Kizer withholds. We can guess that she is giving us a fictionalized perspective on the life of James Wright and the regrettable turn his first marriage took, though some of the details have probably been altered in the interest of producing a more coherent poem. Entirely credible, in any case, is the rendering of the title character. Kizer says, "Once he confessed to us that he had married her / Because he believed he couldn't do better, / Being plain and provincial." If this is true, he pays heavily for having underrated himself and settled for Eleutheria: She becomes that most devastating of enemies, the wife or husband who despises, denigrates, and threatens his or her spouse: "She was no fool; she knew he wanted freedom, / So she began to threaten: 'If you leave me, / You'll never see your boys again'."

When the inevitable divorce comes, she lives up to the threat; not until they are grown does he sees his sons again. The poem suggests that this wound partly accounts for the depth and power of Wright's later poems, just as that same wound may have been connected to his increasing dependence on alcohol. Yet even *before* the divorce he drank, and ". . . sometimes he beat his little sons / Whom he adored, pleading for quiet / So he would have freedom to write." Careful readers will already have noticed that the word "freedom" appears in both citations above, a prompter's cue for us to consider the concept of freedom in its relationship to the story of a man who wants to write great poems, a man overworked and under-paid as a teacher of literature. A fundamental tenet of modern aesthetics is that the artist must be granted complete freedom from any sort of censor-ship, internal or external. On a less exalted plane, it's obvious that free-dom to make any kind of art you choose is meaningless if you lack free time to do your work, freedom from the interruptions of noise, or free-dom from the emotional crises erupting in a failed marriage. The protag-onist of this poem wins free of some of the obstacles to artistic achievement, but, Kizer implies, at an enormous cost.

At the conclusion Kizer describes a final meeting with Eleutheria, the occasion a poetry reading given by one of Wright's sons:

> Of course by then our friend was dead,
> Prematurely, a victim of his hard life
> And that hard woman
> Who had given him his freedom.
> I discovered later that Eleutheria
> Had become a marriage counselor.
> A marriage counselor!
> Do we thank God for irony, or curse it
> When it comes too close?
> We are free to choose. Eleutheria.

The quality in irony we can be grateful for is laughter, even if that laughter comes only in an undertone. And the quality that we curse? Here Kizer focuses on the fact of its having "come too close" as the damnable aspect, which may mean that an ironic fate in this case is the lot of a person close to her heart, a person whose illness and premature death saddens and angers her. Yet irony may also have come too close in another sense, a more private sense, having to do with Kizer's own fortunes as a poet. The hypothesis will have to wait until more is known about her life and its rela-tionship to her work.

"We are free to choose," says the last line, which, in another context, might clang with the tinny accents of uplift. Here the statement forces us to reconsider whether the freedom required for poetry is worth the price.

Apart from its role as the great liberating precondition to artistic achieve-ment, "freedom" may also find part of its essence revealed in the metaphor of the cruel and destructive spouse, even when the spouse's name is not Eleutheria. It may even come to mean freedom from the bonds of earthly existence altogether—Dickinson's "the privilege to die," which was invoked by several twentieth-century American poets in the form of suicide.

Carolyn Kizer, who has expended so much effort on the cause of liber-ation, can't be charged with a sentimental failure to grasp the risks that go with it. She is a moral poet, and by that I don't mean that she is an apolo-gist for self-denial or prudence. Instead, her persistent concern is human character, human choice, human consequences. I'm reminded of a con-versation reported to me by a Mexican friend, a poet, whose father, dur-ing a family dinner, remarked, "Freedom doesn't make men happy." My friend's mother (a Loyalist who left Spain at the end of the Spanish Civil War) answered, "No, but it makes them men." As opposed to subhuman creatures, she meant—just as she intended the term "men" in this sense to apply equally to women. So be it: If freedom is an indispensable pre-condition for all writers who aim high, let those writers read "Eleutheria" and Kizer's other poems about poets before smashing their manacles; and let them acknowledge that serenity and contentment may not be the main result of freedom. Nevertheless, that ideal first formulated by the Greeks still glows with the promise of self-determination and the related project of artistic achievement—anyway, a beacon sufficiently alluring to how many thousands of aspirants who decide to light out for the territory.

TERRY EHRET

"Semele Recycled": A Sacred Tale of Regeneration

There was a muddy centre before we breathed.
There was a myth before the myth began,
Venerable and articulate and complete.

From this the poem springs . . .

—Wallace Stevens

1. "THE POEM SPRINGS"

I have a women's poetry group that gathers four times a year for all-day writing sessions. These marathons are punctuated with laughter and coffee and good food, but our main goal is to get the glimmerings of five or six new poems we can work on for the next few months till we gather again. We each bring something to eat, a poem we've memorized, and an idea for a writing exercise. On one occasion, the exercise involves using a "given" line from an unidentified source. My line is "Meanwhile young boys retrieved my eyes."

This is 1989, a year of intense drought in California. We aren't allowed to shower more than three times a week. We wash our dishes in "gray water," and tote buckets of washing machine rinse water down to the garden to keep a few plants alive. March arrives, and the "storm window" opens, delivering the season's rainfall in the course of a few weeks. Our group meets on the Spring Equinox, a day of slow, steady, engorging

41

rain. By the time I get to "Meanwhile young boys retrieved my eyes," I have composed six loosely connected poems with mythic rain beings, dreams of rain, sounds of rain, descriptions of rainscapes real and remembered. Those "young boys" from the quote become long-legged rain-boys, looking for their saturated woman in a weedy field of star anise and hyacinths, the final scene in what would later become a fertility sequence, titled simply "March Rains."

Jump ahead two years to the fall of 1991. I open my mailbox one afternoon to find a card from a judge who liked a couple of my poems she'd come across in a poetry competition. "I'm having a Lady Poets' lunch next Tuesday," she writes. "I hope you can come." The card is signed "Carolyn Kizer." *The* Carolyn Kizer. I'm flattered, stunned, terrified, but of course, I figure out a way to get there. And on Tuesday I'm sitting in the living room of Carolyn's Sonoma home, a quiet and very nervous guest at a critique session with poets Shirley Kaufmann and Diana O'Hehir. When Carolyn asks to see what I've been working on, I pass around an updated draft of "March Rains."

After I read it out loud, both Kaufmann and O'Hehir admit they are struggling to find the meaning—a fair assessment. The poem lacks any narrative thread, and leaps with associative disregard for the reader from the personal to the mythic and back. Then Carolyn speaks up.

"Well, it's clear to me this is a poem about wetness and arousal. You know, vagina juice."

2. "VENERABLE AND ARTICULATE"

Now, she is absolutely right, though my Catholic-school-trained tongue would never have put those two words together, nor would it have uttered them in polite company. But Kizer has never been one to let polite company get in the way of what needs to be said.

After the group leaves, Carolyn confides to me that seeing my efforts to shape a writing life and career in the midst of working and mothering three small children reminds her of herself 30 years back. Then she gives me a copy of her book, *Mermaids in the Basement*, and shows me "Semele Recycled." At the beginning of the sixth stanza, I spot her line about the young boys and the eyes which had made its way into my poem. She inscribes the title page with a brief personal note, "In Sisterhood, Motherhood, Childhood, all of it." That night while consoling my one-year-old who is up with an ear infection, I prop open the gift to study "Semele" in its entirety: one of the most horrible and sensually thrilling poems I have ever read.

The story underlying "Semele" is the myth of Dionysus, the dismantled god whose scattered parts must be reassembled by the searching wife/lover. Semele is Dionysus's mother, and it becomes her job to reassemble the scattered pieces of the god. In one form or another, this myth recurs in all cultures with a focus on agriculture and vegetation. The dismantled god is the vegetative god whose death and resurrection symbolize the life cycle of the reaped and planted crops. One expects and usually gets a tone of solemnity and high tragedy in poems treating this mythic theme. In Kizer's poem, we get instead a morbid fascination with decomposition, a surprisingly warm humor, and a lusty, stinky celebration of the body's pleasures.

The poem begins with a lover's complaint: "After you left me forever / I was broken into pieces / and all the pieces flung into the river." The most striking difference is that these words are not spoken by Dionysus, but by Semele. When I later asked Carolyn why she had conceived of Semele as the dismembered deity, she replied that the idea had come to her after undergoing some minor surgery. She was thinking about all the women who've had hysterectomies and mastectomies as ways to cure their cancers. "If cancer of the penis were as common as cancer of the breast and uterus, and if the only way to cure the disease was to cut the penis off, you can bet the medical profession would find another cure fast," she laughed. John Wayne Bobbitt notwithstanding, in modern life women are far more likely than men to experience this sort of dismemberment, and to go into their middle and later years with their sexual parts cut off and tossed away. And so in telling the myth of Semele, Kizer decided to reverse the sexes. It is, ironically, also a very ancient twist.

The second novelty in Kizer's treatment of the myth is her shift in tone from high tragedy to romance and comedy. In classical drama the role of tragedy is to transform and enlighten, but it takes the lusty belly-laugh of comedy to complete the alchemy of regeneration. "Semele Recycled" transforms the tragedy of the male hero into a comedy rooted in the ridiculousness of decomposition. From its opening lines, it's clear there is no dismembered phallus to weep over. The narrator's voice belongs to a female body re-membering its dismembered parts, even after those parts have been changed beyond recognition.

> A grizzled old man who scavenged along the banks
> . . . found my torso, he called it his canoe,
> and, using my arms as paddles,
> he rowed up and down the scummy river.
> When catfish nibbled my fingers he scooped them up,
> and blessed his re-usable bait.
> Clumsy, but serviceable, that canoe!

Here and throughout the poem, Kizer uses comic irony and understatement to offset the grisly, morbid details of Semele's disintegration. However, in the next two stanzas the imagery of the poem turns increasingly grim. The torso's trail of blood in the river attracts carp and eel; the wind blowing through the mouth and eye-sockets of the severed skull makes eerie mutterings; the young boys who find Semele's eyes use them as marbles in a game; and later, set like jewels in a bride's diadem, those same eyes send the groom staggering away in horror.

This imagery is unsettling. I want to look away, like that unfortunate bridegroom, or skip ahead. I don't expect Semele's casual commentary "Poor girl!", and the reference to her own "sacred slit" sounds crude to my ears, trained to regard the fluids and smells of the body as vulgar. But a good poem ought to challenge and disturb the reader, I think. It's what I want, at least as long as I can trust the writer not to manipulate my reactions simply for dramatic effect.

Why has the narrator insisted on looking with unflinching eyes on her own decomposition? I don't think it is morbid fascination alone. There is something in the torso-canoe, the muttering skull-shrine, and especially those haunting, disembodied eyes—something I almost recognize. So I read on, trusting the poem to take me further back toward the "muddy centre" which, while deeply disturbing, is also deeply familiar.

3. "THERE WAS A MYTH BEFORE THE MYTH BEGAN"

Older than the story of the dismantled god in all its recurrences, including the Christian one, older than our religions of suffering and death and gods nailed to the cross for eternity, older and more primal is a religion of sacred sexuality when the corn king and queen used to lie down in the empty furrows of the field and make love. While Western religion focuses on the sacrificed, dismembered deity and the atonement we must pay for the guilty part we have played in it, "Semele Recycled" recalls us to a different spiritual tradition with roots in the sacredness of the body and the nourishing divinity of the Earth.

In Riane Eisler's book *Sacred Pleasure* (two words the author claims have not been put together in Western religion), she explores the "ancient traditions vividly expressed in prehistoric art that earlier scholars often found too embarrassing to deal with, and in some cases to even fully see." We can find vestiges of this sacralization of sexual pleasure, which men and women were invited to repeat in their own beds, in the hymns of Innana, in the love-priestesses of the Sumerian narrative of *Gilgamesh*, in Indian erotic iconography and Tantric Yoga, in the stories of Isis and Osiris, Cybele and Attis, the mysteries of Eleusis, and even in the Celtic May Day celebrations.

This embarrassingly wet, smelly, fecund imagery permeates "Semele Recycled," especially in the final stanzas of the poem, brimming with "vagina juice." What begins as a tragic complaint and descends into morbid humor becomes in the end the mystery of a body re-membering itself out of the compost pile, joyously aroused by rumors of the lover's return and the close resemblance between the odor of death and the odors of sexual excitement:

But then your great voice rang out under the skies
my name!—and all those private names
for the parts and places that had loved you best.
And they stirred in their nest of hay and dung.
. . . [O]ur two bodies met like a thunderclap

in mid-day; right at the corner of that wretched field
with its broken fence posts and startled, skinny cattle.
We fell in a heap on the compost heap
and all our loving parts made love at once,

while the bystanders cheered and prayed and hid their eyes
and then went decently about their business.

When I first read "Semele," I interpreted it as a personal testament to faith and regeneration: the miraculous resurfacing of eros after the heart has been dismantled. I was at the time resurfacing from a long stretch of postpartum depression complicated by a move to a new town, the anxiety of a shaky marriage and unemployment. Each time I read the poem, it not only helped me to let go of the infinite, small deaths I felt diminished by each day, but more importantly, it reminded me of the power to nurture and protect myself. And on this emotional level, the narrative of the goddess-hero strengthened and consoled me. Yet the more I studied "Semele," the more I came to understand it as a political poem, both in the assumptions it challenges, and in the spirituality it proposes.

In the introduction to *Sacred Pleasure* Eisler says:

> [I]t is not coincidental that so much of our traditional religious imagery sacralizes pain rather than pleasure, or that the capacity to inflict pain, rather than to give pleasure, has been idealized in so many of our epics and classics. . . . I beg[i]n to understand that to overcome the pain and guilt, the exploitation and alienation, the tragic and often comic obstacles that have so embittered both women's and men's lives will require fundamental changes not only in how we view sex, spirituality, and society, but in how we view the human body, power, pleasure and the sacred.

"Semele Recycled" aims to do just that: alter the way we speak of sex. And in so doing, Kizer challenges the historical notions of the dirtiness of sex and its separation from the sacred, notions I know I have unconsciously internalized. Most women have. I suspect this internalization lies at the heart of our self-disgust so often revealed in depression, eating disorders, mutilation, and the various ways women devise to punish themselves for being human.

4. "A MUDDY CENTRE BEFORE WE BREATHED"

Our cultural and religious disgust with the odors and the fluids of the body is, I believe, misogynist at its roots. Consider this: we come into the world through the door of the mother's body in blood and wetness and stink. Sex shares in this "defilement," which has disturbed male writers and thinkers over the years from St. Augustine to Jonathan Swift. Yeats, for one, wrote "Love hath pitched his mansion in the place of excrement." And death, our final encounter with the bloody, wet and stinky, underlies so much of our philosophical and spiritual anxiety. Platonic idealism pushed away from the sacralization of the body and the wisdom of the sensual with its allegorical retreat from the dark cave of origins. Later Christianity insisted on the empty womb as well as the empty tomb, inventing a god who is not born of sex, and who gets up and leaves the tomb before it has the chance to take him back. This cultural rejection of the body and of earth is apparent more recently in the Heaven's Gate cult, whose leader encouraged his devotees to discard their earthly "containers" and transcend as pure consciousness.

The spirituality of "Semele Recycled" is clearly *not* about transcendence, but about immanence, striving not so much to rise above the earthly body as for the body to be truly of the earth. Semele's reassembled body overcomes death, but her inner parts still remember "fermenting hay" and the "comfortable odor of dung." And it is this deep-body memory that gives Semele, indeed all women, the power to nurture and heal themselves.

Mermaids in the Basement, the collection in which "Semele" appears, is subtitled *Poems for Women*, and it is in this light I'd like to consider the conclusion of the poem, the body's remembrance of "its bloody labor, / its birth and rebirth and decay." Following the notion that the rituals of the sacred marriage sacralize fertility and pleasure rather than pain and death, I have always been struck by the fact that the poem's final line is not the expected "birth and *death* and decay," but "birth and rebirth and decay." The unconventional word order places syntactical and rhythmic emphasis on *rebirth*, a one-word key to the poem's spirituality.

The voice I hear speaking these last few lines is different from the one that has just addressed the beloved, celebrating their erotic resurrection. Semele seems to be speaking to herself, or perhaps to women like herself whose bodies carry both the miraculous power of rebirth and the dark mystery of death. I also have the sense that the poem's persona and the author's voices merge in this stanza, so that we hear not only Semele speaking but Kizer, too, addressing her women readers and her women friends.

More than anywhere else in the poem, the diction in this closing stanza reveals Kizer's fundamentally feminist orientation toward the cycles of body and spirit. Her intimate woman-to-woman voice, speaking of labor, birth and rebirth, calls to my mind some of the earliest sacred images we know of, images repeated in Anatolian votive figures found at Catal Huyuk of the full-bodied woman, the mother and child, the merged or embracing double females. I think of the same rounded female shape encoded in the architecture of ancient temples in Sicily and Malta: the form humans worshipped as divine thousands of years before we ever conceived of god as a man. Kizer's poem, like these archeological fragments of our lost spiritual origins, insists on a "bloody labor" of female wisdom and experience—a bond women share with one another and with the earth itself, forged "In Sisterhood, Motherhood, Childhood, all of it," and which may be, like the "muddy centre before we breathed," even more primal than sex.

WORKS CITED

Eisler, Riane. *Sacred Pleasure*. San Francisco: HarperCollins, 1996.

Kizer, Carolyn, "Semele Recycled." *Mermaids in the Basement*. Port Townsend: Copper Canyon Press, 1984. 70–72.

JACK FOLEY

Review: "In Hell with Virg and Dan"

Harping On: Poems 1985–1995
by Carolyn Kizer

ECCO PRESS recently asked Carolyn Kizer to contribute to its volume of Dante translations. Kizer responded by translating *Inferno*, Canto XVII, into what she calls "antique hipster":

> "Yo, Dan, just give a look at this repulsive creature
> Called Fraud, the wall-buster; He's the prime polluter,
> The poison in his tail's an added feature."
> Then Virgil gave the high sign to that stink
> Of rottenness, to make a three-point landing on the shore. . . .

It is an amazing effect—a little like translating *Paradise Lost* into baby talk. Dante's "*Ecco*" (like the press), usually translated "Lo," becomes here "Yo." "Wall-buster" is an accurate rendering of "*rompe i muri,*" but it carries overtones of "ball-buster," a term with which a "pro feminist" like Kizer is surely familiar. "The prime polluter" (Dante's "*colei che tutto 'l mundo appuzza*") brings us even more definitely into the twentieth century with its ecological concerns, but a moment later the end rhyme of "creature/feature," alive with echoes of American television, returns us to at least the suggestion of *terza rima*. Virgil signals the monster, "that stink / Of rottenness," to make a landing, and we go on with Dante's story.

Kizer's version was, she tells us, "quite properly rejected for irreverence and 'not fitting in'" by the editors at Ecco Press. She published it under the title, "In Hell with Virg and Dan," first in the magazine *13th*

Moon and then in her new book, *Harping On*. A note to the poem states, "I just don't care for Dante's obsessions with shit and revenge. For me, he ranks up there with St. Paul as one of the most destructive literary geniuses of all time." One wonders whether the people at Ecco Press had ever read Kizer's "Running Away from Home," published in her Pulitzer Prize–winning book, *Yin* (1985). In it she writes of "those Rosary scars" and asks, "After Spokane"—her home town—"what horrors lurk in Hell?" The poem ends with a brilliant, anguished passage:

> It's never over, old church of our claustrophobia!
> Church of the barren towns, the vast unbearable sky,
> Church of the Western plains, our first glimpse of brilliance,
> Church of our innocent incense, there is no goodbye.
>
> Church of the coloring-book, crude crayon of childhood,
> Thank God at last you seem to be splitting apart.
> But you live for at least as long as our maimed generation
> Lives to curse your blessed plaster bleeding heart.

Not a lost but a *maimed* generation. That same term returns in Kizer's famous "Pro Femina": "I take as my theme 'The Independent Woman,' / Independent but maimed" (*Mermaids in the Basement*). *This* is the person Ecco Press asked to translate a passage from Dante. What the press got was, evidently, more than it could deal with—a version which was also a *sub*version. Dante's poem survives Kizer's "irreverent" treatment, but her translation raises questions which stay in your mind for a long time. What exactly is "Fraud" here? Is Dante's reputation a kind of fraud? Is he part of the historical condition which, Kizer thinks, caused an entire generation of women to be "maimed"? What is the relationship of an intelligent, literate *woman* to a tradition represented by *men* like "Virg" and "Dan"? Is Dante a prime mover, as he was for Ezra Pound and T.S. Eliot, or is he a "prime polluter," "one of the most destructive literary geniuses of all time"?

"In Hell with Virg and Dan" is only one poem in *Harping On*, and a translation at that. But its style is typical of the attitude towards language which one finds throughout the book: its sheer *aliveness*. Someone once praised Kizer for a particular "political" poem she had written. Kizer's husband, John, immediately remarked, "*All* her poems are political." Though Kizer praises Anne Sexton and Sylvia Plath for their "raw confessional

poetry," that is not the kind of poetry she herself writes. She is an enor-
mously *public* poet; her turf is precisely the intersection point of the pub-
lic and the private—which is one of the reasons she is one of our finest
satirists. *Harping On* begins with a poem dealing with "Franco's grandiose
memorial, / The Valley of the Fallen," and in the course of it the poet
speaks a curse: "*Franco, I spit upon your grave.*" Typically, the poem starts
with a personal anecdote. It's 1946, and Kizer is wondering why her "new
friend, Maisie," married a man "Who, when she was pregnant, knocked
her down, / Stole money from her purse to spend on drink, / And still
harasses her with drunken calls." The answer is: "'Well, you see, / He
fought in the Abraham Lincoln Brigade.'" "'Oh,'" Kizer responds, and
adds, "I would have done it too." We are barely into the book and we
are already dealing with memory, politics, and gender relations. The tone
here is comic and ironic—does Kizer mean that she would have married
the man or that she would have fought in the Abraham Lincoln Brigade?—
and the irony depends on the intersection of two contexts: in one, we
honor men who fought against Franco; in the other, we vilify men who
treat women in such a way. For Maisie, unfortunately, the same man exists
in both contexts. One might expect the pro femina Kizer to assert, "I don't
care how many wars he fought in, he's a monster to treat a woman like
that." But she doesn't—though of course both we and she understand
that the man *is* a monster. *Both* contexts are valuable: "I would have done
it too." The book is alive with such shifts. Is Dante a hero of poetry or a vil-
lain of religion? Clearly, he is both, and what is said about him depends
entirely on which context you are emphasizing. This is one of the exhila-
rating aspects of *Harping On*: it is never possible to predict what Kizer will
say about anything; she is constantly shifting perspectives.

Another poem, "Anniversaries: Claremont Avenue, from 1945"—one
of the finest in the book—ends with a rhetorical burst which not only
describes our current situation but is a marvelous example of how to man-
age a loosely pentameter line and the subtleties of free rhyming:

It's 1985: in pain, my Mother-in-law has died.
Appraisers from Doyle pick through her possessions:
old furniture blistered by sun and central heat.
Twenty-One Claremont is no longer ours.
Recollections are blistered and faded too:
My husband's boyhood toys, my fragments of Chinese.

Mothers have disappeared. Wars come and go.
The past is present: what we choose to keep
by a process none of us can ever know.
Now those little girls are grandmothers
who must remember, after fifty years
the doll, the chill, the tears.
Greatness felled at a blow.
Memory fractured. Black and white apart.
No sense of direction, we Americans.
No place to go.

The rhetorical mastery of that passage—its sheer power of mind—is to some degree a commentary on its negative content. An "American" who can make something as beautifully structured as that certainly doesn't lack a "sense of direction."

In "A Song for Muriel" [Rukeyser], Kizer complains,

No one explains me because
There is nothing to explain.
It's all right here
Very clear.
O for my reputations [sic] sake
To be difficult, and opaque!

Kizer's verse is deliberately "clear." It does not cultivate what Pound in *Mauberly* called "the obscure reveries of the inward gaze." But its "clarity" does not mean it is in the least simplistic. *Harping On* ranges over a vast array of subjects as this "dreadful century staggers to its close." "I was dead certain," Kizer writes, "that uncertainty / Governed the universe." "I'm blue," she writes, "Boo-hoo. / Got those End-of-the-Century blues."

The poems veer back and forth between the elevated and the "low," between the historical and the personal, between the strictly rhymed and metered and something looser, freer. The poet's primary task is to "bear witness," but, at the same time, poets are "always, always ourselves our own mirrors," "selfish and narcissistic and obsessed as ever." Not for nothing is Pope invoked twice in the book and not for nothing is Voltaire mentioned at its conclusion. Kizer is in part, like her father (whom she calls "Mr. Rational") an eighteenth-century rationalist. But she is a rationalist who is living in a century of surreal horror. Unlike her mother, who agreed with Einstein, she agrees with Heisenberg in the debate about the universe: is it orderly or chaotic? But Einstein's and her mother's opinion is honored too. In that vast collision of contexts which is the field of Carolyn Kizer's poetry, satire is one, but not the only, option. The poems are frequently very funny, but they are also very touching and personal, and various other things besides. They are evidence of a mind which stays wonderfully open to its own potential contradictions. As W.B. Yeats wrote, translating the epitaph of another great satirist, Jonathan Swift, Carolyn Kizer's verse "serves human liberty":

> Imitate him if you dare,
> World-besotted traveller; he
> Served human liberty.

One might add: *So does she.*

RUTH SALVAGGIO

Kizer's Politics:
Poetry and Feminism

CAROLYN KIZER tells us that she grew up in "an intensely political household." Her mother was a social activist who, among other things, "ran the first federally sponsored drug clinic in New York City" and was "an organizer for the I.W.W." "Politically," Kizer says of her mother, "she was a radical. . . ." Her father, a more distant influence on Kizer's life, was a lawyer with his own kind of "war chant: truth, justice, equity, freedom, and law."[1] No surprise, then, that Kizer herself has been intensely involved in politics and that politics has infused her poetry. As Director of Literary Programs for the NEA, for instance, the anti-war Kizer accepted funding from a pro-Vietnam war administration, reasoning that "the worse things are politically in a country, the more you need a strong arts program."[2] And she openly identifies herself as a feminist, dedicating her collection *Mermaids in the Basement* to "my dear friends everywhere, feminists all."

The connection between Kizer's politics and feminism, I believe, is a crucial one. It not only helps explain the social aspect of Kizer's poetry as being much more than traditionally "public" or "classical." Even more important, it helps us understand how women poets are mixing aesthetics and politics—and how the political movement of feminism is at last finding expression in the voices of women poets. This is good news for feminism. It may even be better news for poetry, which has long served as a vehicle for the expression not only of individual feeling, but more precisely of the subjective feelings of men. Women poets, of course, must also write

55

their subjectivity, and in fact the recent emergence of women's voices in poetry has involved just that kind of expression—what Kizer herself calls "the world's best-kept secret: / Merely the private lives of one-half of humanity."[3] But in addition to speaking for themselves, women poets are also speaking for others. They are reminding us that neither feminism nor poetry can remain isolated from a world in which otherness has too often been ignored and even suppressed. Writing both *as* other and *for* others, they open poetry to multiple voices. And they do this in different ways. Muriel Rukeyser leaps directly into political subjects in her poetry. Adrienne Rich, in her recent collection, *Your Native Land, Your Life*, speaks through the experience of diverse others. And a growing number of African American, Hispanic, Native American, and international women poets, especially from Third World countries, are expressing their social experience in strikingly political contexts—poets such as Paula Gunn Allen, Audre Lorde, Rosario Castellanos, Cherri Moraga, and Nellie Wong.

Carolyn Kizer joins in with these multiple voices by making both women and poetry into large subjects. I take the word "large" from Kizer's poem "Dream of a Large Lady,"[4] for here we find just that engagement with otherness that underlies both her politics and feminism. The poem opens with a woman climbing down a ladder from a gun emplacement. Unable to dislodge the gun, this large lady unpacks her lunch, and consumes "a single / hard-boiled egg / leaving the shell / not as litter but as symbolism / on the sullen gun / in its grey rotunda." She then meets another woman, this one with orange hair, who likes the large lady's poetry and invites her in for tea. The large lady accepts, and in this mood of acceptance and reconciliation, Kizer ends her poem describing the large lady's vision:

> With a sigh, she puts aside the memory
>> of the grey gun she could only decorate
>>> but not destroy.
>
> Though clear in her eye she holds a vision:
>> the thin, ceremonious shell
>>> of her eaten egg
>
> painted by the sun against the sky.

I see this "large lady" as Kizer herself, a woman poet who tries to "damage the gun," to buck the controlling powers—military, capitalist, patriarchal. At the same time, I also see Kizer reflected in the "orange lady," a woman who admires poesy and sips tea. Each engages the experience of the other. But particularly the large lady, who wants at once "to contemplate / the blue view / and to damage the gun," epitomizes what I take to be Kizer's own vision of largeness—an expansive vision that allows both the aesthetic and the political a place in poetry. There is a quiet aesthetic moment. But there is something else, that almost incongruous vision of the egg shell and the fun. "Clear in her eye" the large lady sees the world aesthetically, but she also sees it with what Lillian Robinson calls "the keen eye of politics."

This vision is surely part of a "poetics of generosity," a poetics described by Judith Johnson as Kizer's full engagement with a "multiplicity of energies" that signals the re-emergence of woman's subjectivity in poetry. Johnson argues that such a poetics is "central to feminism," for it not only reconstitutes the lost voice of woman as poet, but shows women—and Kizer herself—to be fully engaged in "life's furious contradictions."[5] Recovering her voice, the woman poet refuses to partake in the controlling discourse of a masculine poetic tradition, refuses to assume the role of speaking subject who controls the discursive object. She splits the subject-object dichotomy, and opens poetry to multiplicity.

Kizer's "large lady," it seems to me, shows us the essential political dimension of this generosity and engagement. For this lady not only speaks, she acts. And through this lady, Kizer has infused herself into the poem's action. It is, of course, not real political action, since the lady cannot really dislodge the gun. Nor is it descriptive of some actual political event. But what does happen here is something very important: Kizer is bringing together women and poetry, poetry and politics. The "orange lady" and "large lady," I would suggest, represent the very aesthetic and political merger that is taking place. Their drinking of tea mixes the two forms of experience that have long remained antithetical in poetic tradition, and that are now coming closer and closer together in an emerging feminist poetics. For even if the large lady "could only decorate / but not destroy" the gun, there remains the final vision of the "ceremonious shell" in the "grey rotunda." Here is the sign, the emblem, of Kizer's political aesthetics.

But politics is always more than a sign, and Kizer is no mere sign-carrier. What distinguishes her political vision—what marks it as "feminist," as I will be explaining later—is that she herself becomes part of the action. Never divorced from the object of her writing, Kizer is a subject intensely involved in her poetic politics. She does not comment from a safe distance, but always infuses herself in the experience. In "Race Relations," for instance, she sings in her "white oasis" while an unnamed other works and bleeds. Unable to change this very situation which is the object of her description, she becomes part of it—"sentenced to wait" through "our love-hate duet."[6] In "Poem, Small and Delible," she describes a group "picketing Woolworth's," holding signs with words as "baffling, as arcane / As poems." Kizer stands here in the poem, the woman who asked the question, "Who cares, lady?" She stands here as poet and activist, reflecting on the questions, thinking of Gandhi. "They will know who *he* was," she says, "And that Art and Action, mostly incompatible, / Could support each other now and then."[7]

This political vision, intricately linked to the generosity of Kizer's poetry, is also central to feminism. What's more important is that it shows the crucial role Carolyn Kizer plays in shaping a feminist political poetics. This task is a vitally important one—not only for the feminist movement, which has been seeking poetry that voices its political agenda, but for poetry itself, which has long needed to recapture its lost social imperative. In 1978, Lillian Robinson borrowed a phrase from an anonymous woman poet, "the keen eye of politics," to write about "Poetry and the Feminist Movement." Exploring a diversity of poems by women, she identifies the "new voice," the "new set of concerns and preoccupations" that charac- terize women's poetry.[8] Yet while celebrating the emergence of this new consciousness, she is troubled by the absence of a strong social and polit- ical voice, claiming that "the personal aspect is the only dimension of the question that feminist poetry has been able to reach at all." Her sum- mary of what is lacking in women's poetry leads me directly to a discus- sion of what Carolyn Kizer offers. Robinson explains:

> The poetry of the women's movement has failed to challenge a charter assumption of bourgeois literature: the notion that literature in general and poetry in particular exist for the expression of the private, individual, and subjective element in supposedly univer- sal human experience. . . . But ours is a movement that is only half certain where it is marching, and poetry is more often relegated to the "cultural events". . . the thing we drop into when the real polit- ical work is over. It needs to be more than that.[9]

Kizer's poetry is more. It is, like the lady she describes, "large." It not only encompasses the political, but places women in the feminist politi- cal world, and in so doing re-places poetry in its political context.

But why insist, as I do, that Kizer's poetic politics is a "feminist" politics? For clearly she writes on a variety of political subjects, and though she describes herself as a feminist, her concerns would seem to exceed those specifically relevant to women. My reason for identifying such a politics as feminist also has to do with the "largeness" of Kizer's lady, for the most important thing about this "large lady" is that she is a woman—a woman activist and poet who brings her vision *as a woman* to what she says and does. In suggesting this, I am also insisting on the "largeness" of feminism itself, a movement which does not restrict itself to the oppression of women (as if that were not enough), but which sees any form of oppression as intricately linked to patriarchal systems of dominance and control.

This is why it is so necessary to see Kizer's "poetics of generosity" connected to her political poetics. For if her generous poetics is what allows her to split the subject-object dynamics in which male poets have controlled the feminine object of their description, it is Kizer's political poetics that allows her to infuse women's new subjectivity with energy and make the woman poet herself as agent of both "Art and Action." Interestingly, Kizer's poetry is often described as "public" or "classical," and she herself looks to such public poets as Homer and Pope for her heritage.[10] And yet I believe that she is political in a way that these men never could be, for like Sappho—the other classical poet she claims—she writes from the other side of oppression, from the position of woman. She necessarily opens poetry to the voice of the confiscated object, transforms that object in the fury of action where she can not only find her lost voice but also change the world.

Consider, for instance, the way Kizer and Pope deal differently with the politics of writing. From his early *Essay on Criticism* on through the *Dunciad*, Pope shows a special fondness for making fun of bad writers. As a defender of standards and propriety, he never lost the opportunity to demean and belittle his opposition. His life was a constant warfare between those who ridiculed him, and his devastating return of that ridicule. Now look at Kizer's poem "Promising Author,"[11] in which she recalls her time with a writer who is clearly obnoxious—who curled his lip as he "ran down every writer in the place," who "sneered" at his "shabby friends" who lent him money, who "became glib as any Grub Street hack,"

Then demanded help
To write the novel you would never write:

As I turned you from the door
You cursed me, and I cursed you back.

Pope would leave it there. Content to describe the scene from his objective perch, he rarely entered into, never imagined what it might be like to be that person. But listen to the end of Kizer's poem:

Once I believed you were the great white shark,
Slick predator, with tough scarred hide.
But now I know you were a small sea-lion,
Vulnerable, whiskery, afraid,
Who wept for mercy as you died.

Kizer is generous through engagement, enters the mind and body of this "hack," becomes part of the politics of writing. I wonder if only a woman could do this, could know what it's like to be on the other side of propriety, and therefore sympathize. To her, this "promising author" turns out to be no monster, but only a "beat-up scarecrow out of Oz," a man whose bravado can only be tamed by our understanding. Is such understanding "feminist"? I say that, there, it is—that it defines what the woman poet does when she finds her voice and brings that voice to the social arena. She changes the way we think about each other, the way we relate to each other. She enters into the world to change it.

To make generosity political, one must—to use a phrase from Cynthia Ozick—"leap into otherness." The poet cannot be content to find her own voice, essential as that endeavor is. She must do more. She must mix her voice with that of others, bring it into the social chorus. Kizer herself is uncomfortable with the term "public poetry." "I'm not sure I like that term," she says, and then suggests, "Social poetry?"[12] I wonder if her reason may be that "public poetry" carries with it the notion of oratorical speech, of speaking from the privileged position to some uninformed mass in need of edification. "Social poetry," the term she suggests instead, would seem to be more engaging, more caught up in the process of exchange and interchange. So much of Kizer's poetry has involved that kind of interchange, that "leap into otherness." And I believe this is exactly what makes her poetry political. Whether she is in the group picketing at Woolworth's, or participating in a "love-hate duet," or leaving an egg shell on top of a gun and then sipping tea with an "orange lady," Kizer shows us that women poets can do more than remain caught in romantic reverie. They can, and must, become part of a social world desperately in need of change.

And Kizer's world is strikingly social. She describes herself as being in the "Roman" line—with Catullus, Juvenal, and Pope.[13] And yet, to me, she is much more generous than these men. She has their wit and flair, to be sure, and her language is often as crisp and controlled. Yet when she writes in the tradition, even following their forms, the result strikes me as something very different—different because she makes a public situation personal, because she becomes part of a world which they have been largely content to mock from their distanced positions. "Tying One On in Vienna"[14] is a perfect example of what I mean. It has all the exuberance of Juvenal and Pope, all the drunken madness of classical satire. Except that right there in the middle of the poem is Kizer herself, drinking away, "tying one on." If Juvenal and Pope have as their political agenda an exposition of a world gone mad, then Kizer does too—but she not only sees herself as part of that madness, she willingly joins in. There is generosity here, to be sure. But I want to insist that this is *political* generosity—a personal and political engagement with empires gone mad, empires we can only understand when we ourselves are mad, excessive, in love:

> Turks and Hellenes, Mongols, Shakespearean scholars—Hegel!
> Continuity is all!
> Changing the petticoat guard at the palace of Paul;
> Orange groves, All Souls' Day, 4th of July parades;
> Vienna, Spokane, Los Angeles County—even Hamburg. . . .
> And over all others, the face of my lover,
> A man with the brain of an angel!

The phrase repeated in the poem is "an excess of feeling." This is what allows Kizer—drinking, weeping, celebrating—to understand both the personal and the political. The world may be mad, but she is part of it, as we all are. Her "excess of feeling" makes it all tolerable, even joyous. She can "drink to the health of my ex-husband / And other enemies, known and unknown." She can "FORGIVE ALL LOUSY POETS / AS THEY SHALL FORGIVE ME." (Can we imagine this coming from Pope?) And there in Vienna, even political aggression can be forgiven. For Kizer herself is there, in the room, where it happened:

Even the rathskeller door, with its broken hinges
Since the Russian troops hammered it down, looking for girls,
Even the old door, wounded with bayonet marks,
Dances and reels, and my soul staggers for joy,
And we are healed together, noble Viennese landlord!

It is here, too, that we find what Kizer's politics is all about. It is a politics
of love. It is a woman's politics—built on engagement, interchange,
understanding. On a wonderful personal level, Kizer describes herself as
plunging her nose into her lover's navel: "Oh, what a heavenly odor! /
Landlord, hold me up by the hair / Before I drown." The poem ends with
Kizer bringing this personal love to the world:

The soul of the world is a nose,
A nose in a navel. The red sun sets in the navel of heaven.
God save a disorderly world, and the wild United Nations! . . .
And save us all: poets, Mongolians, landlords & ladies, mad
    musicians.

No matter what the subject of her poem—reeling exuberance or tragic
circumstance—we need to understand the willing engagement and pure
love that fuels Kizer's politics. That we should discover this in a woman
poet seems to me no accident. For women have long been the ones who
empathize with others, who "leap into otherness," in a culture where men
assume positions of distance and control. If anyone can bring politics
back to poetry, can transform the political so that it becomes personal, it
is the woman poet whose subjectivity is already defined by otherness. In
her poem "The Death of the Public Servant,"[15] which has all the trappings
of a classical panegyric, Kizer transforms an unknown public figure into a
personal friend. She speaks to this Canadian ambassador who committed
suicide because of charges that he was a communist. She brings the polit-
ical tragedy close to her, and close to us. "This is the day when good men
die from windows," she says, and then addresses him directly—"Now
you, in Cairo." Her public commentary echoes out beyond the personal:

Once there was a place for gentle heroes.
Now they are madmen who, scuttling down corridors,
Eluding guards, climb lavatory walls

And squeeze through air-vents to their liberation. . . .

But Kizer's public message is never far from her personal voice, the voice that makes it all meaningful for her, for us, for the rooms and worlds we live in far away from Cairo:

> I mark the fourth of April on this page,
> When the sun came up and glittered on the windows
> As you fell away from daylight into heaven:
> The muck of Cairo, and a world silenced forever.
> A poet, to whom no one cruel or imposing listens,
> Disdained by senates, whispers to your dust:
> Though you escape from words, whom words pursued,
> Take these to your shade: of rage, of grief, of love.

The message is again one of love. Without that, there's no place for politics in poetry. There's no place for politics at all, unless we believe that all public actions take place in a world of suspicion, hatred, death. If the poet does not leap into the political, then she is doomed to the position of outsider, mocking and criticizing a world which poetry shuns.

Kizer does not do that. Sending "Lines to Accompany Flowers for Eve,"[16] a woman "who took heroin, then sleeping pills / and who lies in a New York hospital," Kizer now makes the personal political, forcing us to merge these two experiences which are both at the heart of this tragedy:

> But what has flung you here for salvaging
> From a city's dereliction, this New York?
> A world against whose finger-and-breath marked windows
> These weak flares may be set.

The question is addressed to Eve, for we want to know why she took the drugs, the pills. But the question is also addressed to all of us, who make our marks on the same kind of windows, seek the same kinds of escape. For we all need to answer such questions if we are ever to understand why. Just as surely as Kizer has entered this poem, we are all implicated in its politics. Closeness matters here in the poem, bringing us into the world of Cairo, New York—or a different New York where Kizer dreams of her friend Nicanor lost in Chile, and of her friend Barbara in Barcelona seeking

the right revolution, the right solution. In "October, 1973"[17] this dream
vaults Kizer into the world of the lost—where politics becomes so inter-
mixed with the personal loss that she can only dream of telephone con-
nections, revolutions, reunions. Kizer is there again, inside the poem,
picking up the phone to hear the personal voice:

> "Dear Carolyn . . . " It *is* Nicanor!
> And the connection is broken, because when I wake up,
> in this white room, in this white silence,
>   in this backwater of silence
> on this Isla Blanca:
>   Nicanor, Nicanor,
> are you, too, silent under the earth,
>   Brother? Brother?

The political is not only personal, it is familial. And how can it be other-
wise? Unless we see ourselves intimately related to these experiences,
then the world will always remain at a distance from the self. Such a sit-
uation has not only been tragic for women—keeping them outside the
realm of what "counts" as human events and history. It has been just as
damaging for poetry itself—separating it from the whirl of social activity in
which the lives of women and men take on meaning and value.

Since I have been arguing that Kizer's political aesthetics—her
engagement with otherness and with others, her insistence on mixing
together the personal and the social—is a feminist act, it only seems nat-
ural that the poem I consider crucial for an understanding of her feminist
politics is "Pro Femina."[18] It is crucial in two ways: first, for the way in
which parts one, two, and three unfold as a powerful social statement
expressed in traditional poetic form; and second, for the way in which part
four, "Fanny," merges the personal and political in recreating "one of the
world's best-kept secrets"—the life of Fanny Osbourne Stevenson while
she lived under the shadow of her husband.

There is something about the first three sections of "Pro Femina" that
reminds me of the spirit and tone of "Tying One On in Vienna." Both poems
are filled with wit and exuberance. Both contain powerful social com-
mentary. And Kizer herself is so much a part of both of them. If Kizer can
learn how to love the world and all its crazy empires in "Tying One On
in Vienna," then what she learns—and teaches us—in "Pro Femina" is that

we can also love ourselves as women, "I mean real women, like *you* and like *me*." Using and at the same time abusing the form of traditional satires directed against women, instead of speaking about women from the privileged position of the male poet, she speaks directly to them and with them—"losing our lipsticks, you, me, / In ephemeral stockings, clutching our handbags and packages." Infused in this feminine world, Kizer doesn't scowl from without or within, but celebrates and forgives. This is a "large" love poem, a love poem in the best social sense.

Of course there's a healthy dose of anger in this poem, an awareness of the "millions / Of mutes for every Saint Joan or sainted Jane Austen, / Who, vague-eyed and acquiescent, worshiped God as a man," or of "Our masks, always in peril of smearing or cracking, / In need of continuous check in the mirror of silverware. . . ." But for all this, the "fate" of women—much like the mad world Kizer contemplates in Vienna—is exuberantly crazy. "We *are* hyenas. Yes, we admit it," Kizer boasts. And with that boast comes just the kind of vibrant engagement that allows us to celebrate rather than shun this feminine world. It is crazy to think that millions of women have worshiped God as a man. It is crazy that we "primp, preen, prink, pluck and prize" our flesh for men who cover their "chicken wrists or meek shoulders" with "a formal, hard-fibered assurance." Once we see ourselves as part of all this, instead of outside and distanced, then and only then can we become involved in the process of transformation. To be political is to be part of, engaged in, the world in motion:

> Give us a few decades
> Of grace, to encourage the fine art of acquiescence
> And we might save the race. Meanwhile, observe our creative
>   chaos,
> Flux, efflorescence—whatever you care to call it!

It is this sense of "creative chaos" and "flux" that is at the heart of Kizer's political engagement. Writing in the tradition of political satires on women, she makes women come alive in the politics of her poem. For all of Kizer's admiration of Juvenal and Pope, her poetry is decidedly different. They criticize from a distance, she celebrates from within. They shun the otherness of woman, she leaps into it. The chaos they condemn is feminine, the feminine chaos she praises "might save the race." Perhaps Kizer's finest accomplishment as a social poet is that she has redirected the energies of classical verse. Bucking the misogynist tradition, yet all the while embracing its wit and liveliness, she brings women to life in the poetic domain. No longer the object of description and figuration, women become subjects of action and change—subjects who can create.

How can women create if they are confined within the dynamics of objectification? "I've been fascinated for many years," Kizer says, "about what women who are the support or nourishment of fathers, brothers, husbands, sons, do. What do these women—Wordsworth's sister, Lizst's sister, Alice James, etc., you name it—what do they do with their creativity if they're terribly creative people, as Fanny Osbourne Stevenson was?"[19] Kizer claims that the poem "Fanny," which she eventually attached to "Pro Femina," was the central part of her collection *Yin*. "I worked on that poem for many years, and I know that it was the focus of that book, the linchpin. . . . Whenever I was pregnant, I always wanted to stay pregnant as long as possible because I enjoyed it. In a sense I think that's true with poems, with the big poem."[20] It is curious, and I think very meaningful, that Kizer should link the issues of women's creativity with her own pregnant engagement with the poem "Fanny"—and that both of these issues would finally be linked in "Pro Femina." For it seems to me that Kizer's concern with women's creativity—"our creative chaos, / Flux, efflorescence"—is exactly what defines her feminist politics. Pregnancy means transformation and birth. To write the story of Fanny Osbourne Stevenson as though the writing itself were a kind of pregnancy is to give birth to this woman and her creativity—to the woman herself and to the work she does. And this, I suggest, is intensely political.

"Pro Femina" ends not simply with the story of a woman, but the story of her creativity, her work. "The curious thing about English feminism," Kizer says, "the interesting thing is, where's the work? I think the class system and masculine dominance is still so prevalent that everybody's still under it. I can't think of any other reason. But it's interesting that in a country like Nicaragua, for example, Ortega's wife is one of the most widely read poets in the country—Rosario."[21] Kizer's remarks are very similar to those of Lillian Robinson who, in putting together a collection of literature by and about working women, found "that the modern literary tradition is remote from the meanings of work in human life, and that poetry is particularly alienated from it." Such observations force Robinson to the conclusion that "feminist poetry's emphasis on the inwardness of individuals distorts the movement's basic perception that 'the personal is political'. . . ."[22] True enough, the personal is political. And yet, as Robinson insists, the political is also personal—and this is especially so for women who suffer the effects of legislation and social policy on such matters as divorce, property rights, and abortion. To keep these issues out of poetry is to keep the world of politics safely distanced from the personal lives of the very women affected by politics.

Fanny Osbourne Stevenson worked continually in Samoa, but it is only the work and writing of her husband, Robert Louis Stevenson, that is remembered or even acknowledged as work. The subject here is Fanny's personal life, but the larger issue is political. It concerns no less than the systematic, historical suppression of what women do and how they create. What did Fanny do? Kizer tells us: "what she did was plant." Asked if "planting" could be regarded as a central image in her poetry, Kizer responds "Oh, absolutely! Of course it's an intensely feminine thing."[23] Allowing Fanny to speak her experience, Kizer gives voice to this suppression:

> Louis has called me a peasant. How I brooded!
> Confided it to you, diary, then crossed it out.
> Peasant because I delve in earth, the earth I won.
> Confiding my seed and root—I too a creator?

If this poem is a tribute to Fanny's creativity, it is a savage indictment of male achievements that constitute the stuff of history. "No one else works much," Fanny says, and then adds, "Of course, RLS is not idle; he is writing *A Footnote to History:* / How the great powers combine to carve up these islands." Fanny, too, is a part of this colonial carving, regarded as a "peasant" by her husband—"Though Louis says he finds the peasant class 'interesting.'"

Through the description of Fanny's planting—the catalogue of potatoes, artichokes, corn, peas, onions, mint root, mangoes, rhubarb, asparagus, coffee, melons, cacao, rubber, sunflower, massio, citron, vanilla, gum, peanuts, grenadilla, ylang-ylang, pineapple—we get a sense of a creation far richer than anything history could record. The contrast between woman's and man's domain is all too clear: "Louis writes to *The Times* / Of 'the foul colonial politics.' I send to New York for seeds. . . . Louis' own seed, / *David Balfour*, is growing. I wrote nothing / From June till the end of this year; too busy planting." The planting, it would seem, is a mixed blessing: at once the source and productivity of her creativity, it is also her prison—like wild tropical growth caging her in. Of her diary, she says, "I stopped writing this. Too hysterical with migraine. / Also, people find where I hide it, and strike things out."

It is only after Louis' death that Fanny can understand what her planting was all about—"an intensely feminine thing," as Kizer would say, but an experience that consumed her in the nourishment of her husband's work. "I will leave here," Fanny says,

> I will live like a gipsy
> In my wild, ragged clothes, until I am old, old.
> I will have pretty gardens wherever I am,
> But never breadfruit, custard apples, grenadillas, cacao,
> Pineapple, ylang-ylang, citron, mango, cacao,
> Never again succumb to the fever of planting.

If planting is Fanny's life and work, the "fever of planting" is her fate as a woman whose work is devalued—despite its richness, its nourishment, its creative energy. This is not Fanny Osbourne Stevenson's personal problem. This is a problem that twists and blocks the creativity of every woman whose labor is regarded as peasant's work. Fanny is "wild" and will "live like a gipsy." She joins the ranks of Kizer's crazy women, "hyenas," who are beginning to know what their hysteria is all about. It *is* crazy that the most fertile work in the world—the work of women and peasants, the work of pregnancy, planting, and birth—is the very work that has been dismissed and ignored.

Kizer doesn't stand outside Fanny's personal world. Nor does she stand outside its politics, safely taking a position pro or con. She puts herself inside it. She makes women's poetry "large"—large in the same way that women's lives are far bigger and richer than any description of their personal plight can convey. Not content to find her own poetic voice, she leaps into the experience of others, takes on the world through a sympathetic, sometimes angry, often joyous engagement. In her poem "Singing Aloud,"[24] she describes her giving way, as she grows older, to singing—in the open, in public. The animals join her, squirrels and rabbits and birds. Song enlarges the world.

> When I go to the zoo, the primates and I, in communion
> Hoot at each other, or signal with earthy gestures.

We must move further out of town, we musical birds and animals
Or they'll lock us up like the apes, and control us forever.

Song enlarges the world. And so does poetry. We can't keep it to ourselves,
Kizer says, as a poet and a woman. She "can't get rid of the tempting tic
of pentameter, / Of the urge to impose form on what I can't understand, /
Or that which I have to transform because it's too grim as it is."

That urge to write and to transform—that is what makes Kizer's poetry
creative, generous, political. In "A Muse of Water,"[25] she takes back water
from the "Masters of Civilization" and returns it to women, to the "water-
carriers of our young / Till waters burst, and white streams flow / Artesian,
from the lifted breast." Transforming this maternal act into public manifesto,
she urges women:

Fasten the blouse, and mount the steps
From the kitchen taps to Royal Barge,
Assume the trident, don the crown. . . .

The message is as personal as childbirth, as political as the crown.
"Rejoice," she tells us, "when a faint music rises / Out of a brackish clump
of weeds." This music, flowing from women like water, enlarges the world.
And Carolyn Kizer is the "large lady" singing this music.

TEXTS CITED

Barbato, Joseph. "'Going Through Life with a Pencil': Carolyn Kizer." *Small Press*,
3 (November–December, 1985): pp. 54–58.

Johnson, Judith Emlyn. "Re/Membering the Goddess: Carolyn Kizer and the Poet-
ics of Generosity" [in this volume].

Kizer, Carolyn. "Alexander Pope: Clearing the Air Around a Giant." *San Jose Mer-
cury News* (August 17, 1986): pp. 21–23.

————. *Midnight Was My Cry*, (Garden City, New York: Doubleday & Company,
1971).

————. *Yin*, (Brockport, New York: BOA Editions, Ltd., 1984).

————. *Mermaids in the Basement*, (Port Townsend: Copper Canyon Press,
1984).

————. *The Nearness of You*, (Port Townsend: Copper Canyon Press, 1986).

Ozick, Cynthia. "The Moral Necessity of Metaphor: Rooting History in a Figure
of Speech." *Harper's* 272 (May 1986): pp. 62–68.

Rigsbee, David and Steven Ford Brown. "Not Their History but Our Myth: An Interview with Carolyn Kizer." *An Answering Music: On the Poetry of Carolyn Kizer*, (David Rigsbee, ed. Boston: Ford-Brown & Company, 1990): pp. 126–147.

Robinson, Lillian S. "The Keen Eye. . . . Watching: Poetry and the Feminist Movement" in *Sex, Class, & Culture*, (New York: Methuen, 1978): pp. 254–309.

NOTES

1. *The Nearness of You*, pp. 64–65, 70; *Yin*, p. 37.

2. Barbato, p. 58.

3. *Mermaids*, p. 44.

4. *Yin*, reprinted in *Mermaids*, p. 101–102.

5. See Johnson, this volume, pp. 97, 120.

6. *Yin*, pp. 26–27.

7. *Midnight*, pp. 66–67.

8. Robinson, p. 262.

9. *Ibid.*

10. Kizer, "Alexander Pope: Clearing the Air Around a Giant," p. 22.

11. *The Nearness of You*, pp.19–20.

12. Rigsbee, p. 135.

13. *Ibid.*

14. *The Ungrateful Garden*, reprinted in *The Nearness of You*, pp. 29–32.

15. *Ibid.*, pp. 23–24

16. *Midnight*, reprinted in *Mermaids*, pp. 36–37.

17. *Yin*, pp. 53–54.

18. Pts. I-III in *Knock Upon Silence*, pt. IV ("Fanny") in *Yin*, reprinted in *Mermaids*, pp. 41–51.

19. Rigsbee, p. 133.

20. *Ibid.*

21. *Ibid.*

22. Robinson, pp. 296, 301.

23. Rigsbee, p. 133.

24. *Midnight*, pp. 10–11.

25. *The Ungrateful Garden*, reprinted in *Mermaids*, pp. 104–105.

MARGARET RABB & JACKSON WHEELER

Kizer's Commandments:
Dicta for Student Writers

IS IT POSSIBLE to say that Carolyn Kizer burst onto our quiet campus in Chapel Hill, North Carolina, much like Athena from the brow of Zeus, fully armed with all necessary literary accoutrements and singing the virtues, visions and vices of poetry? To be mesmerized by the teaching power of Ms. Kizer was to be caught up not only in an intellectually brilliant, somewhat arcane world, but also in the deep humanity at the root of great poetry. The same poet dashing across the rain-dampened lawn in late spring with a huge spray of her own cut roses and a bottle of champagne to celebrate with her students—that would be us 25 years ago—could with her formidable gaze and incisive voice make us all regret that we had not memorized the entire works of Dickinson, Sappho, Catullus, Cavafy, Yeats, Roethke, Auden, Bishop. . . . To be Kizer's student was to be summoned on a very long journey of listening, reading, reciting—to be initiated in the tradition of poetry held both sacredly and profanely. As the beautiful, intimidating guardian at the border she provided us freely with passport and password (which would be spelled "friend" in "Poem for Your Birthday" collected in *Harping On*). All we had to do was work, work, work hard and then harder in the vineyard.

The Tuesday evenings when our honors workshop met at her home on Franklin Street were carefully orchestrated to provide us with experiences miles beyond most undergraduate classes in the seventies. Whenever he came through town from Princeton, we heard Edmund Keeley read his translations of Cavafy, so this voice became familiar and influential. Many

71

Tuesdays Reynolds Price joined us in the small sitting room with Mark Tobey paintings, speaking about narrative, the Bible, or dreaming his characters' dreams—often, amazingly, in response to something one of us had read. From her extraordinary range of poems consigned to memory, Kizer also connected our work with congruent, instructive passages of poems she knew by heart. Once a rather diffident young man delivered his ragged effort; then sweat stained his shirt and he flushed magenta as his lines evoked a long riff of "The Shropshire Lad."

This effect of carrying poetry in the memory was worth both the challenge and the grind; we came to understand that our ears simply had to be trained in cadence, pattern and meter. One evening on the spur of the moment we were asked to call up "Sailing to Byzantium" from our collective memories—and we almost made it. Kizer was also very clear about the importance of elocution and reading aloud, to reveal a weak line or awkward word in our own work. From her responses to our own dearly held failings and shortcomings, a few phrases of advice were repeated often enough to enter our late-adolescent brains and became touchstones for our futures: next line, next poem, next life.

KIZER'S COMMANDMENTS

- There is a difference between opacity and subtlety. Sometimes when we think we are being mysterious, we're merely imprecise.

- If you write about contemporary chaos, do it in a strict meter. The late critic Irving Ehrenpries said, "It's a mistake to write about chaos chaotically."

- Banish antiquities of locution, such as thee and thou, or inverted syntax, or you will have a poem that reeks of the lamp. Dr. Williams reminded us that we are Americans, not 19th-century English, and that we should write in the American idiom.

- Don't use gerunds if you can possibly help it, unless you want repeated –ing's to indicate the tolling of a bell. People think if they use gerunds, it conveys continuing action, or suspended animation, but figure out a way to indicate continuing action by other means. (A smart student said, "What about 'Turning and turning in the widening gyre'?" and Kizer replied, "When you can write as well as Yeats, you don't need to be in this class.")

- Avoid passive constructions. They weaken the poem. Read the masters of active and unusual verbs, from Henry Vaughan to Stanley Kunitz. (Another smart student said, "What about 'To be or not to be'?" and Carolyn answered, "In this case the passive verbs indicate Hamlet's own passivity and indecision, which are at the heart of the play."

- All poets occasionally steal lines, whether consciously or unconsciously, but if you know your sources acknowledge them and pay your debts.

- One reason the Columbia graduate writing program is so good is that you must know a second language; or they will admit you if you have the rudiments of another language and work to improve it. Translating is a wonderful help in learning the possibilities of your own language. Also, it helps stave off writer's block. If you're having a dry spell, just tell yourself you're going into your translation mode.

- Read, read, read. I am shocked to find out how many poets rarely read anybody other than themselves. Become familiar with the Bible and the Psalms, and the unrevised version of the Book of Common Prayer, until its cadences live in your ear.

- Memorize, memorize, memorize!

- Spondees: you can tell a natural-born poet by her instinctive use of the spondee.

- Try all the old forms at least once: the sonnet, the villanelle, the pantoum, the sestina. You don't have to publish them, but you will learn how to discipline your line. We must learn the rules before we can break them.

- Accuracy: if you're writing about the natural world, make sure your information is correct. Just because Yeats didn't know the names of any flowers is no excuse for you. For example, read Fabre's *Life of the Bee* until you're sure that if you're writing about bees you know what you're talking about.

- Revision: A good substitute for a poetry workshop is a bureau drawer. Stick an unsatisfactory poem in a drawer and don't look at it for three to six months.

- Take all the adjectives out of a poem. Usually, you'll find it improved. Then restore only the absolutely necessary ones, like a color, for example.

- Try the poem in different forms. For example, if the stanza has five lines, force it into triplets or couplets. Poetry is not like sculpture. You can always knock off an arm or a leg and put it back. Try taking out a line from each verse, or adopting an arbitrary form which demands that you tighten the poem.

- Try different pronouns. Experiment with moving from I to you or they. Study Yannis Ritsos's poem, "Women." He changes pronouns every two or three lines. The poem begins with "They," moves to "you," then to "she," and back to "you" at the end. By shifting from one pronoun to another, he moves the action of the poem closer to the reader, then to a little distance, ending up close again. This leads to a kind of filmic technique of quick cutting and montage, all in ten lines.

- Don't be in such an all-fired hurry to publish. A good poem will probably outlast you!

We've lived more now, but probably not enough. Some mistakes are easy to stop, but as soon as we are sure we don't have a single -ing form in the entire manuscript we send her, Kizer will read it and suggest adding a few. *What?* we say, stunned by the heresy. Other mistakes have to be repeated over and over. We were fortunate enough to arrive at Carolyn Kizer's house each week for a full academic year. She brought us in the door and pointed us in the direction of our own lives, whispered passwords into the world she has so ardently championed where poetry and experience are one and the same. With her poems and her sustaining presence in our lives during the last three decades, never once giving up on us, Carolyn Kizer continues to give us her distilled wisdom, brilliant wit and amazing courage.

ROBERT PHILLIPS

Larger Than Life:
Mythology and Carolyn Kizer

IN AN INTERVIEW with David Rigsbee and Steven Ford Brown, Carolyn Kizer spoke of the poet Louise Bogan's ability to distance herself from the kind of sentimental love-and-loss poem which men of a previous generation (critics, anthologists, teachers) expected women to write. Kizer cited Bogan's Cassandra poem and her Medusa poem as two examples of how that poet disguised her own feelings by naming them after figures in Greek mythology. "Medusa" seems a poem about stasis, and Bogan suffered terrible writing blocks. The Cassandra poem is about childlessness, though Bogan did have one daughter. (*An Answering Music*, p. 127)

Bogan certainly was aware of this method of composition. In her discussion of Eliot's "The Waste Land" in her *Achievement in American Poetry*, she cites F.O. Matthiessen on Eliot's use of the recurring pattern in various myths, the basic resemblance, for example, "between the vegetation myths of the rebirth of the year, the fertility myths of the rebirth of potency in men, the Christian story of the Resurrection and the Grail legend of purification." (*Achievement in American Poetry*, pp. 74–5)

While Kizer recognized the method in Bogan's work, this is not how she employs myths in her own poems. For one thing, Kizer has been much more "confessional" than Bogan, dealing with her personal problems with unusual frankness. She has written of childhood difficulties and soured love affairs, in poems which are candid examinations of private distress. Further, Kizer is a poet of direct statement, as opposed to Bogan's indirection. Kizer's "Pro Femina" poems, at least the first three of them, are early precursors of Feminist writing and evidence of her poetry of engagement. Later work includes poems against segregation, against the war in Saigon, and against the logging of the redwoods. She has appeared in benefit readings for various freedom causes. By comparison, Bogan writes in code.

Why would a poet so in the world, and of the world, resort to ancient myths and archetypal patterns? One reason is biographical. Kizer attended Sarah Lawrence College, where she studied with Joseph Campbell, a member of the literature faculty. Campbell is the author of the four-volume study of world mythologies, collectively titled *The Masks of God*, and a study of the composite hero (Apollo, the Frog-king, Wotan, Buddha, and many other protagonists of folklore and religion who enact simultaneously the various phases of their common character). It was Campbell who instructed Kizer to bypass accepted versions of myths (versions usually made by males to enforce the male point of view), and to go back to the originals. For instance, Athena springs from the ground in the early version, not from the head of Zeus. This later revision is perhaps an example of womb-envy.

In conversation with the present writer, Kizer has stated that one cannot overemphasize the importance to her work of Campbell's teachings and writing, and the retelling of the Greek myths by Robert Graves (*The Greek Myths*, 1955). Graves assembled all the scattered elements of each myth into one harmonious narrative. He also noted the numerous variants, which may help to determine the myth's ritual or historical meaning. But he also tended to attribute all myths to merely historic origins, which is shortsighted.

Another reason Kizer employs myth could be psychological, to ratify our social customs and human behavior, probing the deeper truths behind our collective attitudes toward fundamental matters of life, death, parenting, and existence.

Still a third reason might be physiological—her own sense of being larger than life, of being of mythic proportions. Her "So Big: An Essay on Size" is a good-humored but serious look at being a large woman. Not one who is circumferentially challenged, but one over five feet ten inches tall in her bare feet—and she usually wears high heels. "I look, as I've often remarked, like a road-company Valkyrie . . .". The essay shows an identification with the White Goddess. (*Proses*, p. 115) As set forth in Graves's study, *The White Goddess* (1948), that would include a belief in an all-important religion, rooted in the remote past but continuing into our time, based on the worship of a goddess, one of whose manifestations is The Muse, to whom (in Graves's opinion), the true poet directs his or her verses.

I can attest that Kizer *looks* like The White Goddess. On the evening of Friday, April 22, 1988, I accompanied her to the Seventy-eighth Annual Dinner and Awards Ceremony of the Poetry Society of America. The occasion was her receiving the Robert Frost Medal. She entered the room wearing a Grecian-looking dress of flowing white chiffon. The White Goddess indeed. And it is a fact that when Kizer was living in Chapel Hill, a letter was delivered to her by the U.S. Post Office addressed simply to,

THE WHITE GODDESS
CHAPEL HILL, N. C.

And it was intended for her.

While she has produced poems on Semele, Persephone, Venus and other female mythic figures, the first poem in Kizer's first book *The Ungrateful Garden* (1961) is a retelling of the Midas story. Kizer's version varies from the widely-known one. As told by Ovid, Edith Hamilton, and others, Midas's request that everything he touch turn to gold backfires the first time he attempts to eat a meal. Midas's meat turns into a lump of metal, his cup of mead becomes solid gold. Thus through his greed he would perish for lack of food and drink. Symbolically, gold may have been chosen by the myth-makers not only for its intrinsic value, but also because it is the metal that does not corrode, and hence symbolizes immortality, the state of which Midas has deprived himself. But in Kizer's version only the out-of-doors is cursed:

Within, the golden cup is good
To heft, to sip the yellow mead.
Outside, in summer's rage, the rude
Gold thorn has made his fingers bleed.

Midas concludes that "Nature is evil," refusing to acknowledge that it is his own stupidity and avarice which have created his situation. Fred Chappell rightfully says this new reading of the old myth is "about the human incapacity to engage with nature in nature's terms." It now becomes a reading of modern man in his transformed environment ("Mother Wit:

Humor in Carolyn Kizer's Poetry," Rigsbee, p. 65). The poem's title also becomes ironic. It is not the garden which is ungrateful, but man and mankind, who have polluted our Edenic garden. Such a reading is consistent with Kizer's poem "The Suburbans," in the same collection, in which she describes a landscape where

> Used-car and drive-in movie lots alike
> Enaisle and regulate the gaudy junk
> That runs us, in a "park" that is no park . . .

Another mythic poem, "Hera, Hung from the Sky," portrays that deity throwing everything away in a moment of arrogance and power, driven by "the dream / That woman was great as man—" And despite her loss, Kizer's Hera does not seem overly regretful. She had suffered much resentment over having a lesser role than that of her lord, and she had resented his condescending praise. She feels her challenge to the order of things was worth the consequence. If she has lost the war of the air, at least she has created a skirmish for Feminism. Like Persephone, in "Persephone Pauses," Hera casts her spirit to the air. Both Hera and Persephone suffer mighty falls, and accept the fact that women can't win all battles. The Biblical Lot's wife suffers no better. These are not only figures from the myth-kitty of world literature; they also are figures of Kizer's view of the role of women throughout the ages, a subject examined in "A Muse of Water," a poem in which women act against their true intimate nature, are strained by labor, and serve as mere cup-bearers to tiny gods,

> Imperious table-pounders, who
> Are final arbiters of thirst.

(These muses suffer much, as does Kizer's selfless Fanny Osbourne Stevenson at the hands of Robert Louis Stevenson, who told her she had "the soul of a peasant." Fanny abandoned her own writing to keep Stevenson alive another eight years. Kizer's poem on this subject took its place as part four of "Pro Femina," a specific section on the fate of women following three generalized ones.)

Knock Upon Silence (1965) moved from the world of mythology to that of Oriental poetry, with sections devoted to poems based on Chinese classical works, translations of Tu Fu, and a diary with poems using the Japanese haibun form. Not much Greek mythology here. However, the original three sections of "Pro Femina" are collected, and in them Kizer addresses the sainthood of Joan of Arc and the life of Jane Austen, as well as those millions of mute or inarticulate females for every articulate Joan and Jane. The myths of Joan of Arc and Jane Austen perhaps are rationalist rather than cosmic beliefs. But they take their place in Kizer's gallery of larger-than-life women.

With her third collection, *Midnight Was My Cry: New and Selected Poems* (1971), Kizer again made forays into ancient myths. The book's title comes from one of the earliest-known blues songs by a New Orleans hooker in the 1870s or 1890s. Her name is unknown. The full phrase goes,

Midnight was my cry
Before death was my creep.

A "creep" is a pimp, and so again from the title forward, the book deals with the victimization of a female by a male. Unfortunately Kizer does not acknowledge the source or the meaning of her title, so few would know. (John Lomax collected New Orleans blues songs and deposited them in the Smithsonian Institution, where Kizer read them.)

In "The Copulating Gods," one of Kizer's fornicators is called club-footed and the other accused of being nymphomaniacal. They are also one poet having an affair with another poet, poets being by nature "super people" and egocentric. As Richard Howard has written, Kizer's couple are also "rather human beings who can speak so . . . only when they are caught in some energy of apprehension, some fit of facture which transcends the fatal et cetera of things." (*Preferences*, p. 148) Kizer's poem concludes, "I know we are not their history, but our myth." The poem was influenced by her admiration for Mark Alexander Boyd (1563–1601) and his "Venus and Cupid." Later Kizer was to publish her own translation of this poem from the Scots, as "Cupid and Venus." (She reversed the order of figures in the title upon the suggestion of editor Ben Sonnenberg.) The poem addresses the impossibility of following love and expecting it to lead you anywhere. Cupid is a bum with a white cane and Venus is a dame "who roars like a rhino as she comes and comes."

Such demythologization is carried over into "The Dying Goddess," in which the lure of Venus is seen as dissipating in our time, and also in "The Old Gods," a poem written after Heine:

The gold green gods who ruled the world in joy,
Now abdicated, crowded out,
Parading through the midnight wastes of heaven . . .

"Wastes" is the operative word here. Written in the voice of a man, pre-
sumably Heine himself, the poem expresses sympathy for the lost god-
desses and dispossessed gods who have been beaten down. The speaker
will take his chance on the side of the losers.

"Voyager" is an attempt to create a combination of all the great quest
myths—*The Aeneid, The Odyssey, Metamorphoses, The Adventure of
Prince Five-weapons* among them. This clearly is a strategy learned from
Campbell. Such archetypal searches, in Kizer's view, end in total futility.
By writing about the vaingloriousness of such male pursuits at the expense
of their faithful Penelopes and children, Kizer may be evoking autobio-
graphical elements. Her prose writings show that she herself virtually
was brought up by her mother, her father being so distant. In "Thrall" she
speaks of a father who

. . . will read for years without looking up
Until your childhood is over . . .

See also "My Good Father," the prose memoir in *The Nearness of You*
(1986), pp. 61–71. There Kizer speaks of "that stranger, his child," and
confesses that for the first six years of her life, her father spoke of her as
"Mabel's baby"—a parthenogenetic attitude to be sure. Kizer also
describes herself as being "a verbally battered" child.

Kizer's fullest exploration of male exploitation of the female came in
Yin (1984), the book which won her the Pulitzer Prize. "Semele Recycled"
is the soliloquy of the daughter of Cadmus and Harmonia after she has
been abandoned by a lover. Again Kizer takes great liberties with
accepted versions of the mythic source, for reasons which will be
presently discussed. Rather than suffering obliteration from the awful glory
of burning light generated when Zeus reveals himself as King of Heaven
and Lord of the Thunderbolt, Semele instead symbolically is broken into
pieces, with all the pieces flung into the river. Use is found for every dis-
card: the torso becomes a canoe, the arms are paddles, the legs become
a roadside shrine, and so forth. Only the heart goes unused, symboli-
cally—a man takes what he wants and disregards the woman's heart. At

the poem's conclusion Semele is reassembled. Yet all is not totally well. Her inner parts remember

> fermenting hay,
> the comfortable odor of dung, the animal incense,
> and passion, its bloody labor,
> its birth and rebirth and decay.

In short, the woman has paid for her resurrection, including bloody labor and spiritual and physical decay. The man in the poem gets away, as they say, Scot-free. Their lovemaking is cheered by the villagers, who are unaware of her past. The poem is about the rebirth of love, but more importantly, about the reconstruction of the female psyche—at a terrible price. When a woman summarily is dismissed by a man, she must overcome her humiliation and literally pull herself together. As Lady Mary Wortley Montagu wrote in "A Caveat to the Fair Sex," a poem Kizer knows well because she anthologized it, "You must be proud, if you'll be wise."

In private conversation with the present writer, Kizer has revealed the inspiration for this poem. It came to her after she'd had minor surgery. She had the thought that it is women who have parts of themselves dismembered, not men. It was Semele who was taken apart, not Zeus or Dionysus. Instead of perishing before the unveiled glory of Zeus—a male sexist notion if ever there were one—Kizer has intuitively conjured up an Urmyth representative of the plight of women. She took the Semele story and stood it on its head.

Kizer's collection *Harping On* (1996) is wonderfully named, connoting both the lyre of Apollo Musagetes—who wears a laurel wreath and leads the chorus of Muses—and The Harpies, those frightful flying creatures with hooked beaks and claws, who always leave behind them a loathsome stench when encountering the Argonauts and others. It is a fact that certain misogynists refer to strong women as Harpies. Since there is no poem in the volume or in the Kizer canon titled "Harping On," I assumed she chose the title for its attendant ironies. There is even a third meaning of hanging onto things, not letting go, persistently nagging. Like Kizer on Feminist themes, some might say.

The book contains only one truly mythic poem, "Fearful Women" (harpies?), in which Kizer exhorts the reader to "Mythologize your women! None escape. / Europe was named from an act of bestial rape."

She reminds us Zeus "refused to take the rap." The poem's allusions range from Europa to Eve to Helen of Troy to Darby's Joan to Saint Joan (once again). Addressing males in general, the poet announces,

> Whether we wield a scepter or a mop
> It's clear you fear that we may get on top.
>
> And if we do—I say it without animus—
> It's not from you we learned to be magnanimous.

Attention should be paid to Kizer's tone here. It is playful and chiding, not strident like Robin Morgan and much of Sylvia Plath. Unlike Plath, Kizer would never call her father a bastard; she would merely point out he didn't know how to act around children. She achieves her goal of defending Feminism without ascending the soapbox or descending to name-calling. "I don't ever want to be hortatory or propagandistic," she told one interviewer (*The Hollins Critic*, June 1997).

Not all her mythic subjects come from myths and legends of the ancient Western world. Some poems are based on legendary mortal contemporaries—Albert Einstein, chosen for his legendary brilliance; Ann London, for her movie-star look. And while equal rights for "one-half of humanity" is one of her central causes, sociopolitics is hardly her single interest. She has many strings on her harp. The quality of women's life is equally as interesting to her as political correctness, as a poem such as "The Blessing" reveals, ranging across three generations of women. Mother-daughter relationships, female and male friendships, manhood, Chinese culture, change and transfiguration in nature, the world of dreams, and the art of translation are just a few of her other subjects and passions. As John L'Heureux has written, "She is a first-class poet; the Greeks would have built her a temple."

SECONDARY SOURCES CITED

Bogan, Louise. *Achievement in American Poetry, 1900–1950*. Chicago: Henry Regnery Company, 1951.

Graves, Robert. *The White Goddess: A Historical Grammar of Poetic Myth*. Garden City: Doubleday & Company, 1948.

Howard, Richard. *Alone With America: Essays on the Art of Poetry in the United States Since 1950*. Enlarged Edition. New York: Atheneum, 1980.

_____. *Preferences: 51 American Poets Choose Poems from Their Own Work & from the Past*. With photographs by Thomas Victor. New York: Viking Press, 1974.

Howells, Georgina. "Carolyn Kizer," *The Hollins Critic*, XXXIV, 3 (June 1997), 11.

Kizer, Carolyn. Conversations with Robert Phillips. Oct. 1999.

_____. *Proses: On Poems and Poets*. Port Townsend: Copper Canyon Press, 1993.

_____. *100 Great Poems by Women*. Hopewell, NJ: Ecco Press, 1995.

Rigsbee, David. *An Answering Music: On the Poetry of Carolyn Kizer*. Boston: Ford-Brown & Company, 1990.

ANNIE FINCH

Carolyn Kizer and the Chain of Women

IT IS THE MARK of a certain point in a young writer's development—arguably the onset of true literary maturity—when she looks up from the eclectic, sprawling collection of classic and contemporary influences she has been ostensibly pulling together for herself for many years, takes a long breath, and is struck by the depth of her indebtedness to a much smaller group of writers. Such a revelation happened to me recently regarding Carolyn Kizer. Since Kizer is approaching her 75th birthday and ready for some long-deserved appreciation, this essay pays tribute to her unique role in American women's poetry. After all, where would I, as a woman poet who feels a close connection to her foremothers in the art, be—and where would so many of us be—without the passionate figure of Carolyn Kizer to link us with our past as women poets?

Kizer might not place herself among the writers she so unforgettably dubbed, in "Pro Femina," "the toast-and-teasdales we loved at thirteen." But she has earned a unique place in my personal canon just because of her sometimes ambivalent but always powerful relationship with such writers. Her poems meet me in the twenty-first century while simultaneously linking me back through a long tradition of emotionally astute, poetically exacting, passionate women poets that includes Phillis Wheatley, Frances Osgood, Emily Dickinson, Alice Dunbar Nelson, Sara Teasdale, Edna St. Vincent Millay, Anna Hampstead Branch, Louise Bogan, and Leonie Adams. Though the exquisitely crafted and classically controlled work of such poets is now beginning to earn a well-deserved reconsideration, it is still a legacy fraught with ambivalence for Kizer, as for most women poets. Responsibility to these poets' concerns has remained a crucial element of Kizer's aesthetic at the same time that awareness of their limitations has spurred her to refute and surpass them.

This powerful tradition of women poets built successful careers writing formal, accessible poems about spiritual and political as well as domestic and emotional themes. I call their techniques "sentimentist" to distinguish them from the more familiar, very different techniques of the romantic poets. Independently of romanticism and modernism, the sentimentists developed and explored their own poetic traditions and techniques: they wrote of a shared, accessible world from an often diffused, uncentered point of view, and they tended to metaphorize the self, instead of nature or a loved one, in their lyrics. As the decades went on and women's positions improved, early twentieth-century sentimentists adapted many of their precedessors' techniques to more powerful and independent attitudes and themes.

But at mid-century the chain broke. The poems of Bishop and Moore preserved some aspects of the sentimentist tradition into the 1970s, in a form so altered by the complex ironic stances of modernism that in their hands the tradition lost much of its original character. Plath and Sexton, both of whom guiltily admired the sentimentist women poets in their youth, died too young ever to admit it. Feminist poets who came of age in the 60s and 70s distanced themselves from the poetesses because of their subject matter, not to mention their form. Finally, in the postmodern climate of the 80s and 90s, the hermetic tradition of Stein and H.D. pushed the sentimentists even further distant on the basis of their accessibility, while the intimate connections between Dickinson and the central thread of women's poetry continued to be ignored.

In the five decades following New Criticism the classic tradition of women's poetry had been torn apart. As Gilbert and Gubar explain in their essay "Forward Into the Past," the price of poetic success for any woman after mid-century has been to despise virtually all pre-twentieth poetry by women, ignoring the intriguing affinities between Dickinson, not to mention H.D. and Stein, and the sentimentists. Yet, in such a climate of uncompromising obliviousness to the serious accomplishments of the vast bulk of women poets, Carolyn Kizer has consistently acknowledged and drawn on the legacy of the women poets who came before her. Kizer's allusions to her foremothers evoke, as often as not, anger, embarrassment, and pain.

Nonetheless, she has kept this irreplaceable inheritance alive, and when the full story of women's poetry has been reclaimed, Kizer's importance as a poet should begin to be even more widely understood.

The complexity of Kizer's relationship to the sentimentists often forces her to play two different roles in some of her poems, as in her description of the "toast-and-teasdales" in "Pro Femina":

> I will speak about women of letters, for I'm in the racket . . .
> Our biggest successes to date? Old maids to a woman.
> And our saddest conspicuous failures? The married spinsters
> On loan to the husbands they treated like surrogate fathers.
> Think of that crew of self-pitiers, not very distant,
> Who carried the torch for themselves and got first-degree burns.
> Or the sad sonneteers, toast-and-teasdales we loved at thirteen;
> Middle-aged virgins seducing the puerile anthologists
> Through lust-of-the-mind; barbituate-drenched Camilles
> With continuous periods, murmuring softly on sofas
> When poetry wasn't a craft but a sickly effluvium,
> The air thick with incense, musk, and emotional blackmail.

Kizer's description here leads to an attack on sentimentists like Teasdale and Millay, both childless, married to older businessman husbands, and eventually suicidal. Yet the number of lines that Kizer devotes to these "conspicuous failures" shows how impossible it is for her to ignore them completely, and her tirade incorporates a note of compassion for the sentimentists who, in attempting to combine heterosexual love with artistic creativity, succeeded only in earning our contempt:

> Impugning our sex to stay in good with the men,
> Commencing their insecure bluster. How they must have
>   swaggered
> When women themselves endorsed their own inferiority!
> Vestals, vassals and vessels, rolled into several,
> They took notes in rolling syllabics, in careful journals,
> Aiming to please a posterity that despises them.

Section 3 of "Pro Femina" ends with a forthright assertion of Kizer's distance from the sentimentists:

But we're emerging from all that, more or less,
Except for some lady-like laggards and Quarterly priestesses
Who flog men for fun, and kick women to maim competition.
Now, if we struggle abnormally, we may almost seem normal;
If we submerge our self-pity in disciplined industry;
If we stand up and be hated, and swear not to sleep with editors;
If we regard ourselves formally, respecting our true limitations
Without making an unseemly show of trying to unfreeze our assets,
Keeping our heads and our pride while remaining unmarried;
And if wedded, kill guilt in its tracks when we stack up the dishes
And defect to the typewriter. And if mothers, believe in the luck of
    our children,
Whom we forbid to devour us, whom we shall not devour,
And the luck of our husbands and lovers, who keep free women.

This conclusion, with its ironic last line, shows Kizer taking up an almost entirely new position from where the sentimentists left off. But it ignores the issue of how such overwhelming change happened in the culture at large—as well as the even more germane issue of how such necessary change can happen and will continue to happen in poetry.

How can a poet like Kizer manage to reclaim the tradition of her circumscribed, neglected literary foremothers without compromising her own strength? The poems themselves can best answer these questions. In "Bitch," for instance, the speaker takes the image of a bitch literally during a scene where she encounters an ex-lover. This inner "bitch," whom the speaker takes very firmly in hand but cannot ignore, might share some characteristics with the stereotypical lovelorn poetess:

At a kind word from him, a look like the old days,
the bitch changes her tone: she begins to whimper.
She wants to snuggle up to him, to cringe.
Down, girl! Keep your distance
Or I'll give you a taste of the choke-chain . . .

The bitch, who is "too demonstrative, too clumsy, / Not like the well-groomed pets of his new friends," "gags" at her mistress's polite hypocrisy while being "dragged off by the scruff," and the poem ends on a note of grudging respect for her.

Another poem, "Dream of a Large Lady," deals with another senti-mentist feminine shadow-figure, a large lady who receives a note from another lady remarking, in poetess-y diction, "I am an admirer of your poesy." In response, the large lady resigns herself to poetess-like behavior:

"Do come to my house near the bay, . . .
we will sit here quietly, in twilight,
and drink a cup of carefully brewed tea."

But nonetheless she cannot forget the fact that her original mission was to destroy a large mounted gun; though she was only able "to decorate and not destroy" it, "clear in her eye she holds a vision: / the thin ceremonious shell" of the egg she left on the gun emplacement. The poesy-loving lady and the poet who has left the egg, a potent symbol of literal and symbolic female fertility, are closer than it appears, since the poet's choice of the egg as sub-versive weapon draws directly on the poetesses' explicit female identifica-tion. The symbolism of "Dream of a Large Lady" offers a clue as to how Kizer has reconciled herself with the sentimentist tradition by acknowledging its power, thus strengthening her own ability to develop beyond it.

On the deepest level of archetypal themes, then, Kizer is interested in reconnecting with the basic female powers—and the sentimentist tradi-tion offers a direct, if compromised, connection with those powers. Sen-timentists like Helen Hunt Jackson or Lydia Sigourney explored themes of feminized nature and a Native American spirituality, and Kizer draws strength from the close connection of these traditions with nature. Natural power in Kizer's poetry is often exaggerated, as in the fecund gardens in the "Fanny" section of "Pro Femina" or the maimed goddesses of "Semele Recycled" and "Hera, Hung from the Sky." Even the title of Kizer's first vol-ume, *The Ungrateful Garden,* suggests on one level an uneasy relation with the view of nature she had inherited from the sentimentists. But Kizer's stories of grief and defeat, outspoken as they are, descend from the sentimentists' depressed laments. Like their precedessor poems from Christina Rossetti's "Song" to Louise Bogan's "Medusa," they are elegies for the loss of female power. The depressed and victimized voices that Kizer mocks in "Pro Femina" were self-directed distortions of anger. Kizer's martyred Hera and dismembered but ultimately triumphant Semele make the sentimentists' historic anger and oppression more con-scious and outer-directed, building on and transforming tradition.

Kizer's ambivalent relation to the most traditional, domestic themes of the sentimentists leads to some of her most amusing and ironic work, and a number of her more serious poems treat relationships between female friends and between mothers and daughters, traditional subjects of the sentimentists. She offers cutting, delicious satire of domestic themes in poems such as "Children" ("the orange crayon that didn't dare write, 'I hate you',") or "Mud Soup" ("Chop the onions, chop the carrots, / chop the tender index finger . . . "). Even Kizer's grouping of poems during the 1980s into two collections aimed at women and men (*The Nearness of You: Poems for Men* and *Mermaids in the Basement: Poems for Women*) evokes the way poems by many sentimentists, Dickinson included, arose out of and for a community of actual people and their emotional relationships.

Not only Kizer's themes, but her poetic strategies themselves are influenced by the sentimentists and throw their tradition into clearer relief. The distinctive voice of "Bitch" and "Threatening Letter," for instance, owes much to the bitter archness of Millay. The persona poem "Afterthoughts of Donna Elvira" uses the form and tone of the sentimentist tradition to arrive at a philosophy characteristic of many early twentieth-century sentimentists: "Whenever we love, we win, / Or else we have never been born." More surprisingly, the remarkable poem "In the First Stanza," based on a 12th-century Chinese women's poem, transforms the poet's self into a natural landscape in the exact manner of a sentimentist such as Sara Teasdale, who in turn was building on the self-transforming technique of earlier sentimentists such as Lydia Sigourney:

first, I tell you who I am:
shadowed, reflective, small
pool in an unknown glade . . .

—Kizer

I am the pool of blue
That worships the vivid sky . . .

—Teasdale

You know me as turbulent ocean
Full of thunder and drama. . . .

—Kizer

I am a wave that cannot reach the shore, . . .

                    —Teasdale

In the third stanza, I die . . .
I beg you to travel my body
till you find the forest glade . . .

                    —Kizer

When I go back to earth . . .
If men should pass above . . .
My dust will find a voice
To answer them aloud . . .

                    —Teasdale

Kizer's poem builds on and develops the key sentimentist technique of self-transformation with an ironic tone and a capaciously surrealistic structure. She answers her foremothers in homage and defiance, heightening and intensifying the grotesqueness and pathos of the poetesses' traditional ways of self-transformation.

"A Muse of Water," the poem Kizer chose to conclude *Mermaids in the Basement,* is a manifesto, a defense of the woman poet whose brimming creativities have been drained by centuries of service as muse, not to mention mother:

So flows in dark caves, dries away,
What would have brimmed from bank to bank,
Kissing the fields you turned to stone,
Under the boughs your axes broke.
And you blame streams for thinning out,
Plundered by man's insatiate want?

In the ironic tradition of female apologia such as Anne Bradstreet's "Prologue," "A Muse of Water" concludes with an ironically humble threat:

Here the warm shallows lave your feet
Like tawny hair of magdalens.
Here, if you care, and lie full-length,
Is water deep enough to drown.

Women have been robbed of their deepest inspirational power, but nonetheless, they hold depths capable of drowning a man who comes to them for inspiration, either as poet seeking a muse, or as reader seeking poetry—and it doesn't take much depth to drown a man. In this conclusion, Kizer turns a Bradstreet-like act of self-deprecation into a chilling and bitter taunt that is also a triumphant assertion of the survival of women's poetry.

At a time when works by women are reprinted most often out of a sense of historical curiosity, Kizer compiled her eclectic little book called *100 Great Poems by Women* only in the name of poetic excellence, editing a true poet's anthology. Among Kizer's hundred are poems reflecting her own taste for satire and political verse, such as Anne Finch's "Trail All Your Pikes" and Sarah Cleghorn's famous and bitter quatrain "The golf links lie so near the mill / That almost every day / The laboring children can look out / And see the men at play"; poems that, like some of Kizer's finest, celebrate friendships between women; and a number of excellent poems that protest women's social and political position over the centuries.

Ever the anti-Teasdale, Kizer made a conscious decision to showcase poems on "gender-neutral" topics: "this anthology is bent on showing what women can write about besides romance and domesticity." But she does not hesitate to include a type of verse that is generally much more devalued these days: public poetry. Kizer's anthology juxtaposes familiar chestnuts, including Emma Lazarus's "The New Colossus," Felicia Hemans's "Stately Homes of England," and Julia Ward Howe's "Battle Hymn of the Republic," with surprising gems from much obscurer writers, many of them anonymous or pseudonymous.

After decades of reading and loving women's poetry, I can honestly say that reading through Kizer's anthology gave me the most palpable sense I have had of how many, many, many women have written poems before me, and with what seriousness, variety, and skill. This is not surprising in view of Kizer's relation with the sentimentist tradition. I am grateful that of all contemporary women poets, she was the one to edit this book, just as I am grateful to her for keeping alive for me a link with women's poetic past. As a younger woman poet who has grown to be nourished by the women's poetic tradition daily, I can't imagine what my own work would be like if Kizer had not had the courage to embrace that tradition in all its sorrow, irony, and desire to please, its beauty, responsibility, and strength.

FRED CHAPPELL

A Swift Education

MY MEMORY has acquired more sinkholes than the most porous acres of Florida, so that I cannot now recall the exact year Carolyn Kizer showed up on the doorstep of our funky, crowded little bungalow on Scott Avenue in Greensboro, North Carolina. Come to that, I can't recall where or how we first met. This was the 1960s; that much I'm certain of—unless it was the early 70s. Anyhow, there she stood and she informed Susan and me that she had come to stay a few days.

We were delighted to see her. A glamorous and formidable figure, she loomed in the hard, hot sunlight tall and erect, even though she carried a large suitcase in each hand. "Here," I said. "Let me." But when I took the case she proffered, I nearly fell over into her. That case must have weighed a solid seventy-five pounds. She'd been handling it as lightly as a furled umbrella. We deposited her bags on our bed and went to the kitchen for glasses and ice and drinks.

We went to sit in the living room and she immediately began to talk about literature. Maybe there was a modicum of polite chitchat, but my impression was that there was none at all—only straight to the point about which poets I admired and why, which ones I disapproved. The only other person I'd met with such fierce intensity about literary opinions was Randall Jarrell, who had died only a short time earlier. But Jarrell was mostly intense about his own opinions for which the remarks of others served as pretext for an imperious airing. Easy to tell that Carolyn was actually interested in what I thought, and if she disagreed with my judgments, she was anything but dismissive.

I had held long converse with grand literary figures before, but none was so widely read in contemporary work or so familiar with those who produced it. She knew all the living poets I had read and many of the deceased. She also spoke casually, and always candidly, of a great many poets I had never heard of, being especially well versed in the bards of the northwest. It was from her that I first heard about William Stafford, about his poems, his career, and his personality which she seemed to admire without desiring to emulate in any way. And I learned of her passion for Janet Lewis's work.

The conversation went on for the next three days without really stopping. There were the ordinary interruptions of family life, of course, and of my teaching schedule, but those hiatuses amounted only to refreshing breathing spaces. When we sat down together again, we would take up precisely where we left off.

At this time I had published three novels, but it came out in the course of our talk that I had a first book of poems coming from Louisiana State University Press. The surprise she evinced at this announcement was the first, and maybe the last, I ever noticed Carolyn to show. Nothing would do but for us to drag out the manuscript and begin to read through it together. She insisted, and she is not someone who usually needs to insist in order to get her way.

I was reluctant, being more than a little shamefaced about a collection of poems in which I had no confidence. They had been composed over a long period of time and so exhibited a spectrum of different half-assed styles. When I tried to explain or, more likely, to apologize, she brushed aside my dithering. "Oh, let's look at the *lines*," she said, making it clear by her manner that going through this book was the one thing worth doing that we could do.

This was my first experience with having my poems "workshopped." I had been teaching a poetry workshop at UNCG for some years, but that was seat-of-the-pants stunt piloting, for I had never attended a serious workshop. When I signed up for one in fiction with Dr. William Blackburn at Duke, he wouldn't allow me to attend. "Use that period to write," he insisted. So I had never endured this particular kind of situation and found that I was just as apprehensive at the prospect as my students were—and are.

She was as extraordinary a teacher and critic as she was as a poet. It wasn't merely that she went over the pages minutely, examining every trope, every line break, every preposition and comma; I had expected that. It was the easy, practiced way she went about it. If you've ever had the opportunity to watch talented amateur billiards players at their game and then to see a professional come among them, you'll know what I mean. She knew her way around the board.

The book was called *The World Between the Eyes* and I don't think she liked it very much, though she may have liked it better than I did. Yet she took it seriously, every poem, and made such expert suggestions that the dull matter actually acquired, if not real polish, some traces of gloss. I have always been grateful for her labors from which I learned so very much.

Probably I learned little about the actual composition of poetry. Our temperaments and subject matter are too dissimilar for me to be able to purloin motives and strategies that would brighten me. But I learned to cast a frosty and murderous eye upon my strophes; I learned the uses of the end stop; I learned some short cuts. Mostly I learned the seriousness that has to go into a poet's self-editing process. Poetry may be composed lightly, even carelessly, in order to acquire an air of insouciance, to give the illusion of improvisation, but it has to be revised with all the careful, stern standards that a sitting judge would apply in a criminal case.

Whether this swift education improved my own work I cannot say; it may have been incapable of improvement. But what I learned from Carolyn Kizer made it possible to understand and appreciate her poems in a new and genuine fashion and that has given me years of durable, numerous pleasures.

JUDITH EMLYN JOHNSON

Re/Membering the Goddess: Carolyn Kizer and the Poetics of Generosity

SINCE THE LATE 1960s I have been slowly feeling my way towards some definition or description of a poetics of generosity, to be to our apparent poetics of parsimony, as an economics of generosity might be to our present economics of scarcity. For this search, Carolyn Kizer has been both moon and polar star, both illumination and guide. In this essay I celebrate not only a prophetic feminist poet, but a leader and foremost exemplar of this newly reemergent poetics, a poetics which is, I shall argue, although not exclusively feminist, central to feminism.[1]

Carolyn Kizer said in 1971 of her own work, "I am a premature Women's Liberationist. I was writing poems on the subject ten years before it became fashionable."[2] She is also a fine crafter of traditional western poetic forms, of haiku, and of the more contemporary open forms. She is a translator, a satirist, a lyric poet, and, as founding editor of *Poetry Northwest* and as the first director of the Literature Program of the National Endowment for the Arts, has strongly influenced the course of contemporary American poetry. Here, without wishing to limit her to the feminism so strong in both the form and the substance of her work, I consider her primarily from the vantage point of my own feminist stance.

The first I knew of Carolyn,[3] some time in the late 1960s, she was the author of a volume of poetry suffused with energy and marked by precision, delicacy, and strength of lyrical feeling. This was a poet who addressed a wide range of cultural contexts and associations and who was willing to tackle great and difficult subjects and to write unfashionable poems. At a time, for example, when the elegantly savage style of Augustan satire had maybe reached its nadir, this poet wrote "Pro Femina," which took the risk of talking about the condition of women long before that was an acceptable contemporary theme, and doing so in a style that for verve, wit, and polished outrage, not to say occasional venom, had not been heard since the satires of Pope. Both the lyricism and the wit, furthermore, struck me as those of a poet confident of her own powers and generous in her trust of her readers and of the poems themselves. This confidence made it unnecessary for her to hide behind either the careful construct of her irony or the pretense of a neuter voice, the first of which seemed obligatory for all poets who came of age in the 1950s and early 1960s, and the second obligatory for women writing at that time, as it had been for the generation that had preceded us.[4]

This forthrightly woman-centered voice and whole-hearted commitment to the immediacy of the poem may have caused occasional misreadings of Carolyn's work. More often, however, reviewers made sensitive attempts to formulate accurate reactions to poems for which the feminist critical context and vocabulary either did not yet exist or were not yet widely understood. Hence one reviewer's courtly characterization of her as "Roman Matron and . . . Oriental Courtesan together."[5] Clearly it is possible, and even somewhat obvious, to read this as an unintentional put-down.[6] Such a reading fails to allow for the effect of characterizing an archetypal, a larger-than-life, a heroically mythic quality of the persona her poems construct. Yes, at times this persona speaks as matron, not simply as ordinary, everyday matron, but as legendary Matron, not housewife but incarnation of The Household, the archetypal character of Matron speaking with the weight of history and of generations of "the private lives of one-half of humanity."[7] At times she speaks as courtesan, not woman up for grabs but woman of erotic power and skill, who avowedly loves men, likes to court and please them, and who expects them to court and please her, too. At times she speaks as quintessential mother, as daughter, as wife (even somewhat balefully as ex-wife), and as friend. At times she speaks clearly and powerfully as citizen of the international community of poets, in the tone and with the authority of a poet who knows herself to have every right to first-class citizenship. And, in many of the poems, she speaks as Goddess, the role that can contain and engender all the other roles. This insistence on woman's centrality both in public and in personal contexts creates a vision of woman as herself a primary rather than a derivative incarnation of Blake's "human form divine," having, like Sir Thomas Browne, her own "peece of divinity in [her]."[8] Such a vision is central to the current feminist enterprise.

Contemporary feminist poetry has been equally concerned with asserting the woman poet's right to write,[9] with reclaiming a lost or obscured tradition of women's poetry, with appropriating and subverting those aspects of the predominantly male literary discourses we find useful,[10] and with negating, de/fusing or re/fusing those aspects hostile to us. Thus, the feminist enterprise has not been restricted to expressions of rage and opposition to oppressive social arrangements. It has certainly included such expressions, but the rage has, in my reading, been secondary, the means to an end and not the end itself. The major enterprise has not been destructive but creative: the task of recapturing, rebuilding, retrieving, remembering, or inventing, if necessary, women's dismembered or disre-membered knowledge of empowerment; the knowledge of being self and not other, author and not mirror, subject and not object. This many-sided project has caused us to propose radical re/vision of the art we inherited: of the forms, the techniques, the conventions, the nature of the language, the themes, the inherited canon itself, the very idea of a canon, the classifications within that canon, the divisions of poets or themes into major and minor, and the position of poet in relation to audience, to poem, and to herself. Although not a radical feminist in the sense of advocating feminist separatism or radical disruptions of conventional biological or linguistic arrangements, Carolyn Kizer has dealt with the basic questions at the root of feminist poetry: how to use the tradition that we learned to love and then found either hated or ignored us, how to re/claim the lost Goddess of poetry and of civilization for our own. In exploring these questions her work proposes extremely useful integrations of western and eastern traditions and re/creates a new, woman-centered vision of woman as myth and archetype of her own subjectivity.

As many recent feminist literary critics have pointed out, male poets take for granted their entitlement to a tradition and a locus for the sub-jectivity of their voices as female poets cannot.[11] The woman poet, typi-cally, even aside from institutionalized denigration, has experienced literary tradition as the presence of an assumed male speaker and as her own absence from a speaking role. She has experienced not only her own absence but the weight of absence as it is incarnated in an entire obliter-ated tradition of voices that do not speak, voices unnamed, unrecorded. This is absence doubled and redoubled, absence squared and cubed, absence that cannot teach her the forms of her own subjectivity. When she looks for a voice to model her own voice upon, she finds nothing but male subjectivity, male presentation of woman in the role of object. Lacking such models, the woman poet, a dismembered female Orpheus, tries to build her voice out of fragments.[12] Some of these are fragments of the male tradition she can use or alter to her purpose. Some are fragments of the image of herself she constructs from piecing together the less gyno-phobic aspects of traditional male visions of Woman. Some are the threads of connection that she weaves with her female contemporaries. As many critics have noted, these connections must be woven anew each generation, because the woman writers of each generation have more often than not been obscured or obliterated from the literary canon before their female successors could make use of them.[13]

Anthropologically and historically, this task of reconstructing a tradition of female empowerment has sometimes involved assuming a prehistoric matriarchy. Theologically it has involved the hypotheses that Goddess wor-ship preceded God worship, that the powers and experiences historically attributed to male deities were prehistorically attributed to female ones, and that female potentiality, immanence, or becoming is as potent as male actuality, presence, or being.[14] Poetically, it has involved using any or all of these approaches to construct a voice that can embody women's power as subject.

Carolyn's process of constructing an empowered voice began, as did that of her contemporary, Adrienne Rich, with an obvious lyric gift, tech-nical "mastery,"[15] and the ability to internalize the voice of the part of the tradition admired in what we might call the Age of Auden. It also began with quiet efforts to subvert this voice. The title poem of *The Ungrateful Garden* (1961),[16] recycles the myth of Midas and the Golden Touch in impeccably neat quatrains. The stanzas are heavily marked with antithesis, repetition of vowel sounds, and alliteration: "*hugg*ed his agues, *lov*ed his *lus*t, / But *d*amned to *h*ell the out-of-*d*oors . . ." (emphases mine). One might note as Audenesque not only the control of parallel struc-tures, alliteration, and consonance in the first of these two lines, but the shift from the ornately rhetorical to the colloquial in the second. Similar constructions are at work in stanza three ("Th*is gi*ft, he'*d* thought, would *gil*d his joys, / *Sil*t up the waters of his grief; / H*is l*awns a *wil*derness of noise, / The heavy *cl*ang of *l*eaf on *l*eaf."). And the tone of the final stanza ("Dazzled with wounds, he limped away / To climb into his golden bed. /

Roses, roses can betray. / 'Nature is evil,' Midas said.") may also carry an echo of Auden or of Eliot, although the particular quality of ironic fury is characteristic of one stream in Carolyn's work, and the use of classical mythology to embody personal concerns derives as much from Louise Bogan as from Auden.

This is, in all its strength, a literary poem.[17] The literary poem has been marked by the use of traditional, frequently classical themes and traditional rhetoric. Modernist poets[18] have typically used the literary poem semiparodically, in tones varying from gentle irony to the most savage contempt, whether for the lexicon itself or for the contemporary culture they could assault by means of it: "Death and the Raven drift above, / and Sweeney guards the horned gate. . . . " or "I'll love you till the ocean / Is folded and hung up to dry."[19] For the woman poet bathed in this lexicon however, there is an additional usefulness in a parodic approach, quite aside from the Modernist agenda. Part of her task is, after all, to define herself as woman and not as neuter or pseudo-man, to separate herself from the tradition which already simultaneously defines her as separate and requires her to obliterate her identity in order to end or at least ameliorate the separation. Here, therefore, the classical themes and rhetoric are used to challenge traditional sets of positions: nature against artifact, flesh against spirit, generosity against greed, "outside" against "within." Thus, the argument moves from Midas's own masochistic cherishing of his "streaming sores" to his final, traditional, and drastically erroneous attribution of his inward and outward condition to the evil in Nature rather than to an evil in himself.

Similarly, in "Streets of Pearl and Gold"[20] the poet gives us the context with an epigraph from Andrew Marvell's "Upon Appleton House," one of the great poems on order and the nature of civilization. She then creates a detailed counterpoint to Marvell's imagery in order to characterize the progress to chaos and heartlessness in our world, and the process by which we use art to restore order ("Not rats or roaches in the wainscot / Nor the old staled odors of man's functioning / But that they were chalice of our history. . . ." and "Paint out the day and you will keep the time. . . .").

Midas' final recourse to his "golden bed" for comfort, even while insisting that "Nature is evil," reads as a flight back to a Nature (and possibly also to Woman as Nature's presence in that bed) he himself has made hostile. The ending of "Streets of Pearl and Gold," with its elaborate play on the Cross and "X of loss" ends in similar comment on the tradition's recourse to woman as nature's surrogate: "So stamp your canvas with the X of loss, / Art mutilated, stained with abuse and rage. / But mark it also as the cross of love / Who hold this woman-flesh, touch it alive, / As I try to keep us, here upon the page." The speaker, however, here involves herself in the effort to fix—both hold and repair—the world in art "here upon the page." And careful readers may note that a reversal of roles has taken place. The male artist/lover who, throughout the poem, has been creating "art mutilated. . . with abuse and rage," flees, like Midas fleeing to his bed, to the "woman-flesh" outside his construction, hoping to "touch it alive." But meanwhile the speaker, attempting her own construction, must "try to keep us, here upon the page." Among its other appropriations and reversals, then, this later poem shows the subjectivity and enterprise of art moving away from its traditional male centers to the female artist, the poet herself.

Not only the treatments of theme in these two poems but their elaborate formal structures challenge the very formal structures they use. The more elaborate the formal rhetoric of each poem, the more it turns on itself, forcing the reader to question what can be attributed to nature, and what to art in the poem itself. Within the poem's formally constricted style and the weight of allusion to prior tradition, after all, be-ringed with artifice, as far from natural spontaneity as it can get, what side is the poet herself on, given that she has chosen to write within such strictures?

It seems clear to me that in these early, formally constricted poems, the poet is following more than the Modernist agenda of contrasting this century's sordid reality with classical myths of transcendence. Although they do so subtly, courteously, gently, even lovingly, these poems of the 1960s deal, without in fact making a big deal of it, in prophetically feminist ways, with the literary tradition and its formal constrictions as specifically male constructions. The use, for example, of formal antithesis in "The Ungrateful Garden" constitutes a challenge to Midas's, and by extension to the tradition's, uses of antithetical modes to structure reality. By parodying and exaggerating these constructions the poem both appropriates and subverts them. That is to say, it lays a claim to a mode that, rather than allowing to exclude it, it will ultimately reject. Midas's misplaced insistence, central to our entire literary tradition, on seeing the world in terms of oppositions rather than of complementarities, of Nature versus Art, rather than of Nature embodied in Art, or of Art in Nature, were later to become central targets of contemporary feminist challenge. The poem implies that the actual evil in Midas consists of both his construction of mutually exclusive opposites and his projection of his own nature outward onto Nature herself. This study of Midas's love of gold and of artifice, his anality (in Freudian terms), and his love-hate relationship with his own earthly body (his sores), and this refusal to endorse his projection of his own inner evil outward onto nature are thus prophetic of later feminist analyses of precisely these cultural constructions and constrictions. And the poem, while making its own uses of a classical theme and technique, wryly challenges and subverts both.

In this light, we can see that even the elegance of the poem's sound constructions subverts traditional uses of such elegance. For example, in stanza three of "The Ungrateful Garden" ("Th*is* gi*f*t, he'*d* thought, would *gild* his joys, / *Sil*t up the *wa*ters of his grief; / H*is* *law*ns a *wild*erness of noise, / The hea*vy* c*lang* of *leaf* on *leaf*."), we can see how much of the consonance and alliteration are in fact analyzed, deconstructed or disassembled rather than exactly repeated configurations. "*Gift*" is taken apart, with its vowel going one way to be recycled in "*gil*d," and "*sil*t," "Wilderness," and its consonants reappearing separated by a different although related vowel in "*grief*." The "*wa*" from "*waters*" is reversed and combined with the "l" from "gild" and "silt" to make "lawns," then reconstituted in its original order but with the vowel from "gild" and "silt" to make "wilderness." I leave it to the reader to follow similar permutations of other sounds I've italicized. The effect of this is to make us hear how the tight artifice that Midas wants to freeze into those very same metallic constructions that will constrict him is constantly slipping, changing, and recycling, even as Nature itself recycles, the sounds the poem's rigid structure pretends to hold changeless. An appearance of rigidity is being used to disassemble, to dismember, to dis/remember rigidity, and thereby to comment ironically not merely on the content of male-centered classical mythology but on the rhetorical forms by which that mythology perpetuates itself. This use of analyzed or disassembled patterns of sound and language is likewise consonant with one vein of feminist subversion of language and thought patterns, deriving originally from Dickinson, and now tending, in one group, toward radical language dislocations and non-linear structures.[21]

One of the ways to subvert or contravene a constricting tradition, of course, is to go outside it, to seek models in another country or another age. The traditions of Chinese and Japanese poetry have been particularly fertile in Carolyn's construction of her voice as both poet and woman poet, partly for their avoidance of abstraction and bombast and for their grounding in the intimate, the daily, and the personal, and partly because they provide her with a method to "refuse rather than cultivate formal distance."[22] "Singing Aloud"[23] is both an example of and a comment on this process. It begins with fine informality: "We all have our faults. Mine is trying to write poems. / New scenery, someone I like, anything sets me off! / I hear my own voice going on, like a god or an oracle, / That cello-tone, intuition. That bell-note of wisdom." The tone is both exuberant and self-mocking; the speaker does not entirely regret her ability to let "anything set her off." But already we hear a note of discomfort with the shaping force of the tradition: she does not feel entirely comfortable with the sound of her voice, in the traditional tones of poetry, "going on like a god or an oracle." She has tried and failed, she confesses, to "get rid of the tempting tic of pentameter, / Of the urge to impose a form on what I don't understand. . . ." In contrast to these traditional vices, age, she suggests, begins to bring her some new virtues. She flees to the actual. Instead of reading her new poems to friends, she shakes branches over herself in the park "so I am covered with petals, / Each petal a metaphor." The image and mood here seem drawn very directly from the vocabularies both of Chinese and of Japanese poetry, particularly in the concreteness with which obliteration of the speaker's former romantic-egotistical stance is suggested by her being covered with petals. Along with the ego of the romantic tradition, she also abandons her dignity. She sings aloud and cavorts, indulging in "innocent folly," accompanied by "squirrels and rabbits . . . with inaudible voices." At the very last, the speaker exuberantly heads for the zoo, where "the primates and I, in communion, / Hoot at each other, or signal with earthy gestures."

This poem is on one level a comment on the poet's own earlier work, on another a successful attempt to remake her own voice, as Yeats did when he turned away from the successes of his earlier style to forge what he called "a poem maybe as cold / and passionate as the dawn."[24] The lush rhetoric, the tight elegance of the earlier meters is gone. The dominant metaphor is not dignified and high-toned, as is even the most sordid element in "Streets of Pearl and Gold," but exuberantly low. Instead of poetic communication pouring from cups of gold it bounds about at the zoo with poet and primate making "earthy gestures," which may well include a few gross ones. The resulting lyric communication is "hooting" instead of speech or song. This new poetic voice is still that of a satirist and a student of myth and history. It is, however, an irreverent and informal voice, sophisticated and confident enough of its control to laugh at its great subjects—history, poetry, and love—and yet serious enough to go beyond laughter. And the elements of the transformation, what one might think of as the theoretical stations of the journey, are the ones contemporary women poets have consistently chosen: forsaking the seductive high tone and rhetoric of the inherited tradition; getting back down to earth and away from abstraction; reclaiming the personal, the trivial, the intimate, the daily, the "primate" concerns as the proper concerns of poetry; exploring not our difference from other animals but our connection with them.[25] In addition, the speaker's characterization of her speech as a "hoot" anticipates and thus defuses possible male denigration of her poetry in precisely these terms.

This corrective orientalization of Carolyn's technique reached its most extended treatment in the long poem "A Month in Summer."[26] The poem, which incorporates attitudes, techniques, and fragments or imitations of Japanese poetry, combines the forms of the prose journal and the haiku. This allows the poet one solution of that traditional problem of the long poem: how to achieve moments of higher intensity and yet vary the tone so that the whole poem is not on the same plane; or conversely, how to allow for transitional passages, or passages of varied intensity, without letting the more relaxed sections seem thin by contrast. In this poem about the slow disintegration of a love affair, the haiku work to focus, to draw together, to construct figures for moments of feeling or intellectual perception, while the journal provides the field, the setting, the ground, from which the polished figures stand out. The net effect of this prose/poem alternation, paradoxically, is to devalorize the self-consciously "poetic" moments and to revalorize the dailiness of life by restoring the moments of perception to their place in the suspended and equal flow of consciousness. This approach, in other words, simultaneously domesticates the archetypal themes of love and loss and heightens or glamorizes the everyday context in which they take place.

For example, the disarming section "Nineteenth Day" wryly admits to "Inertia. / One of the profound consolations in reading the works of Japanese men of letters is their frank acknowledgement of neurotic sloth." Promptly, however, it converts this admission to a statement of pain: "Or the overwhelming impulse, when faced with hurt or conflict, to stay in bed under the covers!" The poet intends us to understand that the speaker is "faced with hurt or conflict" at that moment and is reacting to it like a Japanese man of letters. Because of our cultural assumptions about male and female behavior in the face of grief, this confession both valorizes, by masculinizing, the speaker's behavior and feminizes that of the Japanese men. It also, of course, makes the speaker, however isolated during her separation from her departing lover, part of an international community of letters. By the "Twenty-First Day," the speaker, pursuing gender questions further, asks, "Is it suffering which defeminizes?" She follows this with a haiku in which she describes herself as "neutered and wistful."

The question she has put to herself and us is not merely rhetorical. The suggestion that, far from her suffering making the poet more womanly, it makes her less so, is a radical reversal of the convention that women must suffer to be beautiful.[27] Furthermore, this question of what is woman, what is feminine, has been a constant theme in Carolyn's work, repeated both in traditional and open form poems. "The Dying Goddess," "The Copulating Gods," "Columns and Caryatids," "A Muse of Water," and many more, are not mere exercises in classicism and not merely re/visions of the classical tradition, as discussed above. They are all, in their various aspects, examinations of woman as Figure: as muse, goddess, archetype, idea, object, subject in the process of becoming subject; woman in relation both to the view the traditional, male-dominated culture has taken of her and to the view she must take of herself. Many of these examinations of the Idea of Woman, or of her Idea of Her Self, take place in poems on friendship, for example, the poems to or about Jan. Many take place in mother-daughter poems, involving both the poet's own mother and her daughters. The most elaborate of these is the long prose memoir of the poet's mother in *Yin*, significantly entitled "A Muse." In the remainder of this essay, however, I am going to limit my discussion to the theme of Woman as Goddess, because it both appropriates and challenges the traditional male reifications of Woman.

In a poem that looks at the subject vs. object theme, "The Copulating Gods,"[28] the poet writes of what she seems to treat as a human rather than a specifically female predicament. With her typical combination of humor and gravity, she begins by establishing both the speaker and her lover as archetypal and immortal: "Brushing back the curls from your famous brow, / Lingering over the prominent temple vein, / . . . I ponder how self-consciously / the gods must fornicate." Here the speaker allows her male companion to share the traditional female predicament of being the object of another's contemplation. That is, of course, true of him in his roles as God and as public figure, possibly famous man or well-known fellow poet, possibly target of admiring groupies at poetry readings. It is also true of him in his role as her lover and the object of her thought, doubly true because in this poem, he rather than she is enacting the role of object: she is writing this poem about him rather than he about her.

Yet, significantly, the man to whom this poem is addressed is not in fact object rather than subject, or not more object or less subject than the speaker herself. Not "You" or "I" but "*We* were their religion before they were born. . . ." Although this objectification of lovers or of famous personalities is presented by the deliberate choice of conventional, gendered language as a male activity, both man and woman are equally its victims: "*Men* continue to invent *our* histories, / Deny *our equal* pleasure in *each other*. Clubfoot, nymphomaniac, they dub *us*. . . ." (emphases mine). The poem ends with the speaker's provisional acceptance of this objectification, this subtraction of their positions as subject of their own story: "I know we are not our history but their myth." She then invites her lover to transcend their condition in the traditional way in her arms: "Come, kiss! / Come, swoon again, we who invented dying / And the whole alchemy of resurrection. / They will concoct a scripture explaining this." The lovers swoon into their state as public myth rather than private history; they accept their condition as object or icon, with the concomitant death of their subjectivity. But, by the alchemy of resurrection, the speaker suggests, they will nonetheless be reborn into a transcendent and mythic selfhood as scriptural figures, perhaps as poets, although this mythic selfhood is presented, mockingly, as "concoct[ed]."

It is possible to read this poem as a treatment of the loss of self involved in public life, with particular reference to such figures as The Poet. Clearly, the speaker considers both herself and her companion in those roles. It may also be read as a dialogue with poems like Donne's "The Canonization," in which, likewise, the lovers die out of ego and personhood to be resurrected as exemplars of holy love: "We can dy by it, if not live by love. / And if unfit for tombes and hearse / Our legend bee, it will be fit for verse." Read this way, the poem enters the long tradition of poetry on love, transcendence, and the death of the ego, and on lovers as supra-personal icons for the world, who "did all to you epitomize, / Countries, Townes, Courts. . . . / A Patterne of your love!"[29] Donne's "patterne" becomes Carolyn's "scriptures."[30] And the word "scriptures" itself,

it seems to me, is used here precisely to invoke for the reader the inter-
mingling of sacred and profane love characteristics of this strand in the
tradition. In both kinds of love, the dying of the ego is never an unmixed
blessing. In neither is the transformation from subject of one's own life
to object of another's contemplation painless.

The poem has, however, an additional richness if read as arising out
of the female speaker's specific experience of a specific female condi-
tion: "not our history but their myth." Here the speaker generously insists
on using that experience as a bridge to her male companion. Rather than
exclude him as the adversarial instrument of her reification, the negation
of her subjectivity, she includes him as fellow victim in the reification
and fellow icon in her later transcendence.

The inclusive stance and complex tone, both amused and serious, both
passionate and ironic, in which wit and irony do not diminish the
speaker's commitment to the emotion of the poem, look forward to the
more developed aesthetic stance of later work. This is a poetry which
refuses to be limited to a single, traditional stance, whether of ironic
commentator outside of and distrustful of passion, or of impassioned par-
ticipant. By taking both positions, it simultaneously engages, subverts, and
revises the traditions involving the lover as subject/object. It also, in this
and in the range of readings it opens to us, exemplifies the poetics of
generosity. This poetics neither assumes any scarcity of means for focusing
the poem and holding the reader, nor insists on any need for an exorbitant
and tight-lipped economy in the construction or field of reference of the
poem. Instead this aesthetic assumes an infinity of plentitude in art, as
well as the reader's generous willingness to trust the poem and experience
it in all its scope, its simultaneity of effects.[31] As a feminist technique it
both embodies and goes beyond the less inclusive stances of irony, of
looking askance, "looking out of the corners of one's eyes," at the tradition
and at women's objectification within it.[32]

A more direct examination of the reification of the Goddess as muse
is the subject of "A Muse of Water."[33] The poem is addressed, like "The
Copulating Gods," to a male listener. Since women have traditionally
played the role of muse to male artists, the listener may be a male poet.
The poem may perhaps be seen as the poet's *apologia pro sua vita* for dar-
ing to be artist rather than or as well as muse. The poem begins by estab-
lishing the speaker as a poet without any nurturing presence but her own.
She has, however, a sense of her connection to other women: it is not I but

"*We* who must act as handmaidens / To our own goddess. . . ." as we
strive to "glimpse the muse." Already the traditional terms are being
reversed; women poets are seeking our own muse rather than accepting
roles as muses to men. True, our search for selfhood makes us "Narcis-
sists by necessity," the traditional condemnation of women, that men, no
mean narcissists themselves, have traditionally offered as indictment,
without the examination of the historical context.[34]

Probably, in the context of the poem, the speaker assumes that her
male listener endorses this traditional indictment of women's narcissism.
She therefore presents for his contemplation women in the varied roles
of muses, guardians, nurturers, or even governors and "Virgin Queens,"
not subjects of our own reveries but objects in men's constructs, in the
damaged world "your civilizing lusts have made." The lusts are civilizing
both because they create the civilization we now have and because the
need to civilize as Man has experienced it indeed comes from lust rather
than love for the natural world. The speaker compares this process to the
"Water Music . . . / That men bestow on Virgin Queens" and that the
Queen commands to be played on the royal barge. The Queen, we are
surely intended to remember, has not composed this music herself, but
invokes the work of a male composer, which he "bestows" on her. In this
commanded music, therefore, her purported power is not her own but a
reflection of his.

By the end of the poem, however, the water music the speaker seeks
and commands her male contemporaries to hear is no longer a male cre-
ation on a constructed barge. Spontaneously, it "rises / Out of a brackish
clump of weeds, / Out of the marsh at ocean-side, / Out of the oil-stained
river's gleam." It is no longer the music of men's art but the music of
women's nature. Indeed, from the speaker's tone, man seems singularly
and perhaps restfully absent: "Discover the deserted beach / Where ghosts
of curlews safely wade: / Here the warm shallows lave your feet / Like
tawny hair of magdalens." The beach is deserted, and thus, the ghosts of
curlews may "safely wade," free from fear of predators. This safety is, on
one level, ironic and illusory. That the curlews are ghosts implies both that
they have already fallen prey to some violation of whatever natural safety
they might have expected, and that it is the memory of a state of safety
rather than its actuality the poet has summoned.

In the references to religious ritual and to redemption, the shallows
that "lave your feet / Like tawny hair of magdalens," both enact and

reverse the conventional roles of the Magdalen and the Messiah. This magdalen, significantly non-hierarchal and lower-case, whose name is by this be/heading and de/capitalization demoted from the name of a person to the name of a condition of servitude, lacks, as the first stanza pointed out, her own handmaiden. The concept of a handmaiden for the magdalen is itself a paradoxical reversal of the norm. Forced by this lack to act as "handmaiden to [her] own goddess," the magdalen laves the feet of a male figure now occupying, precisely because she laves his feet, the traditional role of the messiah. The implications of this act are multiple. Because she is "forced to act as handmaiden to her own goddess," and now acts as handmaiden to him, he is "forced to act" as goddess to her. He, through these language constructions, performs the role of muse and inspiration for her while also co-opting the goddess herself in that role. Furthermore, it is her service to him that creates, signifies, and validates his function as messiah.

Thus, indeed she performs woman's traditional service to man, echo and magdalen, both nurturing and validating him, at enormous cost to herself. Her nurturance allows him to replace the Goddess as her muse and establishes him as her messiah. But her nurturance, although it does lead to the traditional death, both does and does not lead to the traditional resurrection and redemption: "Here, if you care, and lie full-length, / Is water deep enough to drown." Is this tender promise one of erotic joy, regretful prophecy, or ironic threat? The tone indeed promises him both a crucifixion and a redemption. The drowning of the self may function, for the male poet, both as death and as baptism into renewed innocence. It is also, in this poem, the death by water of the male ego and of its central place in the female literary tradition. This redeemer, in fact, does not redeem but is redeemed by the magdalen's service to him. Furthermore, this ending is both a return to the original myth of Narcissus with which, we may remember, the poem started, and a reversal of men's traditional use of it against women. In this simultaneous baptism and crucifixion, it is he, not she, who enacts the conventional role of Narcissus, drowned in his reflection of and on himself. Nor is she relegated to the conventional position as his echo; as in "The Copulating Gods," the subject/object relationship is changed by the fact that she, not he, has written the poem and has taken for herself, however gently, the power of the gaze and voice.

The satires and the mixed satire-and-narrative-lyric poems adopt the aesthetic of generosity from a different stance. Like "The Copulating Gods," they function both by including the speaker in the injustices she attacks and by including the enactors of injustice as fellow victims. Thus, "Pro Femina," in its first three sections, forsakes the leisurely, worldly, meditative tone of gentle laughter at and participation in history's errors to adopt a more concentrated tone of satirical exasperation. The first stanza of section one raises again the question of what is womanly or unwomanly, while establishing the speaker in a women's tradition (Sappho) and in opposition to a men's tradition (Juvenal): "From Sappho to myself, consider the fate of women. / How unwomanly to discuss it! Like a noose or an albatross necktie. / The clinical sobriquet hangs us: cod-piece coveters . . . / Juvenal set us apart in denouncing our vices / Which had grown, in part, from having been set apart. . . ." But the poem itself does not adopt and emulate the Sapphic lyric, as, for example, H.D.'s poems did. Instead it appropriates and subverts Juvenalian satire. It does this by accepting the traditional Juvenalian indictments of women and then turning them into both an indictment of men for making them and a boast of women's heroic qualities in enduring them. After disarming the conventional criticisms by doing them much better than they are usually done, the poet can then go on to state her case as a woman and a free intellect. But even this strategy allows due place to the conventional attacks. For example, the line "While men have politely debated free will, we have howled for it . . . ," accepts the conventional role of woman as howling termagant, then throws it back in man's face as being forced on her by his denial of her free will. And the poem, while rushing energetically through its indictment of sexism and its concurrent promise to revalue women's "well known / Respect for life because it hurts so much to come out with it," nonetheless includes its male readers in its promise of charity and redemption. "Relax, and let us absorb you," the speaker soothingly offers, comparing herself in passing to the entire nation of China as it absorbed successive waves of barbarian invaders, and slyly aware of how little she is flattering him by his part in the comparison. "You can learn temperance in a more temperate climate." Like the redemption through drowning of the ego in the previous poem, redemption through absorption is probably pretty far from what the male listener had in mind. It may also be what, traditionally, we should assume him to have feared most from women. To offer it to him, then, whether as promise or threat, is, again, both to accept and to claim as a right a female power men have traditionally seen as evil.

   This is a satire about history and culture, and about what gynophobia does to history and culture. As a satire about history and culture it is in the mainstream of literary tradition. What transforms and transfuses it is its doubleness, the inclusiveness of the poet's vision, as well as its immediate and energetic tone of personal presence. We can see the effects of close study of Pope, Juvenal, and other satirists. The use of such epithets as "indigo intellectuals" or such linkages as "toast and Teasdales," for example, is unkind enough to remind us of similar constructions in *The Dunciad*. The poet, however, unlike Pope, does not adopt the third person, nor the externalized and noncomplicitous tone of exasperated cultural arbiter outside the evils under attack.[35] Instead, she is right there in the center of her poem, not isolated from but a member of the community of women, involved in both the attack and the defense. She refuses to be contained by the prior satiric structures of abstraction or generalization. Resisting stricture and constriction at every turn, inextricably a part of everything she attacks, she rushes off to "get back to the meeting" in every sense. The meeting of roles traditionally separated in satire is precisely what she insists on enacting.

"Fanny,"[36] the fourth section of "Pro Femina," written much later than the other three, engages in an even more drastic subversion of the traditional framework of satire. Reversing the normal structure of Greek dramatic presentations, three tragedies followed by a satyr play, "Pro Femina," in the version printed in *Mermaids in the Basement*, presents the final days of Robert Louis Stevenson in Samoa, from the point of view of Fanny Stevenson, as she nurses him, "[keeps] him alive for eight more years," and frantically tries to counter his impending death with the nurturing force of her gardening. His illness thus becomes the object of her heroic struggle against death rather than the subject of his own tragedy. The use of the first person narrator in this, as in other works discussed above, keeps the subjectivity and selfhood of the speaker firmly before us at all times. The poem both does and does not present Fanny in the conventional female role of nurturer of male genius. We see comparatively little of Louis's struggle for life, or even of Fanny nurturing him. Instead we see her buying seeds, planting them, cultivating the stubborn earth, interacting with "the Reverend Mr. Claxton," with "Mr. Carruthers, the island solicitor," and with "a young thief" who brings her pineapple plants. Louis belittles her efforts, telling her she has "the soul of a peasant," but she continues to assert her own subjectivity as the heroic figure of her own mythology. Although she is far from uncaring towards Louis and functions toward him as earth mother and Goddess, she seems not to do so exclusively for his benefit. The poem's relentless piling up of seasonal and gardening detail creates a displacement of Louis from the center to the periphery both of our consciousness and of Fanny's, so that what this earth mother nurtures is the earth itself rather than any one of earth's children. In fact, the displacement of Louis from the center of her attention represents, on one level, her flight from her role as his nurse and nurturer. This section of "Pro Femina," therefore, while presenting woman in her traditional role as nurturer, removes man from the center of her attention, removes her from the House, and places her firmly outside domesticity and inside the performance of History. Fanny and not Louis seems to enact the traditional colonizing role in Samoa. While Louis "writes to *The Times* / Of 'the foul colonial politics.' I send to New York for seeds." He complains; she acts. It is her action that brings European seedlings to the island, and it is she who in the end bears the historical responsibility for seedtime and harvest, the Biblical symbols of earth's continuation and renewal.

A similar commingling of venom, outrage, and participation in responsibility for injustice occupies the center of "Running Away from Home."[37] This poem begins as a catalog of the small town repressions and hypocrisies of such characters as: "Dear Phil . . . / Whose car had a detachable steering wheel; / He'd hand it to his scared, protesting girl, / Saying, 'Okay, *you* drive'—steering with his knees. . . . " and "Dear Sally . . . / [who] Knelt on cold stone, with chilblained knees, to pray, / 'Dear God, Dear Christ! Don't let him go All The Way!'" Much of this indictment is focused specifically on the role of repressive religious practices in distorting society, "Spooked by plaster madonnas, switched by sadistic nuns, / Given sex instruction by dirty old men in skirts." But this poem is not merely a hilarious letter of attack on Dear Phil, Dear Sally, the nuns, and the dirty old men, or even the rest of its dramatis personae: the "crazed rednecks" from Idaho, the "mad orphans" from Oregon, the "insane salesman" from Spokane, and the "people from Montana [who] are put away." The speaker, furious with grief at the constricted and wrecked lives she contemplates, involves herself, acknowledging fiercely and complicitously, "I know your secrets." Furthermore, the moments of fiery wit are set in a framework of tag ends of literary quotation torn from a literature and a culture in disarray. The mad poets and artists the speaker claims to know flounder both ridiculously and tragically, "in my craft and sullen ebbing," in a wild conjunction of Kraft-Ebbing's science and Dylan Thomas's "craft

and sullen art." Like drunken, suicidal, creatively inept, and sexually tor-
mented Shelleys, they "squint at the light / Staining the white radiance of
O'Leary's cell." Compassion is tragically missing. All this savagery is
funny, but it is also dead serious: "After Spokane," the poet snarls, after
having established herself as having been at one point part of the Spokane
scene (and possibly, by implication, one of Spokane's "insane salesmen"),
"what horrors lurk in Hell?"

   With savage indignation this poem holds up a civilization and its cul-
tural and literary constructs for us to laugh and weep at. But the poet is not
merely attacking derivative or meaningless art, cramped imaginations,
and science wildly out of control—"Mondrian O'Leary" and the "seven-
humped, mutated radioactive Chinook salmon," that "stain the white radi-
ance of O'Leary's brain." She is lamenting the wreckage of lives. The
people she shows us are cracking up both in cars and in madhouses. Their
fates become not merely the casualties but the amusements of a society
that has itself gone mad. The culminating vision of the inmates of "mad
Medical Lake" who become the source of laughter for weekend visitors
is both horrifyingly grotesque and surreal, but it is not unreal. And the
poem itself acknowledges by implication that it has been doing exactly
what it accuses the visitors of doing. It too, after all, has toured the hos-
pital with us, ridiculing "Mrs. Hurley, somebody's grandma, / Eating gravy
with her bare hands." Our bitter laughter throughout the poem is the sign
not only of the speaker's but of the readers' participation in the mockery.
The visitors' reaction of "Just animals, Rosetta. / She's not *your* mother.
Don't let it get you" is implicitly that of both readers and poet, until the
moment when the poem has implicated us so strongly that we see it for
what it is and reject it. The vision of "mad Medical Lake" and its "white
ruin of muscular men / Twisting bars like Gargantua" is not very far as
image from that earlier, more tolerant vision of the poet and the primate
hooting earthily at each other in the zoo. The total stance and vision of the
two poems, however, are worlds apart. "Singing Aloud" is a sunny view of
the poetic ego deflating itself that ends with a moment of ludicrous but
friendly communication with nature. "Running Away from Home" is a
denunciation of a mad world that ends with poet's and reader's anguished
complicity in the madness.

   A similar transformation of focus and expectations, with a similar rec-
iprocity of poet and subject, occurs in "Food of Love."[38] At first we read

the poem as a gleefully violent, half-joking, half-serious treatment of the mutual destructiveness of lovers. The speaker first devours her lover, then turns him into a Sahara, then swells to fill his entire field of vision until he has no choice but to let her absorb and renew him, gigantic desert though he may be. The central trope is the conventional figure of speech —"I love you so much I could eat you up"—here transformed into a literal situation and then developed, as the epigraph warns, "to the bitter end" as if it were an actual event. The original cliché is expanded to "I'm going to murder you with love. . . . / I'm going to hug you, bone by bone, / Till you're dead all over. / Then I will dine on your delectable marrow." This transformation and elaboration of the traditional play in love poetry on "dying," already seen in "The Copulating Gods," places the poem, once again, in a revisionary women's tradition.

In this version of love's mythic death and rebirth, the woman again refuses her traditional role of passive victim. Instead, she accepts, indeed triumphantly boasts of, her role as castrator: "with my female blade I'll carve my name / In your most aspiring palm / Before I chop it down." In the field of sexual combat, she is marking him as her property, her trophy, rather than the other way around. Biologically, this trope refers to her role as depletor of his sexual energy. Socially it refers to her sexual assertiveness, which seems to her lover like a phallic claim ("my female blade"). Culturally it refers to the charged epithets customarily applied to female sexual assertiveness. This assertiveness, as men have traditionally feared, ends by demolishing the lover. He becomes the speaker's "host, my final supper on earth." The word "host" here is richly charged: the lover is the host who entertains the speaker at a dinner party at which he is the meal, the host who allows a parasite to occupy and devour his body. He is, obviously, also the Host as agent of sacrifice and redemption, clearly spelled out in the reference to the Last Supper. The poem, in what looks at first like an atmosphere of exuberant joking, of earthy hyperbole, has ended by revising from a woman's point of view, not only the conventional attitude towards the physiology of sex, but its relationship to that whole deep and concealed process by which, as Wilde put it, "each man kills the thing he loves."[39] And by calling the lover the "Host" the speaker makes him as much the agent of her rebirth and redemption as she is of his when she resurrects him. The relationship, in spite of its apparent inequity, is at least reciprocal, although men might complain, as women

do of similar inequitable but reciprocal relationships, that such reciproc-
ity is not much comfort when survival is at issue. It should, furthermore,
be pointed out that the interaction remains as double-edged at the end
as it was at the beginning. The lover, after his resurrection, will "begin to
die again." While on one level this is a promise of blisses yet to come,
on another it sounds like a threat.

The culminating poem in this body of work is "Semele Recycled."[40]
Here the dis/membered and dis/remembered Goddess speaks again in
that energetically human voice we have come to recognize. This time
she has been dismembered, not, as in the recorded form of the myth, by
her lover's divine radiance, but more realistically, by his departure.[41]
"When you left me I was all broken up" or "I went to pieces" or "I fell
apart," ordinary figures of speech, becomes, "After you left me forever, / I
was broken into pieces, / and all the pieces flung into the river." The
speaker narrates this process of dismemberment not through one but
through two cycles of rebirth. In the first cycle, every individual part,
instead of decaying, is put to some temporary and specialized use by the
people who find it, exactly the way a woman may serve as a wife in one
context; a waitress, secretary, or a model in another; a mother in still
another; a lover or a goddess, a teacher, a housekeeper, an oracle, in still
others. She is no longer a whole human being. She has been broken down
and objectified by the uses others find for her.

These partial uses are painful to her. Some of them exploit or violate her
sexuality; they leave a "trail of blood. . . . [that] attracted the carp and eels,
and the river turtle / easily landed, dazed by my tasty red." They are also not
entirely harmless to the users. The goddess's eyes, when placed in a diadem
by a prospective bride, scare away the bridegroom. This image may suggest
both his terror at the thought of his bride's awakening subjectivity (her "I's"),
and his willingness to let her learn anything from prior women's experi-
ence, particularly since she has overdone things a bit and become "all eyes,"
perhaps through too much insistence on her Self. Her being "all eyes," how-
ever, also suggests the bride's untutored effort at connection, however inap-
propriate and posthumous, with other women. Even in trying to don the
consciousness of another woman she has become a thing, a partial creature
and not a person, like the speaker, whose eyes she has put on and whose
consciousness she has thus partially adopted. Finally the image suggests the
awful effect her encircled innocence, lack of eyes, ego, and connection
with other women, has on both bride and groom. Similarly, the speaker's

genitals, when they are tossed into a trough, have a "radiance" that so maddens the sows that they trample each other in their haste to escape. This may suggest both woman's terror at the consequences of her own sexuality and our traditional socially conditioned failures at solidarity with each other. The sows, in their "greed," see the goddess's sexual parts as a threat rather than as a sign of what they and she have in common. In a bitter acknowledgment of the denial of women's sexuality, the speaker tells us that eventually these parts were discarded upon a compost heap. And, although in this poem the speaker, unlike the earlier speaker in "Singing Aloud," accepts her traditional poetic role as divine oracle, she has no sense of intent. "The breeze wound through my mouth and empty sockets / so my lungs would sigh and my dead tongue mutter," but she herself says nothing. Her sockets are empty; no self resides there. Without her consciousness and her wholeness, she is an empty oracle and her words have no meaning. She is not a whole person but only a bundle of functions and symptoms. Reduced to her complaints, she becomes no more than an occasion for seers, whether medical, psychiatric, or sociological, to find "occupation, interpreting [her] sighs." These, we are probably meant to remember, they interpret as signs of *her* illness, neurosis, or deficiency, as they try to solve their self-created riddle: what do women want.

All this false, uncomfortable, and partial rebirth, this fragmented and exploitative use of the Goddess, is undone when the one worshipper who loves her as a complete being instead of as a scattering of functions recalls her. He remembers her, having previously forgotten and left her; he also literally recalls both the Goddess and her sexual subjectivity: "but then your great voice rang out under the skies / my name! and all those private names / for the parts and places that had loved you best." Her "parts and places" love him; he is the object, she the subject, however reduced to her functions. Yet, she allows him his traditional subjectivity, too: he does the calling and the naming. At this summons, the Goddess's parts, in a typically farcical frenzy, scurry madly from "their various places and helpful functions" to reassemble themselves, including the sexual parts reclaimed from the compost. Pursued by the people who still want to use her varied services, the Goddess and her lover "fell in a heap on the compost heap / and all our loving parts made love at once." So in this second, true rebirth, the Goddess's parts return to their proper uses, their uses as elements of her subjective and purposeful life rather than as objects of other people's consumption. The people who have, like the readers of love's scriptures in "The Copulating Gods," watched this copulation (including, of course, those of us who have just been reading the poem), disperse and go "decently about their [our] business.

This second rebirth, however, is not an unmixed blessing, even though it takes place through and for love, and restores the Goddess to her personhood. First of all, a "recycling" is not the same as a "rebirth." It implies an inescapable use by others rather than the Goddess's centrality to and use of her own life. In this narrative, it is "passion" that has suffered the "birth and rebirth and decay." The Goddess has simply been "recycled." And even though lover and Goddess are purified, having "bathed in the river" and become "sweet and wholesome again," even though they "worship each other in whispers" and in perfect reciprocity, this rebirth is not permanent but cyclical. Not the Goddess as a whole person, but, once again, "The inner parts remember fermenting hay, / the comfortable odor of dung, the animal incense, / and passion, its bloody labor, / its birth and rebirth and decay."

This rich and complex poem can be read as a feminist allegory of the loss and rebirth of women's subjectivity and sexuality, of the fragility of our relationship with man, and of the recovery of a woman-centered mythic imagery for the notions of death and redemption. It can also be read as an allegory of women's recovery of our own dis/membered histories and mythologies. It can be read, like "Food of Love," as a double-edged celebration of the cycles of love and of nature. It can be read as a very great love poem, unique in its lack of complaint, rage, or indictment of the lover (whose periodic departures relegate the Goddess to the compost heap), honest in its speaker's confession that the loss of love feels like the loss of self, and beautifully direct in its celebration of the physicality of love and of woman's own physicality ("my sacred slit / Which loved you best of all").

On one level, this poem reverses the many myths about the tearing apart and rebirth of a male God or mythic figure, whether Orpheus, Dionysus, or Osiris, and of the Goddess who mourns him, reassembles him, or recycles him. Read thus, it joins contemporary revisionist feminism in proclaiming that the men got it all wrong, that not the man but the woman gets torn apart and used in bits and pieces and recycled: it is Woman whose constant death and rebirth in the world's endless uses of us makes the corn grow and the rain fall; it is not the falling down and the rising up of the phallus but our own hard work and loss of ourselves that has kept things going. Yet to reduce the poem to this and to this alone would falsify it. This Goddess is still in love with men, however aware she may be of their misuse of her and of their hostility to her power. She cannot imagine herself without them, however double-edged her love and theirs may be.

This richness, this generosity of effect and of intent, extends into the management of the poem, the effortless transitions from high seriousness to the mordantly witty hyperbole with which the central metaphor of woman's fragmentation is worked out. The accuracy of the allusion to the "trail of blood" of the speaker's sexual flow gives way to the speaker's bitterly boastful description of her "tasty red" and its usefulness for entrapping turtles (entrapment, of course, being one of the conventional charges against both women and goddesses). This leads to the wild farce of such moments as those when the bridegroom runs away from the girl who has become "all eyes." The grim vision of the Goddess's head, speaking "oracles" with the breeze winding through the mouth and empty eyes, the wind-filled lungs sighing and the dead tongue muttering, create simultaneously a tragic and a comic view of the poet's role. From such moments of grim humor or of farce the poem shifts, with no cracking apart at the seams, however much the speaker herself has cracked apart, to the joyful lyricism of such stanzas as those in which the Goddess gets herself together again (another logically literal and comic reenactment of a figure of speech). Even when farcical, the poem is serious, and its highest lyrical moments are likely to shift to farce, then to burlesque stunts, then to expansive transcendence and quiet peacefulness in the final stanza. Nothing is forgotten or undone in this resolution. The Goddess has gotten herself together, but she has kept the terrifying vision of her death and her decay. Clearly the aesthetic behind this poem is not an aesthetic of economy, of parsimony, of the single perception or the unified creation of an effect. This poem works, not out of scarcity, but out of "amplitude [and] awe,"[42] the precise qualities Dickinson complained leaked out of women's lives when they surrendered their autonomy to men. Although every prop, every image, every tonal shift in the poem contributes to a kind of economy by finding a use for itself, like the various parts of the Goddess employed in their "helpful functions," there is more than a minimum, and more than enough, more than contemporary parsimony could find a use for. The poem radiates, glories, triumphs in and through its massive abundance.

Traditionally, our culture has represented life as a series of mutually exclusive polarities: man vs. woman, life vs. death, love vs. hate, destruction vs. creation, enough vs. too much, tragedy vs. farce. The newly emerging woman's tradition exemplified in the work of such poets as Carolyn Kizer and Muriel Rukeyser, without in any way denying or refusing these polarities, re/fuses them, absorbs them, redefines them, reassembles them. In the aesthetic of generosity, life's furious contradictions become neither harmony nor counterpoint, but something for which we have not yet made an accurate technical term. They are not harmony because harmony has heretofore implied subordination of an accompaniment to a melodic line or of the notes played in the construction, deprived of equal autonomy, to the harmonic whole. They are not counterpoint because the strains work not "against" but in balanced junction "with" each other. So it is with the balance of meanings, tones, and methods in Carolyn's poems. One does not negate another. A new approach does not imply the abandonment of a former approach. Early poems and methods stand in happy juxtaposition to more recent ones, the poet's earlier stances recycled throughout the recent collections. Changes of voice are not rejections but true changes of mind, new aspects, costumes, expansions. They do not "counter" or undercut each other as the irony characteristic of this century's poetry in our decades has typically worked to counter or undercut emotion. Instead they balance, reciprocate, mirror, and fuse with each other, allowing each poem the full force of its multiplicity of energies, even when we cannot imagine such materials co-existing in such balance, such full and wholeheartedly enthusiastic correlationship. These are the fragments of woman-centered tradition re/membered and restored to power and wholeness.

The poetics of generosity commits itself to the passions of the poem rather than retreating from them. It trusts the poem's energy. Above all, it trusts the reader, knowing her to be no adversary but a co-creator of the poem's force and as generous in her welcome of the poem as the poet herself. A poetics built on generosity is a poetics built on inclusiveness, on force of feeling and intellect, on trust, and on the will to change and to offer change. This generosity we find in Whitman's democratic fervor, in Dickinson's constantly shifting meanings and in her equation of poetry with possibility, in Hopkins' exuberant orgies of language, in Rukeyser's splendid inclusiveness of the political, the erotic, and the transcendental. In this part of the century we find it in Carolyn Kizer's Goddesses, lovers, muses, and large-spirited voice.

TEXTS CITED

I. Carolyn Kizer's poems have been reprinted in later collections and in varying arrangements as earlier ones went out of print. My notes will cite the earliest book publication and the most recent, and give page numbers for the most recent.

Kizer, Carolyn. *Knock Upon Silence.* Seattle: University of Washington Press, 1968.

————. *Mermaids in the Basement: Poems for Women.* Port Townsend, Washington: Copper Canyon Press, 1984.

————. *The Nearness of You.* Port Townsend, Washington: Copper Canyon Press, 1986.

————. *The Ungrateful Garden.* Bloomington: Indiana University Press, 1961.

————. *Yin.* Brockport, New York: BOA Editions, 1984.

II. When I quote directly from widely available examples of our inherited literary tradition, I will cite author and poem title, but not book, edition, or page number.

III. Texts I find indispensable for the consideration of feminist literary theory as it relates to this essay are:

Brownstein, Rachel. *Becoming a Heroine: Reading About Women in Novels.* New York: The Viking Press, 1982.

Daly, Mary. *Beyond God the Father: Toward a Philosophy of Women's Liberation.* Boston: Beacon Press, 1973.

Ecker, Gisela, ed. *Feminist Aesthetics.* Boston: Beacon Press, 1986.

Gilbert, Sandra and Gubar, Susan. *The Madwoman in the Attic: The Woman Writer and the Nineteenth Century Literary Imagination.* New Haven: Yale University Press, 1979.

Juhasz, Susanne. *Naked and Fiery Forms: Modern American Poetry by Women, a New Tradition.* New York: Harper and Row, 1976.

Moers, Ellen. *Literary Women.* Garden City, New York: Doubleday & Company, 1977.

Ostriker, Alicia Suskin. *Stealing the Language: An Emergence of Women's Poetry in America.* Boston: Beacon Press, 1986.

Rich, Adrienne. *On Lies, Secrets, and Silence: Selected Prose 1966–1978.* New York: W.W. Norton & Company, 1979.

Rukeyser, Muriel. *The Life of Poetry.* New York: William Morrow & Company, 1974.

NOTES

1. To accept plentitude rather than parsimony, emotion rather than unearned irony functioning as denial of emotion, has, of course, been the task of poets

as different from each other as Allen Ginsberg and Adrienne Rich. Feminists may need, however, to formulate the aesthetic as a basic condition of our creativity.

2. Carolyn Kizer, in jacket copy for *Midnight Was My Cry*.

3. Since 1970 I have been a friend of Carolyn Kizer's. I am not going to create a false appearance of academic objectivity by referring to her by her surname. The value often placed on objectivity is counter-productive. Objectivity unmediated by personal involvement falsifies as much as unacknowledged or dishonest subjectivity. In any event, an involvement, a stake in something, whether or not it is acknowledged, always exists. One of my assets as a reader of Carolyn's poetry is precisely my lack of objectivity, my personal involvement, my immersion in her work. I suspect it would be hard to find a poet of her and my generation who had somehow managed to avoid knowing and having a personal involvement with her. Poets become friends much of the time because we feel affinities for each other's work. Those affinities lead to informed readings and then to close friendships.

4. On this subject, Juhasz in *Naked and Fiery Forms* is particularly useful. See her discussion of Marianne Moore, for example.

5. Richard Howard, in a review in *Tri-Quarterly*, reprinted on the dust jacket of *Midnight Was My Cry*.

6. Would this writer, or any, have characterized, for example, a poet like James Dickey as "Southern redneck and all-purpose stud?" If he had attempted such an irrelevancy, would he or Dickey's publisher have felt that the presence of such a comment on a book jacket might tend to sell books?

7. Carolyn Kizer, "Pro Femina: Part Three," *Mermaids in the Basement*, p. 44.

8. William Blake, "The Divine Image"; Sir Thomas Browne, *Religio Medici*.

9. Gilbert and Gubar in their opening chapter, Rich in "When We Dead Awaken," and Juhasz, in her chapter on "The Double Bind of the Woman Writer," have laid the groundwork for all future discussions of this situation.

10. Ostriker. The title of her book tells the story; the book documents it.

11. Juhasz, Gilbert and Gubar, and Moers all deal with this.

12. I have dealt in more detail with the woman poet's use of the Orpheus myth as a focus for her efforts to form a public voice for herself in a paper on Muriel Rukeyser's Orpheus poems at the MLA, and in two papers on the artist Ethel Schwabacher delivered at conferences on Schwabacher's art and journals. My papers examine two related questions: how does the woman artist deal with her fragmentation, and how does her work change when her vision of her public voice changes from identification with Orpheus to identification with Eurydice.

13. Moers, Juhasz, Gilbert & Gubar.

14. Daly.

15. I use this term here deliberately to carry overtones of purposeful control of male traditional poetic forms.

16. *The Ungrateful Garden*, 1961, reprinted in *The Nearness of You*, 1986, p. 18.

17. I don't use the word literary pejoratively but for characterization.

18. Perhaps eccentrically, I refuse to use the term "Modern" to describe a movement of formative poems which were written in the first half of this century, and all the major figures of which are dead. T.S. Eliot et al. are no longer modern in the strict sense. We who write now in this modern time are the moderns, whether or not we follow aesthetics that were modern in earlier decades. "Modernist" is not accurate either, but at least it suggests an attitude associated with a movement in art, rather than asserting a contemporary quality to work no longer contemporary in its origins. Until somebody coins a term that accurately describes the Modernist movement's approach to poetics, I use this term *faute de mieux*.

19. T.S. Eliot, "Sweeney Among the Nightingales"; W.H. Auden, "As I Went Out One Evening." To both poems, I would guess, Carolyn's poem owes something both in tone and in rhetoric, as, in its general use of classical themes, it owes much to Louise Bogan.

20. *The Ungrateful Garden*, reprinted in *The Nearness of You*, p. 53.

21. Women's challenges in this century to the nature of traditional language and linearity were prefigured in early, radical linguistic dismantling by such figures as Gertrude Stein. The current generation of women involved in radical linguistic experimentation includes Susan Howe, Kathleen Fraser, and Lyn Hejinian. This is also an important part of the agenda of an influential group of male poets, but arising out of a different experience of and relationship to language.

22. Ostriker, commenting on Kizer and other poets, p. 12.

23. *Midnight Was My Cry*, p. 10.

24. William Butler Yeats, "The Fisherman."

25. This is not to suggest that contemporary male poets have not also used some of the same correctives; the entire range of so-called "Post-Modern" poetry in this country has been nourished by them. I am suggesting, however, that this correction or shaking of the prior tradition has a particular and specific force, different from its force in men's work, when women do it, because the need is greater in degree and different in kind. To some extent we might argue that the men writing recently may have consciously or unconsciously adopted or converged with parts of the feminist literary agenda.

26. *Knock Upon Silence*, 1965, reprinted in *Mermaids in the Basement*, p. 20.

27. See, for example, Yeats, "Adam's Curse," which, when it deals with Eve's curse, equates suffering with labor, and has the "beautiful wild woman" lament that she "must labor to be beautiful."

28. Reprinted from earlier volumes in *Yin*, p. 20.

29. John Donne, "The Canonization."

30. For a feminist point of view on the drawbacks of this transcendence, some readers may find it useful to read the sections on Clarissa as "exemplar of her sex" and on Sir Willoughby Patterne in Brownstein.

31. Rich, in "When We Dead Awaken," written in 1971, spoke of a "deep fatalistic pessimism" in the poetry of her male contemporaries. At about the time her essay was first published, I attended a literary conference at which a distinguished poet and friend of mine spoke of his resistance to poems that attempted to "over-whelm" him, giving such examples as Hopkins' *The Wreck of the Deutschland*, Thompson's "The Hound of Heaven," and almost anything by Dylan Thomas and Whitman. I though of Donne's "Batter my heart, three-person'd God. . . ." and wondered why this successful man's ego seemed so fragile that he had to pro-tect it carefully not only from the great and generous force of language, but from everything he perceived as most sacred. The pessimism Rich noticed and the self-protective shrinking back from emotion I found so pitiful seemed to me directly related. Subsequent thought has convinced me that the irony and com-plexity that, at their most exuberant in the early part of the century, embodied generosity by welcoming all the intertwined passion and range of possible inter-actions of a text, have somehow become confused, in a dominant aesthetic of our generation, with a fear to commit oneself to passion or range for fear of being judged sentimental. But, if sentimentality is unearned emotion, then this petty and self-protective pseudo-irony, this withholding of justified passion, is the sentimentality of our age. This recognition may have something to do with why June Jordan entitled a recent book of poems *Passion*.

    Muriel Rukeyser, in *The Life of Poetry* (New York: William Morrow & Company, 1974), first published in 1949, analyzes a deeper level of the fear of poetry, and grounds this fear less in a fear of sentimentality than in a desperate fear of emotion and of giving due force to the unconscious life within us. If she is right, then the poetics of parsimony is based upon a basic fear of surrender, a fear of poetry itself.

32. Sigrid Weigl, "Double Focus," in *Feminist Aesthetics*, p. 80.

33. From an earlier volume, reprinted as the closing poem of *Mermaids in the Basement*, p. 104.

34. A useful discussion of this dilemma as it involves visual art and the prob-lem of the gaze may be found in Elizabeth Lenk, "The Self-Reflecting Woman," *Feminist Aesthetics*, p. 51.

35. Pope does use the first person in *The Dunciad*, but in formalized invocations to the muse or similar set pieces. He presents his narrative and his enven-omed character sketches as if they were somehow externalized statements of fact rather than personal expressions of rage. Only the language (what an only!) shows him to be personally involved.

36. Parts one, two, and three of "Pro Femina" first appeared in book form in *Knock Upon Silence*. In *Yin*, those three parts are not reprinted, and "Fanny" makes her first appearance in book form as a poem in a section entitled "Fanny and the Affections." In *Mermaids in the Basement*, published the same year as *Yin*, "Pro Femina" has four sections, labeled "Part One," "Part Two," "Part Three," and "Part Four: Fanny." This, most probably, represents the poet's most recent organization of this material, and the one most useful to me to examine in the context of my argument. There is, of course, no reason why the poet should not continue to present her work in multiple versions, arranged as the context dictates. That constant changing and rejuxtaposition of the lineup from one volume to the next, is, in fact, a basic organizing principle of her work, and signifies a denial of linearity and a refusal of the later self to reject any of the earlier self's modes. [Editors' note: "Pro Femina" was published with a new fifth section as a chapbook in 2000, and the full text is included in *Cool, Calm, & Collected: Poems 1960–2000*, published in 2001.]

37. *Yin*, p. 29.

38. *Yin*, p. 28.

39. Oscar Wilde, "The Ballad of Reading Gaol."

40. *Yin*, p. 13.

41. In the traditional form of the myth, Semele was a human woman Zeus adopted human form to court. She asked him to appear to her in his divine glory. When he consented to do so, his blaze of heat consumed her to ashes. Before she was totally consumed, Zeus tore her unborn infant, Dionysus, out of her body, and concealed the baby in his thigh until the proper moment for birth (another of those mythical reversals of the actual biology of birth, like the birth of Athene from Zeus's head, Eve from Adam's rib, and the practice of couvade). When Dionysus himself became a god, he restored Semele to life and promoted her to Goddesshood. Semele, in her traditional form, is thus a highly ambiguous Goddess for this poet to re/member. This recycling of the myth, in the form she gives it, constitutes a revisionary proposition that the recorded form of the myth is an error, and an assertion that Semele was not a victim of her own vanity but another form of the resurrected deity of renewal.

42. Emily Dickinson, #732 "She rose to his requirement."

KIM VAETH

The House of Madame K.

WHEN CAROLYN KIZER entered a room, she glided in with the authority that stunning women command, in silk caftan, arms extended, her bright hair swept back, her toenails painted pinker than the inside of a conch and would say something like, "The problem with Ronald Reagan is that he doesn't read Akhmatova. If he did, he would know better." A ripple traversed the room. Carolyn Kizer had arrived.

On several occasions, I went on her arm—in a loose manner of speaking—to poetry readings at the women's bookstores in Berkeley and Oakland. A somber hush of disbelief would fall over the gloriously unshaven and Birkenstocked assembly of feminists when Carolyn swung open the door and entered, wearing a three-quarter-length mink and heels. Did the women of the cotton drawstring trousers know that the woman who had just entered the bookstore had written these lines just over a decade earlier?

> So, sister, forget yourself a few times and see where it gets you:
> Up the creek, alone with your talent, sans everything else,
> You can wait for the menopause, and catch up on your reading.
> So primp, preen, prink, pluck and prime your flesh,
> All posturings! All ravishment! All sensibility!
> Meanwhile, have you used your mind today?
>
> —"Pro Femina," Book Two[1]

In July of 1977, I met Carolyn at Centrum, a summer writers' confer-
ence in Port Townsend, Washington. Writers from all over the country
converged for one week on what had been an army compound on the
Puget Sound. Carolyn, joined by Olga Broumas, Gary Snyder and William
Pitt Root, held workshops by day and gave readings by night. All day
until late at night, the compound hummed with poetry which floated up
above the abandoned cannons and artillery fields and out over the Sound.

Drifting languorously from one motley poet group to another, wear-
ing chic capris—Carolyn was the queen of the entire poetic hive that
week. As the crow may or may not fly, the sultry diva of Port Townsend
had come a long way from Spokane.

In those years, Carolyn and her charming husband and paramour, the
architect John Woodbridge, lived in the Berkeley Hills. On a street named
LeRoy, above the detritus of Telegraph Avenue, above the intellectual frolic of
the UC Campus, above Euclid Avenue's coffee and falafel houses. Their
house was perched high enough to see the slate sheet of bay and beyond it,
Mt. Tamalpais. Their frequent travels opened the door for me to hop into my
pale yellow VW Bug and drive from the heart of San Francisco's Mission
District, across the airy deck of the Bay Bridge, to housesit in Berkeley.

One foggy afternoon, Carolyn and I had a long conversation about
Emily Dickinson. I made a few respectful, predictable graduate-student
observations about the poet from Amherst. Mainly, I listened to Carolyn
quote lines and discuss Dickinson's singular, brilliant and revelatory
vision. She dipped into her reservoir: "I stepped from Plank to Plank / A
slow and cautious way / The Stars about my Head I felt / About my Feet the
Sea." Perhaps Carolyn alone could have easily persuaded Emily D. to
leave her house for an afternoon martini at an appropriate, nearby bar.

We had other, equally long conversations about teaching. Carolyn
spoke in great detail about the assignments she gave her students. Her stu-
dents at Princeton, for example, were forbidden to use the pronoun "I" for
an entire semester. "It's the only way to wake them up to the power of
the subjective voice," she said. She would actually discuss workshops of
hers that had flopped! These conversations usually opened into a consid-
eration about *how* to teach—the various and endless ways to offer the
world to students of poetry. Though I was a few years away from my first
teaching job at Goddard College, I stored every morsel for future use.
Soon after these talks, Carolyn dropped my given name and called me
Cherubino. I blushed.

I was invited to housesit when John and Carolyn went on trips to Tucson or to Washington, D.C., that involved poetry events and awards ceremonies. At the time, I lived in an apartment in the Mission District—a futon-on-the-floor, orange shag carpet kind of apartment, located in a great, constantly moving throng of humanity. I was only too glad to leave the hot crush of people and the continual eruptions they made. Each time I arrived at Carolyn's house, its vastness startled me anew. Did Carolyn herself sometimes find its spaciousness discomfiting? I never knew and I never asked.

On my first visit, I entered the front door with the meekness that small town folk exude like perspiration in the big city. Yet perhaps in this particular house, Carolyn had found one that was her true measure. Unlike other houses—typical, boxy American houses where one walked through rooms—Carolyn's house seemed to unfold around one. Each room required a sassy, if not theatrical presence—a profoundly sleight-of-hand effort for Carolyn.

I imagined that as the *Duino Elegies* had certainly waited for Rilke to write them, the house on LeRoy Street had certainly waited for Carolyn to arrive. Could its architect, Julia Morgan—designer of the Hearst mansion—have had a premonition of Carolyn and the poetry that Carolyn would write once she arrived?

In *The Poetics of Space*, Gaston Bachelard claims that our houses are our dream spaces—their shape, their nooks and crannies, their thresholds and gardens work on us unconsciously to elicit our dreams. And in our dreams, lies our poetry. Ah, "Pro Femina," indeed. Only Julia Morgan could have designed the house that would, in time, elicit the poetry of Carolyn Kizer.

The house was so spacious and meandering, that, upon arriving, I would become immediately absorbed with a task not unlike shadow boxing: in which room should I write?

On the right, just inside the foyer, was Carolyn's study. It was open, bright, many windowed, with a square desk at the back of the room and books lining the walls from floor to ceiling. Her desk was perched away from the walls, facing the entranceway, which kept one's back to the windows. Invariably, there were a half dozen poetry manuscripts of friends and students scattered on the desktop, waiting for her penciled remarks in the margins.

I couldn't possibly sit at Carolyn's desk in Carolyn's study surrounded by a thousand of Carolyn's books. I know because I tried. There were books by Michael Hamburger and John Clare. Why had I never heard of John Clare? Could anyone have been as wildly unread as I? It seemed a crime to be a twenty-five year old graduate student with no knowledge of John Clare. There were volumes of Japanese art prints and rows upon rows of poetry in translation. I could stay up all night, each night, and read. Sitting there on the floor, strangely comfortable and uncomfortable simultaneously, I breathed the oxygen coming off of Carolyn's books.

Around the curving corner from the study was the living room. Perhaps I could work better in the living room, notebook perched on knees as I sat in the cushioned window seat overlooking the Bay, the brown or green (depending on season) Berkeley hills, and on a clear day, and there were many of those, Mt. Tamalpais across the Bay in that salad county of Marin. Despite the understated grandness of a Baby Grand, the living room had an Eames feel. The sleek sofas were white, as were the swooping saddles of the chairs. The stereo was close at hand, accompanied by stacks of Bach, Vivaldi, Mozart, Callas and von Stade. In this room, what could one do but crank up "Der Rosenkavalier" or "La Traviata," sit in one of the Eames chairs, gaze at the Bay and wait for deliverance? At least, that's what Cherubino did.

More curvature. Up the winding stair in the main foyer, at the far side of the second floor was the library. Formal, even formidable, with a few small reading tables of somber wood, its Julia Morganesque elegance aside, I imagined that Carolyn did not fully embrace this room. She might have been elated that it existed, of course, but was in no way desirous of working there. Perhaps it was just the knowledge that this room anchored a certain portion of the house, that it was a room large enough to actually stroll through that gave her spiritual comfort. Perhaps she saw it with a utilitarian eye—as a place to hold an occasional fundraiser for the American Academy of Poets or to have a few of the gals over for some five card draw. Even in bright sun, its iron-filigreed windows shadowed the room. I toured this room only in daylight and thought about the 19th century.

Bearing slightly right at the top of the stair was Carolyn's bath that opened into a dressing room. It was yellow and plush. The long, curving bathtub was perched on claws. It begged for bubbles and fortunately, Carolyn had many vials of lavender and lime green bath beads and potions. The small, womb-like dressing room had a plumpish chaise lounge for reading or napping pre- or post-bath. It was also the perfect perch for painting one's toenails, a pleasure, which, ruefully, I did not indulge in those years.

Clearly, regarding the intrepid row of small rosy bottles, Carolyn did. Should one read, paint one's toenails, or nap? I napped.

I had only two significant responsibilities during my stay in Carolyn's house—to feed Mishkin, her haughty, highly cerebral cat that probably knew John Clare stanzas by heart, and to order the large quantities of mail. Great poets receive lots of mail from all over the world. Each day it poured through the slotted front door into a heap. At the plateau otherwise known as the dining room table, I sorted and stacked. It was yet another place I tried to work but its sheer expanse undid me and I decided it was best suited for stacking. Eventually, each day's pile formed a paper range of terraced foothills. I moved on.

The list of potential spots to set up a writing perch was long. A lovely glass and wrought iron table and chairs beckoned from the brick patio and garden behind the house. A desk in the master bedroom up on the second floor serenaded. The bed itself—always a viable draw for certain sensual writers like myself and Carolyn—whispered sweet phrases. In the end, I merely slept in that bed and hoped for no more than a few unorthodox dreams.

The truth is that I never found a place to write in her house. The struggle was not just where to be but rather, how to find my proper place in the great poet's house. This struggle comprised the focal point and sum of all that I learned in and from the house of Madame K. Her house worked on me unconsciously, forcing my own poetic cards. In her house, I could almost hear the blackjack dealer call out, "Ante up." This one circumscribed, repeatedly arduous process of deciding how to inhabit Carolyn's house during each sporadic spurt of tenure proved to be a singularly illuminating struggle that prepared me for other magnificent places—the Guggenheim, Chartres, Emily Dickinson's poetry and the upper plateaus of Tibet. In short, the merry life of a writer.

One of the last, pungent memories I have of being in that house is of the morning after John and Carolyn had returned in the wee hours from one of their junkets to the East. Carolyn was reading the paper in her study. John was making coffee in the kitchen. I was walking down the main staircase toward the smell of coffee. She called out, loudly enough to reach us both—"John Lennon was murdered last night in New York." I stopped on the staircase. John stopped making coffee and turned around in the kitchen. Carolyn put the paper down and rose. We all stood there in our different places inside the vast house—a still, triumvirate of sadness—and were silent for a long time.

NOTES

1. *No More Masks! An Anthology of Poems by Women*, edited by Florence Howe and Ellen Bass. New York: Doubleday Anchor Books, 1973, pp. 174–5.

DOMINIC CHEUNG

Carolyn Kizer and Her Chinese Imitations

IN THE ACKNOWLEDGEMENTS which preface her book *Knock Upon Silence*, Carolyn Kizer confesses the debt she owes to Arthur Waley's translations of Chinese poems.[1] It is from Waley's translations that Kizer derives the material for a group of her own poems which appear in the section of her book titled *Chinese Imitations*. These eight poems are dedicated to Waley, whose translations Kizer has read, she frankly admits, since her childhood, adding that "like so many of my contemporaries, my debt and my devotion to him is incalculable."[2]

Admittedly, it would be difficult to talk about the impact of the Chinese poems themselves on Carolyn Kizer's poems since her "imitations" are essentially imitations of Arthur Waley's translations. However, although the risks of any influence study run high, an examination of the sources available to Kizer is appropriate in order to furnish a clearer appreciation of what Kizer has undertaken.

Waley modestly assures us in the preface of his translations that his Chinese friends attest to the closeness of his translations, "closer, they have sometimes been kind enough to say, than those of any other translator."[3] Nevertheless, certain inaccuracies do exist in Waley's work; quite inexplicably, for instance, the Chinese poem "Reciting Alone in the Mountain" is translated as "Madly Singing in the Mountain."[4] Twice removed from the original, Carolyn Kizer's "Singing Aloud" is evidence of yet another stage in the metamorphosis of the poem.[5]

In another instance, Kizer claims that two of her works are derived from Arthur Waley's translation of *The Book of Songs*, a selection of ancient odes which were composed around the tenth century B.C. In actuality, Kizer's poems are based on the Waley translation of the "Tzu-yeh Songs," ballads written in the third century A.D. The confusion is compounded further by the fact that the fourth of the five "Tzu-yeh Songs" which Waley translated is in fact taken from the tenth-century A.D. "Mo-ch'ou Songs."

However, the effect of these inaccuracies on Carolyn Kizer's poems is minimal since she is engaged in the creation of imitations derived from the Chinese works rather than translating the works from the original. On the other hand, considering the conciseness of the Chinese language and the resulting ambiguities and indirectness such a language poses when employed in poetry, it is rather amazing (particularly for those versed in the Chinese poems themselves) to note that Carolyn Kizer has effectively captured the subtlest nuances of the Chinese works while often bringing latent connotations to full and precise imagistic expression.

It is never a matter of referring Kizer's pieces to the Chinese poems themselves or vice versa since Kizer's works successfully demonstrate her sensitive explorations of material available to her. What she finally voices in her own poems is no longer the solitary cry of the oriental woman, but that which belongs neither to the east nor the west and is not confined in terms of either space or time. Three stanzas of Kizer's "Summer near the River" are modeled after the "Tzu-yeh Songs." The last stanza, which actually belongs to the "Mo-ch'ou Songs" and which Waley mistook as belonging to the "Tsu-yeh Songs," is gracefully combined with the "Tzu-yeh" verses in the form of a dramatic monologue which utilizes all the episodes inherent in the original poems.

The word "Tzu-yeh" is a somewhat meaningless title of one of the largest group of songs from the Six Dynasties of China. According to a historical treatise, one of the original songs was said to have been written by a maiden named Tzu-yeh. The treatise goes on to describe, in all seriousness, the singing of two ghosts in two households of the T'ai-yuan period (A.D. 376–396). Since the ghosts kept singing the words "Tzu-yeh," the historians concluded that Tzu-yeh must have been the creator of these songs!

Carolyn Kizer's version of the "Tzu-yeh" assumes the title of "Summer near the River." In this work, two images immediately present themselves:

the image of summer and that of a flowing river. Traditionally, summer symbolizes passion, the season of ripening love. In Kizer's poem, it is a season when life forces surge strongly but are counteracted by the cold determinism of the river, a symbol of the relentless flow, the clearly defined course of life. Where summer presents a wide variation of color in nature, the river, on the other hand, suggests a certain fixedness by virtue of its defined path.

The river and summer are thus two antithetical images which Carolyn Kizer uses, tying them together through the use of internal rhymes such as "Sum*mer* n*ear* the ri*ver*." By persistently stressing the grief which is inherent in the symbol of summer, the poet is able to extend herself into the realm of dramatic details. The first two stanzas:

> I have carried my pillow to the windowsill
> And try to sleep, with my damp arms crossed upon it
> But no breeze stirs the tepid morning.
> Only I stir. . . . Come, tease me a little!
> With such cold passion, so little teasing play,
> How long can we endure our life together?
>
> No use. I put on your long dressing gown!
> The untied sash trails over the dusty floor.
> I kneel by the window, prop up your shaving mirror
> And pluck my eyebrows.
> I don't care if the robe slides open
> Revealing a crescent of belly, a tan thigh.
> I can accuse the non-existent breeze. . . .[6]

In Arthur Waley's translation of two of the "Tzu-yeh Songs" we read:

> I have brought my pillow and am lying at the northern window
> So come to me and play with me a while.
> With so much quarrelling and so few kisses
> How long do you think our love can last?
>
> I will carry my coat and not put on my belt;
> With unpainted eyebrows I will stand at the front window.
> My tiresome petticoat keeps on flapping about:
> If it opens a little, I shall blame the spring wind.[7]

A word-for-word translation of the Chinese original reads:

carry — pillow-north — window — lie
you (man/boy) — come — to — me (woman/girl) — play/tease
little — joy — more — clashes
to pity each other — can — how long

carry — gown — not — tie — sash
lightly — brows — out — front — window
gauze — dress — easy — wavers
little — exposure — blame/accuse — east-wind.

When compared to Waley's translation of the Chinese work, Kizer's verses are, psychologically, much richer in their depiction of the dejected woman. The opening lines, "I have carried my pillow to the windowsill / And tried to sleep, with my damp arms crossed upon it," direct our attention immediately to the meaning associated with the heat of summer. Physically confined to her chamber, the woman's discomfort is heightened by the oppressive warmth which, in turn, creates a sense of stasis since "no breeze stirs. . . . / Only I stir." On the psychological level there is the same sense of oppression which is manifested by physical reality. Thus when the woman moves towards the window, she is not only seeking physical relief from the "tepid" morning, but, locked in her own ego, is trying to establish contact with the outside world. By providing her own details, Kizer thus amplifies the emotional tenor of the original work without departing from the basic thrust of Waley's "I have brought my pillow and am lying at the northern window."

Although each stanza of Kizer's poem is in fact an independent poem, she has managed, by reversing the order of the original poem, to melt the disparate elements into a single unified poem. The invitation "Come, tease me a little!" followed by "With such cold passion, so little teasing play, / How long can we endure our life together?" for instance, successfully prepares us for the actions which follow in the next stanza, where the woman, having failed to engage the man in a "little teasing," rises and slips on his dressing gown. Kizer's own use of the pronoun "your" with regard to the man's dressing gown, may, at first glance seem immaterial. Several suggestions are implied, however, by the woman's use of her companion's dressing gown. The malaise which is created by the heat in the first verse is now paralleled by emotional lassitude: the woman does not bother to dress, but merely slips on her companion's dressing gown, allowing the untied sash to trail on the floor. It might have been suggested, too, that by wearing her companion's robe, the woman subconsciously strives for the physical contact which is not in the offing from the man whose passion is "cold" and who is so little inclined toward the "little teasing play."

By having the woman wear her lover's robe, Kizer effectively sets the stage, so to speak, for the crucial closing lines in the second verse where the woman says, "I don't care if the robe slides open / Revealing a crescent of belly, a tan thigh." Elsewhere in her poem "Hiding Our Love," a modification of Wu-ti's "People Hide Their Love," Kizer again uses the seemingly casual detail as a means of bringing certain facts to light without overt reference to them. In Waley's translation of Wu-ti's poem we read:

> Round my waist I wear a double sash
> I dream that it binds us both with the same-heart knot.[8]

In Kizer's version she says:

> The sash of my dress wraps twice around my waist
> I wish it bound the two of us together.[9]

In Wu-ti's poem, the sash is a symbol of platonic love, the illusory bond between two hearts. In Kizer's poem, the sash is utilized to convey two levels of meaning: a separation between lovers has affected the woman; that the sash can be wound twice around her waist suggests that her health has failed and that she has grown thin. By winding the sash around her waist, the woman, undoubtedly, is reminded of the binding power of love, hence her words "I wish it bound the two of us together."

Similarly, in "Summer near the River," the trailing sash, a seemingly small detail, is utilized to convey several levels of meaning. Where the sash in "Hiding Our Love" is a symbol of woman's desire to be bound in love, the trailing sash in "Summer near the River" suggests a deteriorating relationship, a slackening of love on the part of the woman's companion. It is also a means of leading into the last lines of the verse where the robe slides open, blown apparently by a non-existent breeze to reveal the "crescent of belly [and] a tan thigh." The untied sash in Kizer's poem is parallel to the fluttering gauze dress worn by the lady in the Chinese poem. In both instances, the seemingly casual dishabille is an attempt at seduction, but where the sliding robe reveals belly and thigh, the diaphanous gauze dress is allowed to flap open in the spring wind and perhaps "open a little."

The defiance of Kizer's "I don't care if the robe slides open / Revealing a crescent of belly, a tan thigh" is absent in the Chinese poem. The woman's defiance as well as the subjunctive mood in which she states that she "can accuse the non-existent breeze" is weak because there is only the remotest possibility that a breeze would stir the "tepid morning." In the Chinese poem, whatever the "wavering" dress reveals is not mentioned and neither are reasons given as to what causes the dress to "waver" in the first place. The attention is thus drawn not to what the opening dress reveals, but rather, to why the spring wind is being used as an excuse for the dishabille and not the gauze dress or the deliberately unfastened sash.

In Kizer's poem, we learn of a waning interest on the man's part and the woman's suspicion of his infidelity later in the poem. Laying the blame on her "non-existent breeze" for the exposed belly and thigh thus lends a poignant air to the situation in the poem. For although she is aware of the "cold passion," the woman's pride is maintained sufficiently to the extent that the efforts to win back the man must appear casual and not actively sought. True desperation over an impending loss cannot be revealed, hence the feeble lie, that a wind, and a non-existent wind at that, has caused the robe to fall open.

In the third verse of "Summer near the River," the woman's pride is affirmed in the midst of her fears over her vagrant lover. She reveals that:

I am monogamous as the North Star
But I don't want you to know it. You'd only take advantage.
While you are as fickle as spring sunlight.[10]

Her love and desire to hold on to her companion cannot be revealed to him for in contrast to her steadfastness he is "as fickle as spring sunlight."

In comparing her lover to the spring sunlight, Kizer once again stays close to the astrological imagery used in the Chinese poem. In the "Tzu-yeh Songs," fidelity and faithlessness are described in terms of the North Star and the sun:

Where I am the dawn star of the North
Never shifting for thousands of years,
You bear the heart of the bright sun
East in the morning, west at dusk.[11]

(my translation)

As an archetype, the sun is a representation of truth, righteousness and supremacy. Used in the "Tzu-yeh," the sun conceit is similar to the image employed by Donne in "A Valediction: Forbidding Mourning." In Donne's poem, lovers are bound as one by their love. As two separate entities, the poet sees himself as the active half which, when it "far doth roam," "leans and hearkens after" "the fixed root," which "in the center sit."[12] In the "Tzu-yeh" and "Summer near the River," the path taken by the sun each day from east to west suggests not only the man's infidelity, but perhaps his natural inability to remain constant. For just as the sun may pass through northern skies at certain times of the year, it must, inevitably, move on its own established course leaving the Northern star which never shifts in a thousand years. The very inevitability of such a course in nature only heightens the harsh reality which exists in terms of the human lover relationship.

It is not until the last two verses of the poem that Kizer introduces the image of the river, and where the passion associated with summer is identified with the man who is seen "striding towards the river," while the woman petulantly exclaims, "The cat means more to you than I." When he returns "reeking of fish and beer," the woman notes that:

There is salt dew in your hair, where have you been?
Your clothes weren't that wrinkled hours ago, when you left.
You couldn't have loved someone else, after loving me![13]

In her distress at the sight of her returning lover, all of the woman's senses are brought into play as she smells the beer and fish, notes the wrinkled clothes and salt dew in his hair.

The river is mentioned again in the closing lines of the poem when the man embraces the woman, causing her to say, "for a moment, the river ceases flowing."[14] The river, as we have previously noted, is a symbol of unrelenting fate. Specific applications of the symbol are made in turn to the man and the woman in "Summer near the River." The man, for instance, strides toward the river, and figuratively the act may be seen as the control he has over his life and fate. The woman's fate, on the other hand, rests on the man himself, her happiness and peace of mind depend on his uncertain love. Fate, like the relentless flow of the river, has already decreed a change in the relationship, but in the moment that the man embraces her, the woman feels that what is foreordained cannot possibly occur. In the light of her present ecstasy, the future without him is stalled, hence "for a moment, the river ceases flowing."

In the Chinese poem, the stilled river is placed in context of a separation between a woman and her lover. She sees him off on his journey, going "with him as far as Ch'u-shan." When he, against all social conventions, embraces her in public, she ecstatically says:

For a moment you held me fast in your outstretched arms.
I thought the river stood still and did not flow.[15]

Here, as in "Summer near the River," a parting of the ways is in the offing, harshly determined perhaps by fate. The breach of socially accepted behavior is sufficient reason for the woman's ecstatic "I thought the river stood still and did not flow," but in terms of the river as a symbol of predetermined factors in life, it would seem that here, as in Kizer's poem, the ecstasy can, and does momentarily, halt the tide of fate. In the Chinese poem, the moment is crystallized by the illusion of the river's stillness, and the setting of mountains surrounding the embracing pair is fixed in a perfectly harmonious whole. While Carolyn Kizer's poems are not exact translations, they do utilize the substance, stylistics and subtle nuances of Chinese works. Where basically oriental allusions with no English equivalent appear, they are used as points of departure for Kizer's own personal experiences without jeopardy to the essential details of the original Chinese works. The graceful artistry of Kizer's poems lies on the strength of the balance she has struck between her vision and that which is inherent in the Chinese poems, for her poems are never merely accurate copies of the Chinese poems, nor are they simply a vehicle.

It cannot be said that Kizer lacks originality in what she has undertaken to write, since what she has taken from the Chinese is synthesized by her own passion and sensitivity. The extent of this synthesis is seen in a comparison of her lines from "Winter Song" with those of Arthur Waley:

(1) So I go on, tediously on and on. . . .
     We are separated, finally, not by death but by life.[16]

        (Kizer)

On and on, always on and on
Away from you, parted by a life-parting.[17]

        (Waley)

(2) How can you and I meet face to face
     After our triumphant love?
     After our failure?[18]

        (Kizer)

The way between is difficult and long,
Face to face how shall we meet again?[19]

        (Waley)

In the lines quoted above, we see that Waley, like many established sinologists, has tended to present the original poem as closely as possible. With Carolyn Kizer's renditions, we sense for the first time an attempt at exploring the poems for meanings which go beyond the linguistic representations. With her lyric temperament and acute sensibilities, Kizer peels away at different layers of metaphor, exhausting words and allusions of their ultimate meanings. Thus, although her works may be deemed interpretative, they, on occasion, exceed even the Chinese poems themselves, for the vibrancy which Kizer has infused into them.

NOTES

1. Carolyn Kizer, *Knock Upon Silence* (Seattle and London: Univ. of Washington Press, 1968). These are the words found in the beginning of her acknowledgments: "I have been reading the poetry of Arthur Waley since childhood, and, like so many of my contemporaries, my debt and my devotion to him is incalculable."

2. *Ibid.* In her notes following the poems, Kizer has singled out each poem's originality as follows: "The first three poems in the book are written in the style of Po Chü-I. 'Hiding Our Love' is modeled on a poem of the Emperor

Wu-ti. 'Night Sounds' and 'Summer near the River' are based on themes in
The Book of Songs."

3. In preparing for an illustrated edition of his translations, Waley confidently
    states, "Since the translations made over twenty years ago my own knowl-
    edge of Chinese and the general study of it in America and Europe have
    made enormous progress. In arranging the poems for this illustrated edition
    I have corrected a certain number of mistakes. . . . There is a great deal that
    specialists might quarrel with, but not much, I hope, that will be definitely
    misleading to the general public. . . ." See Preface, in *Translations from the
    Chinese by Arthur Waley* (New York: Vintage, 1971). Incidentally, the earliest
    edition was published by Alfred A. Knopf, Inc. in 1919. Therefore, the trans-
    lation made by Waley twenty years ago must have been sometime around
    1900.

4. *Ibid*, p. 197. The title of this poem has also been adopted for a posthumous
    volume in memory of Arthur Waley's works. See Ivan Morris, ed., *Madly
    Singing in the Mountains: An Appreciation and Anthology of Arthur Waley*
    (New York: Harper & Row, 1970).

5. Kizer, pp. 4–5.

6. Kizer, p. 11.

7. Waley, p. 35.

8. Waley, p. 104. A clarification is needed here. The Wu-ti who wrote this
    poem is Liang Wu-ti (A.D. 464–?), or Emperor Wu of the Liang Dynasty.

9. "Hiding Our Love," Kizer, p. 8.

10. "Summer near the River," Kizer, p. 12.

11. The original Chinese poem can be found in Kuo Mou-ch'ien, ed. *Yüeh-fu
    shih-chi* (Taipei: Shang-wu, 1968), II, 521.

12. *The Complete Poetry and Selected Prose of John Donne*, ed. Charles M. Cof-
    fin (New York: Random House, 1952), pp. 38–39. Other examples that
    demonstrate love triumphing over the inconstancy of the sun can be found
    in Donne's other poems like "The Anniversarie," and "Song: Sweetest Love,
    I Do Not Goe."

13. Kizer, p. 12.

14. Waley, p. 35. The original poem can be found in *Yüeh-fu shih-chi*, II, 574.

15. Waley, p. 35.

16. "Winter Song," Kizer, p. 14.

17. "Seventeen Old Poems," Waley, p. 37.

18. Kizer, p. 14.

19. Waley, p. 37.

HAYDEN CARRUTH

Afterword

I CAN'T and won't pretend that I am able to write about Carolyn Kizer or her work "objectively." She has been a friend of mine for more than thirty years. She has been of such significant help to me—in many ways, which I won't elucidate—that I cannot imagine my life as being anything but *far worse* without her. I mean this literally, although in the whole thirty years I doubt that we have spent that number of days in each other's actual company.

But indeed the entire poetic community is in her debt almost as much as I. When she was editor of *Poetry Northwest*, the magazine she founded in Seattle in the 1950s, she published the first work of many young poets, and she opened her pages to older poets who were experimenting in new modes. When the NEA was established in 1966, she served as the first director of the literature program and had much to do with getting the program off to a good start, meaning primarily a fair and sensible distribution of grants, something the program has not always sustained in the years since then. She was also active in the general discussions preceding the establishment of the NEA itself, which was the first federal venture into the arts since the controversial awarding of the Bollingen Prize by the Library of Congress to Ezra Pound in 1948. Now that we are used to the presence of the NEA in Washington it is easy to forget how vexed was the whole question of governmental participation in the arts at that time. As a reviewer and literary journalist, also as cultural attaché to the American embassy in Karachi and USIA lecturer, Carolyn has done a great deal to bring attention to American poetry both at home and overseas. She and Donald Hall have done more in this respect, though in different ways, than any other poets alive. As a visiting teacher at many universities, she has brought her enthusiasm for poetry to many thousands of young people.

Carolyn's poetry is various and brilliant. Like some other romanticists she is a confirmed neo-classicist, and her characteristic mode is a witty, intelligent eroticism that puts her in a direct line of descent from Catullus. But she has mixed in a fair-sized dash of the classical Chinese masters, too, their slyness and good sentimentality. As a person of our century she is sufficiently neurotic and metaphysical. Her writing has a flexibility that permits her to turn from public satire—and how few have even attempted this in recent times!—to personal meditation or lyric celebration with scarcely a shift of voice. Her work delights me. Obviously it delights many others as well because it has won a large audience, and for her efforts she has been rewarded with many honors and distinctions.

She wears her laurels well. Carolyn Kizer is a great lady. She combines the role of great ladies of the past with that of a responsibly liberated woman of the present, and does it magnificently. In her home in California she is arbiter, impresario, author, friend, succorer, facilitator. This could be a great burden to her, and no doubt it sometimes is, but she is so absolutely honest and just and generous in all her dealings with the literary world that she is relieved of the mess in which lesser players of the literary game find themselves. Unlike them, she can repose ultimately in the acuteness of her sensibility and the goodness of her work, her own personal genius. This is what will sustain her prominence in the literature of America for a long, long time to come.

Poems
for
Carolyn

MARIE PONSOT

Inviting Carolyn Kizer

Because I'm seldom where I should be, I am
—with great kindness—invited late
to party with this crowd of Kizer fans
gathered to fete her.

What'll I wear? I long to go, intent
On dancing to her tune of joy come true—
Which plays, in Carolyn's embodiment,
Wickedly, newly.

My closet hangers droop: no spiffy dress,
No chic trou'. Too late to shop. Clothes should propose
The body's pride in presence at the dance.
Carolyn shows it

In every tone she sweetly wears or writes,
Gorgeous in her lovely lines and bones,
Dressed as if by angels glad to recite
Garment Te Deums,

Te Deum stanzas, verse transformed to liturgies
Of wit. So here I come in sneakers, trusting
That her forgiving eye refigure me
(mercy, not justice!)

How crucial her courage to our tasks, how dear
Her wit, her work, the word-world she saves us in.
There's no one like her. Make silence. Hear, hear.
Carolyn, begin.

ROBERT CREELEY

Bub and Sis

For Carolyn Kizer

Let the dog lie down with the dog,
people with people.
It makes a difference where you fit
and how you feel.

When young, I was everybody's human,
a usual freaked person,
looking for love in the dark,
being afraid to turn the lights on.

It makes a great difference
to have a friend
who's a woman,
when you're a so-called man,

who can talk to you
across the great divide
of mixed signals
and wounded pride.

Small thanks in the end
for that maintaining sister,
but what she says
is what you remember.

KELLY CHERRY

On Some Qualities in Her Self and Poetry

For Carolyn Kizer

Some qualities command a stage: beauty,
For instance, such as must be seen up close
And center (no understudy cutie
Who muffs her lines before a half-filled house),
For presence is another quality
In poetry, the poem's assumption of
Itself a measure of vitality.
In part, this is to say a certain gumption
Lends poetry its wit. One must be brave
And risk catcalls, the tomato and the boo,
The silence no bit of stage business can save.
The serious poem will manage much ado
About everything, and not only because
Attention to the world deserves applause.

LUCILLE CLIFTON

Sisters

For Carolyn Kizer

In the parade,
you are the best
procession.

I follow your voice
through the fog
to arrive where
I wanted
to be.

We are greeted
by a grandstand
of old women.

Sister,
they make music,
and you win
first prize.

TERRY STOKES

Because You Are Always There

For Carolyn,
With Love

Children. We used to talk about our children
After coffee, & what to do, what to do.
Rochester, Brockport, in the dead middle
Of creepy winter, the friends, frozen in time,
Look at that ass, you said. I did, fell in love.
Your taste in women was as perfect as some
Nouveau cuisine. No, you would never compare

Knockwurst, & people. Too enlightened for
Idiocy like that. In Cincinnati,
Zapped a fool, held my baby daughter, Nadja.
Evidently, you still had important info,
Rare spiritual info, to pass along to this caveman.

C.L. RAWLINS

Drifting in Montana

For Carolyn,
After a poem by Tu Fu

Dry grass and heaven's breath upon the banks,
waves chuckling on the hollow hulls, tied fast.

Stars spring up from ridges, black above
thirty miles of lake, one reflected moon.

Can love rise from the word alone?
A poet wakes to spoken dreams,

Apart. Dogs bark and drunken laughter
drowns the owl's dark flute.

Flathead Lake

CAROL MUSKE

Haiku

Prague rain. Sweeping past
Kafka sleeping under stone:
Carolyn's red scarf.

AGHA SHAHID ALI

I Dream It Is Afternoon
When I Return to Delhi

At Purana Qila I am alone, waiting
for the bus to Daryaganj. I see it coming,
but my hands are empty.
"Jump on, jump on," someone shouts,
"I've saved this change for you
for years. Look!"
A hand opens, full of silver rupees.
"Jump on, jump on." The voice doesn't stop.
There's no one I know. A policeman,
handcuffs silver in his hands,
asks for my ticket.

I jump off the running bus,
sweat pouring from my hair.
I run past the Doll Museum, past
headlines on the Times of India
building, PRISONERS BLINDED IN A BIHAR
JAIL, HARIJAN VILLAGES BURNED BY LANDLORDS.
Panting, I stop in Daryaganj,
outside Golcha Cinema.

Sunil is there, lighting
a cigarette, smiling. I say,
"It must be ten years, you haven't changed,
it was your voice on the bus!"
He says, "The film is about to begin,
I've bought an extra ticket for you,"
and we rush inside:

Anarkali is being led away,
her earrings lying on the marble floor.
Any moment she'll be buried alive.
"But this is the end," I turn
toward Sunil. He is nowhere.
The usher taps my shoulder, says
my ticket is ten years old.

Once again my hands are empty.
I am waiting, alone, at Purana Qila.
Bus after empty bus is not stopping.
Suddenly, beggar women with children
are everywhere, offering
me money, weeping for me.

[Note from the author: I was very inspired when I read
"October 1973" by Carolyn Kizer. The poem stayed
with me for a long time and it eventually led to the
strategy I adopted in this poem.]

ANNIE FINCH

A Carol for Carolyn

It is easy to be a poet,
Brim with transparent water.

—Carolyn Kizer, "In the First Stanza"

I dreamed of a poet who gave me a whale
that shadowed clear pools through the sea-weeded shade.
When beached sea-foam dried on the rocks, it would sail
down currents that gathered to pool and cascade
with turbulent order.
She brims with transparent water,
as mother and poet and daughter.

The surface is broken and arching and full,
impelled by the passions of nation and woman.
The waves build and fall, the deep currents pull
toward rocky pools cupping the salt of the human.
The ocean she's authored
brims, with transparent water,
for poet and mother and daughter.

MAXINE KUMIN

Pantoum, with Swan

For Carolyn

Bits of his down under my fingernails
a gob of his spit behind one ear
and a nasty welt where the nib of his beak
bit down as he came. It was our first date.

A gob of his spit behind one ear,
his wings still fanning. I should have known better,
I should have bitten him off on our first date,
and yet for some reason I didn't press charges;

I wiped off the wet. I should have known better.
They gave me the morning-after pill
and shook their heads when I wouldn't press charges.
The yolk that was meant to hatch as Helen

failed to congeal, thanks to the morning-after pill
and dropped harmlessly into the toilet
so that nothing became of the lost yolk, Helen,
Troy, wooden horse, forestalled in one swallow

flushed harmlessly away down the toilet.
The swan had by then stuffed Euripedes, Sophocles
—leaving out Helen, Troy, Agamemnon—
the whole house of Atreus, the rest of Greek tragedy,

stuffed in my head, every strophe of Sophocles.
His knowledge forced on me, yet Bird kept the power.
What was I to do with ancient Greek history
lodged in my cortex to no avail?

I had his knowledge, I had no power
the year I taught Yeats in a classroom so pale
that a mist enshrouded the ancient religions
and bits of his down flew from under my fingernails.

Interviews

MICHELLE BOISSEAU

Intensity and Effect:
An Interview with Carolyn Kizer

KCUR/National Public Radio
March 3, 1997

MICHELLE BOISSEAU: How about the title of *Harping On*? How did you decide to throw your hat in with such a bold title?

CAROLYN KIZER: I had it in mind for a number of years. I loved the idea of being a harpy, being a nag along with the idea of the *harpist*, a sort of muse figure. A painter friend of mine Salvatore Federico did the cover, and it worked out awfully nicely.

MB: It's a picture of a somewhat . . . a male figure, or would you say it's androgynous?

KIZER: Oh, androgynous. She has snakes in her hair, but that doesn't really come out terribly clearly. But you know, a harpy—in a pure definition— is a creature with a woman's head and the lower features of a bird—bird feet and little wings. But I didn't want that on the cover—that's going too far. Maxine Kumin and I talk about being harpies, starting our own coven one of these days, and allowing in a few select witches.

MB: The whole effect is bold, especially when you begin the book with a poem about the Spanish Civil War which defines you and your generation in terms of your politics, your response to Franco, the Lincoln Brigade— that revolution seen by someone young at the time as the sexy thing to be involved with.

KIZER: Of course, I never thought of it that way. I came from a political family, and I think it comes out in the poem, and it certainly didn't occur to me that it was sexy. A lot of the reviews of *Harping On* have called me a leftist which I think is pretty funny. If you think Franco was a monster, are concerned about ecology, and are a feminist, that means you're a leftist. I don't know what's happening to terminology because it seems that's just being a human being. The part of the poem that does incorporate my politics and that of my parents comes at the beginning:

My new friend, Maisie, who works where I work,
A big, pleasant woman, all elbows and peasant skirts
Has a young child, and debts, and struggles on her own.
Not twenty-one, I am her confidante.
Gallant, intrepid, she soldiers on;
But in the ladies' restroom, or when we munch
Our sandwiches at our adjoining desks,
Her bitterness erupts: the bum! the bum
Who, when she was pregnant, knocked her down,
Stole money from her purse to spend on drink,
And still harasses her with drunken calls
In 1946.
One day I have to ask,

"Maisie, why did you ever marry him?"
Gazing into her large pale-blue eyes
That brim with rue: "Well, you see,
He fought in the Abraham Lincoln Brigade."
"Oh," I say. I would have done it too.

I think it's one of the very few poems in which the ladies' room figures in the opening and closing passages. [Both laugh.] The rest of the poem is concerned with Franco's death and The Valley of the Fallen, Franco's grandiose tomb near the Escorial in Spain. It's a monument that he built to himself, built with slave labor, by people who had fought against him in the revolution. As I say in the poem, the workers may have had to build the tomb, but at least they got to bury him.

MB: It's interesting how the poem sets up a frame. Political elements, sexual politics, and reinterpreting the past, all come up in other poems. The poem seems to set the book up with—I don't know—self-irony, perhaps.

KIZER: That's my big number. [Laughs.] When I wrote "Pro Femina," I used to get cards and letters from young women troubled by the line "the luck of our husbands and lovers who keep free women." They wanted to have that explained. I finally got tired of this and had a little stamp made that said, "Irony, irony, irony." That was a great help, and where I was teaching at the time all the professors wanted to borrow it to help grade papers. It got quite a workout. Stanley Kunitz said of me that I was "unforgettable, savage, tender, hilarious." Savage, tender, hilarious. That's the best description of myself I've ever heard. [Laughs.] But there has always been a savagery in my approach to my work and to myself.

MB: That's part of the harping, isn't it?

KIZER: Oh, absolutely.

MB: In the fourth poem in the book, "Gerda," you examine yourself in the third person. The mother gets set up as a villain, but she shifts, and has many manifestations. She's permitted a kind of grand parade of personalities in that poem, and in "Index, a Mountain" and "Pearl," even in "The Valley of the Fallen," where she is "My Red—and red-haired—mother."

KIZER: My mother was a many-faceted person. And a very neurotic person, and I was crazy about her. I miss her still. I still dream about her. She was an amazing human being.

MB: She read your poetry, right?

KIZER: Oh, from the beginning. I mean, she made me into a poet. There is no question of that. I think it was her own balked creativity that made her neurotic. In fact, I don't understand how people can live who don't have some kind of creative outlet. I would find life unbearable. I'd also find it unbearable without a sense of irony. [Both laugh.]

MB: As an ironist, you strike me more as an early 17th century ironist. Multidimensional. The irony seems to have a moral ingredient, an ethical requirement.

KIZER: I think I get that from my father. Somebody said to him once, "Oh, Mr. Kizer, you're such an 18th century gentleman," and my father said, "17th century, my dear fellow, 17th century." He didn't have a strong sense of humor, but he had a wonderful and delicious sense of irony. But his was not directed at himself the way mine is at myself, most of the time.

MB: Is that a particularly female thing, do you think?

KIZER: I don't think we're famous for it. We're supposedly famous for not having a sense of irony. That may be one reason I rather specialize in it.

MB: Seems like the more intellectual, or intelligent, a woman, the grander the irony.

KIZER: I would never call myself an intellectual, but then I don't know any intellectuals. I don't think they exist anymore. Perhaps Edmund Wilson was the last, or perhaps Nabokov. We don't produce Renaissance people anymore. It may be partly the failure of our educational system, or simply that life has become so complex and difficult that people don't have enough time to learn everything they need to know. Also the scope of learning has increased so much. In the time of John Donne, say, you could know almost everything there was to know about science. You'd had Greek and Latin in school, as part of your working vocabulary. I don't mean just language, but vocabulary, the way your mind works. You could know almost everything about music. You might not have known much about art, or painting, if you were English, but you could be intellectually fulfilled in a way that I don't see much of these days.

MB: Or wisdom. I wonder if there would be your poem "Medicine," which seems to argue against over-specialization, or the blindness of over-specialization.

KIZER: I suppose so. But I think of it more as the great failing of medicine in our time, using patients as guinea pigs. I read a piece in the paper the other day which, as an ironist, struck me rather forcibly. Some scientists wanted to do a study on whether estrogen kept you from having Alzheimer's, and the person writing the article was saying, It's really distressing that we can't get women to do a blind testing because they don't want to give up estrogen. Too bad! [MB laughs.] Do you find that as hilarious as I do, in a morbid way?

MB: Yes, it's disgustingly marvelous.

KIZER: My poem "Medicine" is in hexameters, a good classic meter but very rarely used in English. I used it in "Pro Femina." I decided I wanted a classic meter, the kind used by Juvenal and Catullus. I looked for models in English, but there really aren't very many. A couple by Swinburne, Arthur Hugh Clough—he sorted of cheated, though, by sticking on an extra syllable at the beginning of the line. "Medicine" is a little hexameter poem in triplets. It ends,

When the man loved by you and me appealed to your doctor
To know why you couldn't have your way and be let go,
He said, "I couldn't just stand and watch her die."

Later, when it was over, we spoke to a physician
Grown grey and wise with experience, our warm friend,
But ice when he considers the rigors of his profession,

And repeated to him your young death-doctor's reply,
We heard the stern verdict no lesser person could question:
But that was his job: to just stand there and watch her die.

MB. I want to ask you about the rhyme in that poem which I find very interesting. It sometimes announces itself, and sometimes retreats. Or it begins retreating and ends announcing itself.

KIZER: I have a theory about rhyme. Maxine Kumin and I carry on a continuous conversation about poetry, and send each other drafts of our poems. I have a new poem about St. Augustine and Kierkegaard. It's in 12-line stanzas of 14 stanzas. I think it's extremely funny but never mind. Maxine wanted me to have a regular rhyme scheme, and so I wrote her Kizer's theory of rhyming: When you want to intensify the effect, you use more rhymes. It creates a kind of emotional tension. In "Medicine" I don't know whether I did anything very consciously or not. I try to observe what my old teacher, Theodore Roethke, said once: "You have a great facility for rhyme, so work against it. Bury the rhymes in the line. Don't have them clicking along at the end if you can help it." And I've tried to do that, but it has become pretty automatic by now.

MB: I often tell my students that the trouble with poetry in the late 20th century and trying to rhyme is that so many of the rhymes have been discovered so we have to move into slant rhymes.

KIZER: Oh that's so true. I don't know if you remember a poem of mine to my husband. I wrote it after he was complaining that when we got married he thought I'd write a lot of poems to him, and I hadn't written any. And I thought, Oh boy, I'd better get busy! [Both laugh.] In that poem, "Afternoon Happiness," I comment to my husband about rhyme. That's kind of fun:

Much as I want to gather a lifetime thrift
And craft, my cunning skills tied in a knot for you,
There is only this useless happiness as gift.

It takes 30 years of practice before you can rhyme, as I did in that poem, "funny" with "Cyril Connolly." [Both laugh.] I think that's one thing that serious poets are constantly in search of, new rhymes, new slant rhymes, anything but "moon" and "June." There again, that poem is full of rhyme. It's buried in the line.

MB: Yes, you hear them, especially when you read it out loud.

KIZER: Exactly.

MB: I wanted to ask you about the NEA. You were the first Director of Literary Programs. I wonder if, with that kind of experience, you could characterize the way you see that poetry has changed. There's a retrospective quality to this new book—

KIZER: Well, my dear, it's retrospective because I'm old. It's easy! [Both laugh.] What you say reminds me of "Fin-de-Siècle Blues" where I mention the names of the men I've known who've died of AIDS.

Maurice, Tom, Tony, Gordon, Jim, Peter, Bill,
bitterly I mourn you
and I wait for the next beloved name.
The red-neck senators who would starve the Arts
are a less-efficient scourge.

With AIDS on one hand, and Jesse Helms on the other, the poor arts are in a sad way. But we survive. We always do. Actually, I worry more about theater and dance. The NEA almost single-handedly, through the Director of Dance, a wonderful woman named June Eyrie, caused modern dance and ballet to take off in this country, by subsidizing dance companies. They've always hung on by their teeth; they've never had any money. You saw that Martha Graham's company just had to cancel its season?

MB: Yes.

KIZER: Dance companies are folding all over the place, and nobody seems to make the connection between the kind of subsidies that dance began to get in the late 60s compared to the dearth now. It's very serious business.

People, for some reason, aren't as willing to subsidize dance companies as they are perhaps local theatrical groups, and so on. I think a lot of the programs that I started at the NEA have been very useful, such as the Poetry in the Schools program—when it's properly administrated. And, of course, it was turned over to the states, so some states do it well and some states do it poorly. Initially, it was to help young, college-educated writers in that transitional period between getting a book out and getting a name, during that hiatus of sorts that takes place when you have very little income. Also sending poets and novelists into Black colleges was very useful. Those colleges didn't have any creative writing teachers back in the days when I was at the NEA. Now that program's being revived. But if I was going to start all over again with a literary program at the NEA, I think I'd move more toward the Swedish system of subsidizing writers to go into prisons and hospitals and some sort of permanent subsidies for elderly and ill writers so they'd have some sort of economic security in their later years. I'm afraid what happens to individual grants is that it becomes a kind of horse race. On literary juries there is a lot of trading off, of "I'll support your lover, if you'll support my wife." That kind of thing goes on, don't think it doesn't. But the arts will survive.

MB: How about the New Formalist movement?

KIZER: I get a great laugh out of it. And I have to tell you many of them aren't very good. They have tin ears. I picked up an anthology the other day, and I was pretty horrified. Compared to honest-to-God formalists, like Jim Merrill and Dick Wilbur, these people don't know their stuff. I find it amusing that they are now preening themselves on their formalist qualities. All that means is they don't read anybody over forty. [Laughs.] Or take Marilyn Hacker. She'd probably rather die than consider herself a New Formalist, but she writes the most elegant formal poetry. No one can touch her in that department as far as I'm concerned.

MB: She plays with the rules in very witty ways, doesn't she?

KIZER: Wonderful. I particularly enjoy her ballads. "The only Jewish Lesbian in France" is the ballad line I love. In a ballad she quotes as a refrain, "The Jew squats on the windowsill"—that piece of anti-Semitism on the part of the late T. S. Eliot—and just demolishes it. She's another accomplished ironist, by the way. She's one of the people I correspond with. To talk shop is something delicious, and I love doing it.

MB: How about your poem, "Song for Muriel"?

KIZER: Oh, that's to the late Muriel Rukeyser. But it's also about me, obviously. It's just a song, beginning, "No one explains me, because there's nothing to explain." And ends:

> Once I am dead
> Something will be said.
> How nice I won't be here
> To see how they get it wrong.

MB: Were you thinking of something in particular about Rukeyser that you thought they were getting wrong?

KIZER: I very much admire Elizabeth Bishop, but there's a huge Bishop cult, and Muriel has never had her due. I think because she is so lucid. And she was a threat to men in a way Elizabeth wasn't.

MB: Right, talk about leftist.

KIZER: Yes, indeed. Heroic. Though she was threatened with having her leg cut off at the hip because she had bad diabetes, the dear old lady went over to Korea, and stood in the snow outside the prison where the young Korean poet, Kim Che Ha, was incarcerated. It took all the courage in the world for her to go there in winter to get him out of prison, which she did.

MB: That's the kind of poetry persona we identify more with Latin America, or with Eastern Europe. She put herself so much into the public light.

KIZER: I suppose one could say the same of Akmatova. But she's an icon in a way that Muriel isn't. What I was really getting at was the kind of critic, who shall be nameless—but you can guess who I mean—who specializes in translating difficult or boring poets like John Ashbery and Archie Ammons. You've got to have something that needs explanation in order to make that kind of career as a critic.

MB: So poets who, in a sense, build into their own work the code by which it can be read—instead of having it external—don't get that kind of critical attention?

KIZER: That's very shrewd. You can explain the most difficult passages yourself. You don't have to wait for somebody else to do it. You do it in the work. Absolutely.

MB: Or there's a decision made that this passage is complicated, and I'll have to take you through here, this tricky sonnet of Shakespeare's.

KIZER: Yes. I recorded all of Shakespeare for my father when his eyes were failing when he was in his late 90s. It was a marvelous experience. When you're reading a poem aloud, you cannot read levels of meaning. You have to read one meaning. That was immensely rewarding. In *Harping On* I translated a couple of poems by the German poet Ingeborg Bachmann who was very difficult. I translated them in order to understand the poems. It's one of the best ways other than reading them aloud to get a grip on what somebody's talking about.

MB: Was that the approach you took with the Chinese translations?

KIZER: I've always felt an affinity with the Chinese poets. To me the most important relationship in life is friendship, and that's the most important in the poetry of the Tang dynasty, my specialty. Also the ironic stance appealed to me. I like these guys. I'm really devoted to them. And I drank a lot while I was translating them because they did a lot when they wrote the poems in the first place.

MB: There's a quiet irony, a sort of smiling irony.

KIZER: "A Present for Tu Fu from Li Po" is a translation I wrote because I'd read a very bad translation of the poem which irritated me so much that I did it over again. I have a poet friend who said when we were young that irritation is a stimulus to poetry. Now, I was totally idealistic and naive, and I was horrified by this statement that something as petty as irritation could produce poetry. But I discovered he was right.

MB: Sort of like a little burr that rubs and rubs, and produces—

KIZER: Exactly.

MB: Your poem "An American Beauty" fits in here. I think it takes a deep friendship to be able to call someone a pedant and get away with it.

KIZER: And in "Poem for Your Birthday" I tease another friend about waving her arms in the air when she's had a couple of drinks. Again that's something you only do with a close friend. "An American Beauty" mentions my friend Ann London, who wrote the legislation for the Equal Rights Amendment. The poem is written in double Sapphics, she said proudly. [Laughs.]

MB: Which is important to know, and it's probably a fitting form for the poem.

KIZER: What you have are two five-feet lines, a two-foot line, a five-foot line, and then another two foot-line. Which you probably wouldn't hear, if I've done it well enough. My dear friend Maxine objected to my rhyming John Lennon with Grendel. I thought it was rather neat myself.

MB: Never been done before!

KIZER: Or again. Let me put in a good word for one of the real joys of writing poetry, and that's revision. I'm a real revision junkie. I've probably published less than I might if hadn't revised everything about forty times. But I'm not sorry. My drafts are absolutely ghastly. They're shamefully bad, and in the process of revising a poem thirty or forty times it starts coming out pretty well. When you're young, you really hate revision. You do it because you have to, if you've got any sense. Then the more you do it, the more you like it—I'm with Alexander Pope on that. Many younger poets nowadays feel they've got to have a book every two years, or be forgotten, so they publish everything as fast as they can. I've got news for them: they're going to be forgotten anyway. [Laughs.]

MB: I played for one of my classes a tape of your reading "Bitch" because I wanted them to hear that, though it's a dramatic poem in the classic sense, you deliver it with a normal conversational tone. To manage that, and to manage something in double Sapphics and intricate rhymes seems to me can happen only through the kind of precise revision that you're requiring of yourself.

KIZER: I may be so hooked on it that I revise even when I don't need to, but I hope not. "Bitch" is a poem that makes me a little nervous, it's so popular. I showed an early draft to the poet Donald Finkel, a dear friend of mind. And he said, "There are too many puns, take them out." I said, "But audiences love it." He looked at me coldly and said, "Yessss." One of the best pieces of criticism that I've ever had, in one word. So I did what he said. Now "Bitch" is a poem in which I decided to pick one simple metaphor and run it into the ground. That was the way it started. I think we all have some kind of totem animal within us. Mine is tigers. I really have tigers in my basement. I'm not really a dog person, but it turned out this was going to be a dog, my alter ego, or doppelgänger.

MB: I think it's popular because it boldly takes on exactly what so many people feel.

KIZER: It is a poem I made up out of whole cloth. Of course, everyone assumes it's autobiographical, but they always get it wrong.

MB: A nun couldn't write that poem, however.

KIZER: Well, a nun I haven't been. Alas.

WILLIAM HOLLAND

An Interview with Carolyn Kizer

Voyages
Fall 1967

THIS INTERVIEW took place when Carolyn Kizer was Director of the Literacy Programs of the National Endowment for the Arts.

WILLIAM HOLLAND: What percentage of American writers would you say realize the program exists?

CAROLYN KIZER: I think that very few people know about the program or its purpose. Thank goodness, because we are very understaffed. We are very short of administrative funds to help run the program.

WH: How much help do you have?

KIZER: I have one assistant, who is also my secretary. The staff of the whole Arts Endowment is between twenty-five and thirty people. (And we have half-a-dozen shared staff with the Humanities Endowment.) So when people come to me, as they do, indignantly saying, "Why don't we know about these programs?", I say first of all, we are not running a propaganda agency, but an arts agency. We have press conferences and we send releases to the newspapers and it is up to them whether they print them or not.

WH: How many people do you think know the purpose of the programs, or even what they are?

KIZER: I think a lot of people understand that we have an individual grants program. That seems to be getting across to the public. I'm constantly amazed at the number of people that act as if that is all we do. Last year we gave out twenty-two grants amounting to $10,000 each, and except in the case of three people who were critics and biographers, where the grants were given jointly by us and the Humanities, they all went to novelists and poets. I'm not even sure that we will continue an individual grants program because it is not really clear in my mind that we are doing something that couldn't be done just as well by the existing foundations like Rockefeller and Guggenheim. If we do continue, I think it will be radically different from any program envisaged thus far. I feel we have to think very hard about the underlying philosophy of an arts program or any federally sponsored program: what can they do that private agencies and private philanthropies are unable or unwilling to do?

WH: I know that you are busy not only from 9 to 5, but very often in the evenings and weekends as well, and I'm just curious—why does the program take up so much of your time?

KIZER: First of all, I think that we might approach it from a typical day in the life of an arts bureaucrat. My day begins with about forty-five letters which have to be answered. Some of them are referrals from the White House. Any citizen in this country—and you would be amazed at how many do—can write to the President to say that they are artists or writers and they need help, or have medical problems, or that they have not fulfilled themselves or something. This mail has top priority—this is what gets done before anything else.

Second are the letters that come in to Roger Stevens, the head of the Arts Endowment and the Arts Council. I prepare answers for his signature to people who write in with questions about the Literary Programs, or with criticisms or suggestions. This could include answering newspaper comments as well.

Then we get down to *my* mail, which consists largely of appeals for information from writers, but also includes people who are making specific applications for grants for themselves or for a project. This can consume about half of the day before you even get started thinking about the larger programs.

WH: Would you describe some of these programs?

KIZER: First I want to say a word about how the whole thing works. I think people are pretty confused about that. A year ago November, Congress passed the enabling legislation for twin agencies, the Endowment for the Arts and the Endowment for the Humanities. For each of the agencies there was an advisory body, a Council for the Arts and one for the Human-ities. People who belong to the Council for the Arts are illustrious, glam-orous people—people like film stars, dancers, museum curators and people of that kind—Gregory Peck, Leonard Bernstein, etc.—who discuss and vote on programs. The Endowment is the "working" staff, composed of the paid help like me, who develop and carry out the programs. The current members of the National Council of the Arts involved in litera-ture are the novelists Harper Lee and John Steinbeck; and the poet and for-mer director of the Iowa Writers' Workshop, Paul Engle; Lawrence Halprin, a landscape architect from San Francisco whose wife is a well-known dancer, and who is extremely interested in the avant-garde, I'm glad to say, and knows quite a bit about it; and Nancy White, the editor of *Harper's Bazaar*.

It is much easier, I should say, for Council members to give advice in the area of music and theatre than it is in literature, because in these areas you clearly have existing institutions clamoring for aid—symphony orchestras, repertory theatres, and dance companies, all of which run deficits (and the better the company, the larger the deficit). In literature, there are not these well-established public groups. Therefore, a good deal of ingenuity has to be exercised in developing the programs. We have had some inspiration from the British Arts Council, and I have looked with some interest and curiosity on what's been happening in the Scandinavian countries, but by and large we are pretty much on our own in this area. We have done some unique things that are still very much in the experi-mental stages that have never been attempted by any government so far as I know.

I would say that the first among these is the program we have to sup-port literary magazines, which is called the Coordinating Council of Lit-erary Magazines. The Board of Directors consists of William Phillips of the *Partisan Review*; Reed Whittemore, formerly of the Carleton *Miscellany*; Robie Macauley, formerly of the *Kenyon Review*, now the literary editor of *Playboy*; Jules Chametzky, editor of the *Massachusetts Review*; William Roth, who among his many duties and obligations is on the Board of Regents of the University of California; J.R. de la Torre Bueno, who is with the Wesleyan University Press; and Carl Stover, the President of the National Institute of Public Affairs. The National Institute of Public Affairs is managing this for us because the Coordinating Council of Literary Mag-azines does not yet have its tax-exempt status. The Council represents the interests of about thirty-five of the leading literary magazines in the country and it is engaged in devising programs to support literary magazines and the people who write for them.

WH: You're responsible for it?

KIZER: We are responsible for funding it and making its existence possible. We have given $50,000 to the C.C.L.M. I should explain here that the funds for all of our group projects, by Congress's wish, must be matched, so that we can only put up 50% of the funds needed. Aid to magazines is not limited by membership in the C.C.L.M., but is going to extend to the smallest, most far-flung and experimental types of magazines. Unfortunately, it is a little premature for me to discuss the specifics of the program, but I do think it is the first time in history that the Federal Government has suggested backing the activities of virtually all the outstanding literary magazines in a country.

The C.C.L.M. is going to carry on some experiments not only in aiding special projects which magazines develop, and taking care of special financial emergencies, but in direct subsidies. As you know, most of the literary magazines do not pay their contributors. This works a great hardship on the writer, obviously, and an even greater hardship on the magazine, when its best writers are funneled off into working for the more affluent magazines who perhaps don't have the literary reputation, but do have the payroll. I don't think writers themselves are very happy with this situation. A writer wants to appeal to his peers and be read by serious readers and writers rather than be buried by girlie pictures and advertisements in glossy magazines. But he has to if he is going to live on what he writes. Furthermore, the editors of the little magazines know where the young talent is.

The private foundations tend to support writers that are part of what I have called the Eastern Seaboard Grants and Gravy Train: the writers who congregate around New York, who are well-known to editors and publishers, have the right connections and glide from Fulbright to Guggenheim, to a *Prix de Rome*, to a Rockefeller grant. Many writers have lived on these for many years and some of them have produced very little, considering the long, free ride they have had from the private foundations.

It seems to me you could make a very good case for the obscure writer who is either so young that he hasn't yet come to the attention of the great foundations or is so difficult or unfashionable that he has been overlooked; or the young writer who perhaps is married and has a couple of children to feed, or is a graduate student and has no visible means of support and would like to spend his time in writing—this is the kind of writer whom you could assist if you were editor of a little magazine and had the money to give to him.

WH: I've heard a lot about the anthology of the best writing from American literary magazines. Could you describe that program?

KIZER: Well, it is now winding up its first year. Hopefully, the first volume of the *American Literary Anthology* will be out in the spring. Most of the leading New York publishers have asked to take turns publishing this anthology. This program, administered by George Plimpton, has been widely misunderstood because there was a garbled press announcement that said that we had given him $55,000 to run an anthology of the best writing. We haven't given Mr. Plimpton anything of the sort. We did give him something around $9,000 to cover the expenses involved in corresponding with 600 literary magazines, Xeroxing the best stories, poems and essays from these magazines, paying readers—enough readers to sift through 5$1/2$ tons of literary magazines and decide which were the best candidates to submit to a set of juries in poetry, fiction, essay and criticism—and paying four juries consisting of three writers each. From the $9,000 Plimpton only took a fee of $500 for the administrative work. The $45,000 remaining went in direct prizes to the winning writers included in the anthology and the editors who picked their work.

Every author of a prose work who appeared in the anthology received a $1,000 award, and the editor who published his work received $500 for his magazine. I don't think this has ever been done before—that the editor's perspicuity in discovering a writer has been acknowledged. In poetry, each author was awarded $500 regardless of the length of the poem. The editor who chose it received $250 for his magazine.

The choice of the judges was very wide-ranging. It included quite obscure magazines such as the *Brown Paper Review* and *Hollow Orange* and a magazine called *Salmagundi*, which is said to have a paid-up subscription of 80.

WH: Were these basically East Village publications?

KIZER: No, all over the place—all over the country—not just New York but San Francisco, the South, Chicago and all over the mid-West. Of course, if you've ever worked with a literary magazine, you know that $500 might just pick up the annual deficit if the magazine is small enough and obscure enough.

Another program which has been among our most successful, although very few people seem to know that the Federal Government is involved in it, is the program that is being run by the Academy of American Poets called "Dialogues on the Art of Poetry." This consists of gathering together the teachers of English in a particular city and having them addressed by famous poets like Auden, Robert Penn Warren or Denise Levertov. The second half of the program, "Poetry Reading in the Classroom," consists of younger poets going into English classrooms and talking to the children about poetry—about their own poetry. We carried out this program in New York, Detroit and Pittsburgh and are going to extend it to San Francisco, Los Angeles, Chicago, Minneapolis and a whole cluster of cities in the Southwest including Tucson, Albuquerque, Denver, El Paso and others. We are hoping very much to get into classrooms where there are large proportions of Mexican-Americans and American Indian children who have been largely muffled in their creative and responsive expressions and in their appreciation of literature. We have concentrated on high schools in slum areas in many of these cities.

The response in New York, for example, has been very, very gratifying indeed. One member of the New York Board of Education has said that directly or indirectly, the program has touched the life of every high school student in the New York City school system. At their request, we have made additional appropriations to the Academy to go back to 200 more high schools with this program. I think the really touching thing about this program is the response from the children. Many of these children barely knew, if at all, that there was such a thing as a poem or that living men wrote it or even—wildest fancy of all—that *they* might conceivably be able to write. The children developed a strong sense of loyalty to the poets who came to talk to them. Children from various high schools fiercely defended their own particular poet—a "my poet is better than your poet" sort of thing. I thought at one point maybe we should issue letterman sweaters!

And, of course, as you would expect, not only is the world of poetry opened to these children, but the possibilities of self expression, and that perhaps is the most important of all. Not that they are all going to become poets, but they can find out that it is possible for them to pick up a writing implement and gain some relief from the burdens and pressures of their lives, and the problems which are screaming for some kind of personal expression. This has been most satisfactory and I am most happy about it. I haven't heard any adverse comments on it at all.

We are also interested in developing, as we can, writing organizations which exist in this country, although they don't exist in a very impressive form as yet. The leading writer's organization in this country is P.E.N., which stands for Poets, Playwrights, Essayists and Novelists. We gave them $40,000 to put on the first International Congress of P.E.N. to be held on American soil in their forty-two year history. We also helped make it possible—and this is one of the things that a Federal Agency can do that no one else can do—for writers such as Pablo Neruda and Ignazio Silone and writers hitherto barred by the McCarran Act, to come to this country for the first time, because they were accredited to an International Congress. I think the incredible reception which Neruda received in New York alone almost justified our participation in the P.E.N. Congress.

For the first time, Neruda, one of the world's greatest poets and the living poet who has most influenced young American writers, appeared on American soil, and several thousand people turned out to hear him and hung from the balconies and cheered themselves blue.

There was also a wonderful afternoon with all the Latin American writers talking to each other and about each other. A very curious situation exists right now in Latin America: writers from various countries have very little opportunity to communicate with each other. Mail is censored, custom regulations are such that it is almost impossible for a writer to send his book to a fellow writer or to a magazine in another Latin country. So this was a very good thing. Not only that, but many of the Latin American writers of great distinction live in Paris and are clustered around a couple of émigré magazines in Paris because living conditions for them at home are so difficult. This was also an opportunity for them to come together with other Latin American writers and to diminish the alienation and the sense of isolation that they must feel in being far from their homelands.

I might add that we are putting a considerable amount of money into the Center for Inter-American relations, to support the translation and dissemination of work of Latin American writers; and this is going to be an increasingly important program. We hope that when plays by major Latin dramatists have been well translated, we may be able to help support regional productions. It is perfectly natural for us to take Latin America as the first step in an international program of this kind. I don't see why we shouldn't expand major translation programs into other areas in the world as well.

So much for the programs that are off and running. I would like to mention several new ones that have just been adopted or are just getting started now. One of them is aid to independent publishers.

WH: Things like Alan Swallow was doing?

KIZER: Yes, right. We have a long tradition in this country of isolated, icon-oclastic individuals with their own printing presses and their own ideas of what constitutes literature, who have for many years supported the avant-garde and who have maintained very high standards of produc-tion—printing, typography, layout, art and so on. The press of the late Alan Swallow, who died largely of overwork and connected ailments last year at the far too early age of 51, is the most well-known. Jonathan Williams of North Carolina, and some of the many distinguished presses that are located in Iowa City—Stonewall Press, Cummington Press, and the Prairie Press—also turn out some fine work.

The first step that has to be undertaken in this is to see that all these presses acquire a non-profit tax-exempt status because, again, our legis-lation forbids us from giving assistance to commercial profit-making enter-prises. They seem to be acquiring this without too much difficulty. Among the presses that we are helping are Jonathan Williams, whose imprint is Jargon Books; Dave Haselwood of the Auerhahn Press, and George Hitch-cock of the Kayak Press, both in San Francisco; and the three Iowa presses I just mentioned. The smaller grants have been made to James Weil of the Elizabeth Press in New York; Diane di Prima of the Poets Press in New York; and the Talisman Press in Georgetown, California.

The other current project in which I am particularly interested is a program which will take poets into disadvantaged colleges in the South. Many of these colleges have never had speakers from the outside or vis-iting lecturers of any kind. Many of them have budgets which preclude any kind of fancy arrangement. A number of poets—of whom I am one—who have toured in the mid-South have wanted very badly to appear in these colleges. One or two poets have tried it—namely Edward Field and Galway Kinnell. The novelist John Hawkes has gone too. The reception has been poor for a variety of reasons, most of which are fairly easy to figure out. John Hawkes once gave a lecture at Tougaloo—I heard it was brilliant—to four students. Now that is a tragic waste.

So we wanted to devise a program that would make some kind of con-structive contribution to these students. It seemed important to us that it have local origins and indigenous administration, and therefore it occurred to me that it might be a good idea to administer it through the Woodrow Wilson National Fellowship Foundation, which has a series of two-year internships at these colleges, and that if the interns were willing to conduct and administer it locally, that it might well be worth doing. I made preliminary inquiries with them and they said their interns were screaming for something of this kind.

We are planning to send Negro and white poets together to stay for a period of at least a week. They'll conduct preliminary sorties into classrooms and discuss American writing and American poetry in general—what it's like and what it means. They will also give at least two public performances—one for the college and one for the surrounding community. At some point in their stay at the college, they will involve local writers connected with the school itself and writers living nearby. After the public performances the writers will go back to classrooms and discuss writing and review student work in private. This is really a kind of pilot program. We are putting $30,000 into it, but many other federal agencies are extremely interested in its outcome. I don't see any reason why dancers, actors, and so on should not follow in the wake of this.

By the way, in the middle of this particular program, we have scheduled a poetry festival in Atlanta at which all our circuit poets will be able to meet with the local poets that they have encountered, and we hope that it will be a wonderful and interesting meeting of students and lonely isolated writers, both Negro and white.

There are also funds for an evaluation conference; I know it will be valuable to get all the poets and interns together and discuss how the programs succeeded and how they failed. It might make an interesting publishable account, it seems to me. Later, we could possibly expand the program into something really comprehensive. I should say we are very limited in funds. Our total budget is going to be 4½ million for programs and 2 million for states. By contrast, the National Science Foundation has about 440 million dollars—and let's not forget that it is only 17 years old. It is not as if it had been there always. I've heard that all of the Federal appropriations for arts would run the war in Viet Nam for 38 minutes. I think that is a useful statistic.

WH: Four times your budget is the amount Senator Robert Kennedy said Americans will spend on pets this year.

KIZER: Do you remember when we lost that bomb over Palomares, Spain? That rather unfortunate episode? It cost 24 million dollars to retrieve it, which again is almost six times what the Federal Arts budget is. So what does this mean for us? It means that we must concentrate at this point on experimental pilot programs, which presumably we later pass on or give away to other agencies more equipped to fund them on a broad scale.

I think this program with developing colleges is probably one that some agency will take over. I say this with a little sadness, knowing that this is the way it has to be. I think that one of the wonderful things about being in on this program at the very beginning is that it is so personal. You are so involved with everything; with every phase of the project; with everybody in it; with every writer; with every teacher; with everybody who writes to you. Of course this is inevitably going to fade away as the program gets bigger.

But I do think that the arts program is capable of expansion without losing quality. It is capable of keeping its human aspects. The other day I went in to my boss Roger Stevens and said, "I hope you can fork up $407 to help survey the high school libraries in a certain city, because, of the money that they are getting from the Office of Education to expand their libraries, not one penny is spent on poetry." They haven't even bought a single anthology. Of course, I'm looking forward to doing this on a nation-wide basis—looking into the buying habits of libraries. This seems to me crucial for our literary future in this country. Beyond that, I want the Federal Arts Agency always to be able to take seriously a program which envisages spending $407. As long as we can keep that kind of humanity and that kind of personal quality in an arts program, then I think we are on the right track and we are doing our job.

WH: Another point I'd like to include: everyone knows how busy you are and you have said that you haven't had a chance to write.

KIZER: I finished a book just before I took this job. I didn't feel that I was going to have another book immediately and I felt that whatever I did next was going to be a radical departure from anything I have done. I thought that if we were going to have a Federal Arts Program, it ought to be run at least in part by artists. I still feel this way, and I think Roger Stevens feels this. My fellow directors are people who are not bureaucrats; they are people who are professionals in their own fields. I don't suppose the situation will last forever.

But I think it is wonderful that we are starting off this way. I don't plan to give up writing, but let's just say it's in abeyance. I think something is going on inside my head that I don't know about yet—which is usually the way it is with me. When the moment comes when that imperative makes itself known, then I will make some sort of arrangement to do something about it. I am going to Chapel Hill for five weeks in the spring as Writer-in-Residence, and I'm looking forward to that more than I can say. I hope that will be enough time to develop something significant—at least it will be enough time to give me a rest.

WH: Are there any more hints that you can give about what you just said? For instance, has the tremendous complexity of literary life that you've dug up since you've been in this job afforded you insights into American culture, and the D.C. subculture that must finally express itself in some sort of creative work?

KIZER: Of course editing a literary magazine was pretty good preparation for this job. I would say that my knowledge of novelists and novels isn't what it should be, but I was extremely well-prepared in terms of know-ing people in the literary world. Perhaps not what New York thinks of as the literary world, but this is a Federal program, and it concerns people in the whole country. One of the things that worries me about the job is it is so time-consuming, I don't have time to do the amount of reading that I have done all my life. I keep up pretty well with magazines and period-icals, but in terms of solid reading of books and being able to have four or five hours in the clear in which to concentrate on something—that just doesn't happen any more. So in some ways I feel that I am disquali-fying myself by the very act of participating in the job, but again this is something that can be rectified by some time off. I like Washington, per-haps better than I should. I have always liked Washington. I think that is the key to living here. My interest in politics and international affairs goes just as deep as my feeling about poetry.

The literary world, as it is presently constituted, at least in the big cities (and I don't include Washington because it just doesn't act or *feel* like a big city) is pretty hermetic, often pretty airless as a result. When I go to New York cocktail parties or a weekend in the Hamptons, I find I resent very much some of the remarks that people make to me: If they don't come right out and accuse me of it, they strongly imply that I am personally venal, self-aggrandizing, and probably crooked. But the most annoying gambit is the one that begins, "I know you won't do this, but . . ." And they proceed to recommend a program that is already in existence, or that has been considered, examined, and rejected, for very good reason, long since. The most depressing facet of this work is the paucity of really good, creative suggestions from outside. And the second most depressing aspect is the article which describes a program that has hardly begun yet and omnisciently tells its readers why it is going to be done so badly that it is bound to fail.

WH: What other types of criticism do you receive? Why do you think that the programs are attacked?

KIZER: It comes from both directions. It's a cliché that as long as you are getting it from both directions, you know that you are doing more or less the right thing. We're told on one hand that because we're a federal agency we're reactionary, we're chained to the whims of Congress, and we're going to support only established procedures and establishment projects.

Then from the other side, we are told that we are supporting radical or innovative programs which shouldn't receive a penny from anybody, or that what good writers need is to starve and all that. You know—why not let him die of T.B. at the ripe age of 24, then you *know* he's good? We get a lot of that. So I would say that a very high proportion of the kind of criticism that we get is quite irrational, from the kind of person who is not listening, doesn't want to listen and isn't interested in what I have to say. He is interested in the sound that he makes.

Of course, the best public relations in the world cannot be effective with a person like that. I think the only thing to do is blithely to go on with the work and wait for the results to speak for themselves.

WH: What sort of congressional relations do you have? When you run into problems, how do you handle them?

KIZER: I don't handle congressional relations personally, although we have somebody in the agency that does. Once in a while a Congressman will refer someone to us that they think worthy of a grant and we process that just as we would anything else. I confess that I'm so caught up in the work that even here in Washington when someone at a dinner party asks, "Just exactly what do you do in the Federal Arts Program?", I tend to say: "Look, I have just been thinking about it for eleven hours and I would rather talk about something else." I think sometimes I offend people. It isn't something that you can discuss in ten minutes. It is all too complicated. Perhaps if this interview turns out well, I will buy a whole lot of copies and carry them around in my handbag and when people ask me what I do, I will take one out and give it to them. Wouldn't that be just wonderful!

WH: Great!

KIZER: But really, as long as I can say to myself that I am doing what I think is right, without having my behavior modified by fear of anybody inside of Government or outside, that's all I want. In other words, you have to live in a perpetual state of uncertainty. After all, if you look at it in the long range, life itself is a pretty uncertain thing. That is something that none of us likes to remember. There is no such thing as security. But I have found with this job that I can live uneasily but cheerfully because it's highly speculative, and highly creative. That is the important thing.

BARBARA THOMPSON

Carolyn Kizer: The Art of Poetry

The Paris Review
Spring 2000

CAROLYN KIZER was born in Spokane, Washington, on December 10, 1925, a birth date shared with Emily Dickinson. She graduated from Sarah Lawrence College, studied at Columbia University as a fellow of the Chinese government and, in 1946, became a graduate fellow at the University of Washington, Seattle. In 1948 she married Stimson Bullitt, by whom she had three children; they divorced in 1954, and that same year she began studying poetry with Theodore Roethke and, later, Stanley Kunitz. In 1959, with two colleagues, she founded the quarterly *Poetry Northwest*. Her first collection of poems, *The Ungrateful Garden*, appeared in 1961. She received the Pulitzer Prize in 1985 for *Yin: New Poems*. In addition to her collection, *Harping On* (1996), she has published a book of translations, *Carrying Over* (1989), and a collection of essays on poets and poetry, *Proses* (1994). She was appointed a chancellor of the Academy of American Poets [editors' note: and subsequently resigned].

Thirty years of conversation—a good deal of it about writers and writing—preceded this interview. I first learned of Carolyn Kizer in 1965 in Rawalpindi, Pakistan, where she was a Specialist in Literature, from a Punjabi poet who had heard her give a reading and hastened to a telephone to reproach me for missing it. "She is a goddess!" he said. "She is mighty!"

We met the next night at a dinner party in the tiny, embroidery-crammed living room of a Bengali painter. Statuesque, honey-blond, with a rich and powerful contralto, she was an ideal standard-bearer for the English language in those competitive poetry recitals (mushairahs) beloved in the Indian subcontinent. She seemed to have read and remembered everything, not just reams of William Carlos Williams and Theodore Roethke and Stanley Kunitz, but also wonderful poems no one else had ever heard of: I wonder how many poets in Pakistan still hear in her voice Ruth Pitter's "But for lust, we could be friends . . ." and Bernard Spencer's "Yachts on the Nile."

In 1966 she came back to Washington to the National Endowment for the Arts (she had been appointed the first Director of Literary Programs), sharing with her daughters and a large Persian cat named Myshkin a townhouse whose wall to the garden was a pane of glass against which willow trees inclined. She has always been, as she says, "house lucky."

For the last seven years she has lived with her second husband, architect John Woodbridge, in a white Victorian farmhouse surrounded by huge acacia trees, just outside the city limits of Sonoma, California, with a mature rose garden, tennis courts and a swimming pool; inside, tall rooms are filled with books and works of art. Kizer writes in a handsome study painted a pale mauve "to go with the muted colors of Northwest paintings"—in her twenties she began buying the work of Mark Tobey, Morris Graves and other Northwest painters.

We began our taping in dressing gowns on a sunny morning in the library. Music played in the background, Vivaldi maybe. We settled into deep leather armchairs overseen by Mark Tobey's portrait of Kizer's father. His gaze is both stern and benign. As she says, "It could be a painting of an Adams or a Jefferson rather than a man who started life on a bankrupt farm in central Ohio."

BARBARA THOMPSON: I know you've written about this, but could we begin with the beginning, how you became a poet?

CAROLYN KIZER: I began writing poems when I was about eight, with a heavy assist from my mother. She read me Arthur Waley's translations, and Whitman, and Robinson Jeffers, who have been lifelong influences on me. My father read Keats to me, and then he read more Keats, while I was lying on the sofa battling with asthma. A sort of intellectual seduction: there I am, lying on the sofa breathing with difficulty, while Father pours Keats into the porches of my ear. If Daddy had only read Keats's letters! They're so wonderful, but Keats is someone you can't let yourself be influenced by. There's that interesting group of poets who are fatal to your style:

I'd say Keats, Gerard Manley Hopkins and Dylan Thomas. The Waley led me to my own interest in Chinese and Chinese translations, which has been a major theme in my life. And Whitman, of course, I idolize, though I'm more attracted to metrical verse. Meter is as natural as breathing or the heartbeat. I think my childhood asthma had a lot to do with my consciousness of the breath unit: in a sense I've never really taken breathing for granted.

I wrote poetry off and on in high school, when I could manage to get out of gym classes and sports—using my allergies as an excuse—and climb the hill behind school till I found a nice place to settle down with a notebook, and look at Spokane spread out below. As I remember, the first real poem I wrote was about the wheat fields between Spokane and Pullman, to the south. Mother used to say that Spokane was "a walled town," quoting Ralph Adams Cram; these walls, to her, were the wheat fields to the south, the forests to the east and north, and the desert of the Grand Coulee to the west. I forget what were supposed to be the virtues of a walled town, but it was a metaphor for my mother's claustrophobia— trapped in this extremely provincial town after living all her adult life in New York and San Francisco (until she met and married my father in her forties). I know that I, too, felt that isolation, with radical parents in an arch-conservative city—and I also felt trapped, but by the excessive concern of elderly parents with one lone child. Poetry, then, was chiefly a means of escape from a huge, rah-rah high school, from Spokane and from them.

BT: But you don't think of poetry as escape now, do you?

KIZER: No, I think what I really want to escape from now is what is happening to my country—the anger, the fear, the knee-jerk conservatism. Which is probably why we bought an apartment in Paris a few years ago. As a child of the New Deal, politically active since I was twelve or so, I never thought I would feel this way! Now poems seem to be social commentary as much as anything; principally, they are focused on human interaction, which one would think is more of a novelist's concern.

BT: Influenced by . . .

KIZER: I would put Flaubert first, not only the novels, but the incomparable letters that he wrote to George Sand. And Henry James.

BT: How do you see these influences emerging in your own work?

KIZER: Well, I think if there's a major theme in my work, once we get past the love and loss of the early days, it is the impact of character upon character, how people rub against one another and alter one another. A poem of mine called "Twelve O'Clock," which was published in *The Paris Review*, was based on that principle of Heisenberg's that you can't look at a subatomic particle without altering it. Equally you cannot meet someone for a moment, or even cast eyes on someone in the street, without changing. That is my subject.

As for James, he is the master of timing. If I may go from the sublime to the ridiculous, so was Jack Benny. And Arturo Toscanini, with whom I was saturated as a young girl. It's that significant pause, that caesura, the time-out to breathe, which is why we need to hear poetry as well as see it on the page. Because we don't get the full sense of its music if we just look at it. It's always a revelation to hear a poet read his or her work.

BT: What was the importance of your time at Sarah Lawrence?

KIZER: I didn't learn much about writing at Sarah Lawrence, but I learned a lot about the sources of poems—dreams, myth, history—from the really great teachers, Joseph Campbell, Charles Trinkhaus, Bert Loewenberg and a young Australian anthropologist named Harry Hawthorne. In class he would fix us with his beautiful blue eyes, and begin, "Now, gulls . . ." and for a moment all of us would preen our feathers and flutter our wings. . . . Later he went off to Canada to study the Doukhobors, a strange religious cult of Russian descent whose form of protest was to take to the streets stark naked. I've always wondered what happened to Harry, and to them.

BT: And during your fellowship at Columbia?

KIZER: I concentrated almost exclusively on Chinese studies and, as I remember, didn't write poetry at all, except to attempt some Chinese translations. But nobody taught me how to make a good poem out of a bad poem until I encountered Theodore Roethke ten years later. During my first marriage I wrote one poem, which was published in *The Atlantic*—and which I hope no one will look up—and had three children in three years. When that marriage broke up, I went to study with Roethke at the University of Washington. I was then in my late twenties, living in Seattle. I had never taken myself seriously as a poet, and at that point the poetry didn't deserve it. But then, most women poets of my generation didn't dare take themselves seriously, because the men didn't take us seriously—I was almost middle-aged before the idea penetrated. But Ted took poetry seriously and himself seriously, and taught me to do so eventually.

It was an extraordinary class, with James Wright and Jack Gilbert, among others, and the poets David Wagoner and Richard Hugo—Ted's former students—were around too. There was a shortage of gifted women, although we received a heavy dose of women poets in class, especially Louise Bogan, Leonie Adams and Ruth Pitter (the neglected English poet who died last year at ninety-five). But you can see by the names I've mentioned that I was in a nest of singing chauvinists. Ted, and Stanley Kunitz, who took his place a couple of years later, were always willing to talk shop, but my peers were different. The men would be having conversations about craft, and if I said something they would go on as if I hadn't spoken, as if I were wallpaper. It was upsetting. But they were very much worth listening to, particularly Jim Wright, who could recite reams of poetry from memory, and several acres of the prose of Samuel Johnson, getting every word right so that those Johnsonian cadences were preserved. Then when he was really drunk he went into the German and recited Hölderlin! But we all went in for memorization, to one degree or another. I wish that more students did it today.

BT: How did the guys react to your poems, then?

KIZER: Often with great generosity. Dave Wagoner, that splendid poet, was a fine and helpful critic. But a few years later when I wrote "Pro Femina," the poem for which I may be best known, the reaction was extremely negative. The poem is in hexameters, not a common English meter; it was used by the great Roman satirists and social critics like Juvenal. I wanted a classic meter in which to write a feminist poem, having been turned on by reading Simone de Beauvoir's *The Second Sex*. I hunted for examples in English poetry and all I could turn up at that point were a couple of Swinburnes, Arthur Hugh Clough and one by Edmund Wilson. What a trio! So I was virtually on my own. But the negative reaction of my men friends was such that I nearly threw the poem away. It was my good fortune to be saved by two classical scholars who turned up then: Rolfe Humphries and Robert Fitzgerald. They loved it—not the subject, perhaps, but the meter! I fear my peers were jolted by the subject matter—but the irony is that within a couple of years one of them was teaching it at Reed College.

But it's with a sharp pang that I recall those days. Ted is dead, Jim is dead, Dick is dead. Stanley, bless him, is still with us. I remember the first day of Stanley's class I went to pick him up at 10 A.M. (he was fifty then) and he greeted me at the door with a martini in his hand. I thought, He won't last long. And he has celebrated his ninetieth birthday! He still makes a wicked martini. Perhaps that's preserved him.

BT: He and Roethke were close, were they not?

KIZER: Absolutely. Ted revered him, quoted him and stole from him. Stanley has always been too tactful and modest to mention how much influence he had on Roethke, and Lowell as well. I remember Bill Matthews quoting from Ted's essay "How to Write Like Someone Else," where the subtext is that everybody borrows from everybody, and anyone who pretends he hasn't—consciously or unconsciously—is lying. Ted pretends he is addressing beginning writers, but he is really admonishing his colleagues for acting like Romantic poets (to quote Matthews) "who pretend they made everything up out of the winey air."

Over twenty-five years ago there was an anthology called *Five Poets of the Pacific Northwest*: Wagoner, Hugo, Kenneth Hanson, William Stafford and me. The book was dedicated to Roethke, who had died recently, and there was a memorial reading in Portland in which we all took part. Each of us got up in turn and tried to say what Ted had meant to us, until it was Bill Stafford's turn. Bill said, in effect, that he hadn't been influenced by Roethke, that Roethke didn't teach him anything, that he didn't know him very well and didn't really care for his poetry. So Dick Hugo got up and said, "Thank you, Martin Bormann."

BT: Egotism, claiming he never learned anything from anyone.

KIZER: That's the "warbling woodnotes wild" school. And of course, most male poets are very competitive. They have sharp elbows. I remember that when Ted died Robert Lowell and James Dickey did a memorial to him on TV. When they read from his poems it seemed to me that they picked the weakest poems they could find. Lowell read a very minor poem, "The Geranium." To quote Bill Matthews again, he says it's a poem about Roethke firing his cleaning lady. Ted admits to being foolish, and I felt that Lowell was trying to make a fool of him when he read this poem. It was difficult for men of that generation to be generous with each other. It's easier for us women to be generous—with the exception of Sylvia Plath, who was so competitive—because we are still giving each other a helping hand. Also, in the West generally we tend to be friendlier and more generous with each other, men and women. I remember Jim Wright, who had just come from Kenyon College, being amazed at how easily we shared new work with one another. He said that people at Kenyon were much more anal, and clutched their work to their bosom as if they feared someone was going to pinch their deathless phrases. Kunitz, fresh from New York, said much the same thing.

I remember the day that Ted got the Pulitzer. He'd started class, and someone came in, whispered something to him, and he left the room. He came back looking stunned and tried to pick up where he'd left off; and then he stopped dead and said, "I've just won the Pulitzer." We all stood up and screamed with joy. In an odd way we all seemed to feel that we shared in the work of the rest, that success for any of us belonged to all of us. I still feel much that way. When Louise Glück won the Pulitzer I was elated for her, and with her, and hastened to fire off a note of praise and joy.

BT: It's interesting that you remember so many details of those years with Roethke. We're talking about things that took place thirty to forty years ago.

KIZER: Yes, it seems as if in some ways those were the defining events of my life. Of course, some of them were terribly painful. Roethke was ill, off and on, during those years. I could always tell when he was going mad because I would get a couple of dozen long-stemmed American Beauty roses. Lillian Hellman would receive a Chinook salmon sent air express. When the women he was fond of received these presents, instead of being pleased we would burst into tears, knowing too well what was to come.

BT: The onset of mania?

KIZER: By then it would be much more than an onset. The most dramatic time—in the late fifties—I came to the campus to learn that Ted had just arrived at Parrington Hall. He'd run all the way from his home, which was several miles away on a hill overlooking Lake Washington. He had perspired so heavily that his clothes were soaked. I remember he took a pack of cigarettes from his breast pocket and it dripped with sweat. We were all terribly upset. He had one of those heavy railroad flashlights in one hand and in the other a mammoth bottle-opener, both of which could have been formidable weapons. I was never afraid of him, but the students were paralyzed. So we called on the late Daniel Weiss, the brilliant Jungian scholar who was also a black belt in Judo, to stand by. In the classroom Ted did what he always did when he was going mad: he wrote his name on the blackboard, *Theodore Heubner Roethke*. He pronounced his

name with a German accent. Then he went outside to a little raised plat-
form in the middle of the quad where the flagpole was. He made an inco-
herent speech to the passing students who either ignored him or laughed.
Meanwhile someone had called the police. When they came, Dave Wag-
oner and Dan Weiss and I led Ted to the police car. I know we all felt
like Judas. Ted had been belligerent and noisy, but when the police were
about to put the handcuffs on him he held out his wrists like a little child.
As they drove off, Dave and I collapsed against the wall of Parrington Hall,
weeping. Ted wasn't a violent man; he was a gentle person, but big peo-
ple—as I know to my cost—are often seen as threatening.

BT: Could you speak a little about Roethke's methods as a teacher? I know
you have adopted them as your own.

KIZER: He taught us close analysis, to spot the soft underbelly of the poem
and to trim it ruthlessly, including the author's favorite passages. He
pointed out that the poems of tyros often don't start at the start, but spend
a stanza or two cranking up before beginning. He taught us what we dis-
liked at first but what for me became joy in later life: rigorous revision. In
his magisterial biography, Maynard Mack points out that Alexander Pope
was quite aware, as most working poets are, that "the lines which seem
to the reader or critic the most spontaneous, graceful and natural are often
the ones laboriously revised, far into the night, with an obligato of curses
and an outpouring of sweat." Pope once called the process of revision
"the greatest proof of judgment of anything I ever did." With practice, revi-
sion itself becomes a creative act. "One learns dispassion, judgment,
and a certain limited faith in one's powers of discrimination." I believe that
with my whole soul, and Roethke did too.

BT: Not to equate spontaneity with poetic genius?

KIZER: Ah yes, those who think that their first impulse is so wonderful
that they cannot alter it—in the words of a student I had at Stanford, to
revise "would be to violate the integrity of the poem." But what you do
through revision is to *find* the integrity of the poem. I've always believed
that the poem inside is perfect; I have a very clumsy retrieval process for
getting it out. It's like trying to remove a baby from its mother with a pair
of faulty forceps, getting it out without bashing its head or knocking off
one of its ears.

BT: Do you still revise a lot?

KIZER: Yes. Pope also said you should keep a poem for two years before trying to publish it—which I do. I also have long poems hanging around in notebooks that are unfinished and that I drag out and work on from time to time. It keeps me from worrying about writer's block. And of course my Chinese translations are another way of doing that. I just say to myself, I'm going into my translating mode.

BT: Let's talk about translation. What's its chief value, aside from keeping your hand in?

KIZER: It allows you to explore the possibilities of your own language. I remember in Pakistan once some intellectual said to me, "Ah, but our language is so much richer than yours. You have only one word for *love* while we have dozens." And I said, "Oh, yeah?" and I began to rip off similes, much to his amazement. I think I got off at least two dozen without pausing for a breath. And that is the fascinating thing about translating. That there is a word, if you can just find it, for everything. I've got two poems of Ingeborg Bachmann that I've been working on. They are impossibly difficult. If you want to figure out what a poet is telling you, trying to translate her is the best way to find out. I sent my versions to an eminent German scholar at Reed College who's a good friend of mine, and he pointed out all the things I hadn't seen and didn't know; so now I'm going to go at it again. I've got the rhymes, and the basic plan for the poem. Now all I have to do is get the nuances and subtleties, the subtext.

BT: What do you do with an element like sound patterning?

KIZER: In German I damn well abandon it! I think of poor Heine saying, "My God, to think I was cursed with this vile language!" Perhaps with German even Hopkins might be a help: you could be freed up to invent compound words.

The problem that most translators have, especially professionals translating the whole body of somebody's work, is that they fall into "translatese": the linguistic pattern of the language that they're translating from, sometimes to the extent of putting verbs at the end of the sentence. It's very seductive. The better you know the language, the more seductive it is. I don't have a general theory of translation; I think I have a theory of translation for each poet that I translate, because each language requires such different things. Each poetic voice is so different from every other poetic voice. The thing you have to do is become that person for a time.

BT: Are there dangers in falling in love with another poet's voice?

KIZER: It's like an actor trying on a new role, finding another voice that's within you to express something. I have a poem called "In the First Stanza," where I got the idea and, I think, the voice from a twelfth-century Chinese woman poet. She did exactly what I had been told in workshops not to do, which is telegraph your punches. She tells you in one stanza what she is going to do in the next. I fell madly in love with this idea and tried it, and it worked out very well. Of course I have done many imitations of classic Chinese poems, particularly by Tu Fu, and I've also translated Tu Fu. In the noble Tu Fu poem "The Testament," Roethke's influence was a great help; there are lines that are very Roethkean, like "I find the grasses dying with the year." That sounds like Roethke to me, both the rhythms and the way the language goes. Ted gave me a voice that I heard as the voice of Tu Fu, but I also think the reason I'm good at Tu Fu is that I feel a real affinity for him. You have to fall in love with that other poet, really.

BT: You've had a wide range of poetic influences—Eastern European, Oriental, as well as the whole line of poets in English. But weren't painters important to you, as well?

KIZER: In some ways painters have been more important in my life than writers. Painters teach you how to see—a faculty which usually isn't highly developed in poets. Whether you take a walk in the woods with a painter, or go to a museum with one, through them you notice shapes, colors, harmonies, relationships that enhance your own seeing. Also, male artists always have had the qualities that modern women find lacking in most men; these guys know how to cook, change a diaper, take responsibility for entertaining and educating their children. Of course part of this is due to economics: most good painters are poor. But mainly it's because they are tactile, earthy; like Antaeus, they have their feet firmly in the dirt.

BT: You met Mark Tobey and Morris Graves while you were still in your twenties.

KIZER: One morning the doorbell rang, I was clutching a very young baby to my breast who was dribbling on a totally impractical trousseau dressing gown. When I opened the door, there was this towering person. He looked like Jehovah, or Jesus or St. Jerome. It was Morris Graves. I literally reeled backward as he strode into the living room. I can't remember how I met Tobey. It seems as if he was always there, like a father. I saw him at least once a week for years. Mark was also a very articulate person, unlike many good painters. He would say things like, "Cubism is the great unfinished business of painting." Once he was describing the renovation of a fine old theater: "Then the orchestra rose out of the pit like the devil's liver!" Mark used to give free lectures at the Seattle public library. Smart young lawyers and businessmen would bring their brown-bag lunches and listen enthralled. Mark, with a blackboard, would sketch in the lines of a great classical painting, Rubens or Tiepolo, say, and show how it could be broken down into a composition by Picasso.

BT: I love your Tobey *World Egg*.

KIZER: I bought that when I was pregnant, because it was just the way I felt at the time: as if I contained multitudes! I was married to a very rich man at the time, but like many people who inherit wealth, he was frugal to a fault. But my dear mother gave me a tiny allowance—twenty-five dollars a month—to hire a cleaning lady. Instead I bought paintings from Mark, on time. Whenever I looked at my paintings I thought, I scrubbed bathrooms for these! Of course, when I was divorced it was handy, because all the paintings were ones I had paid for, so I got to keep them.

One reason I have some astonishing little paintings by Tobey is that I became a sort of repository of paintings for him, of things he wanted to keep around to look at. Painters will tell you how painful it is to give up their work, particularly if a given piece contains the seeds of work as yet unpainted. Mark always felt free to hang around my house and look at his own work. My Tobeys are superb, my Graves's less so, because Morris was much more expensive, even then. Mark was dreadfully hard up. I remember carting around major paintings of his, endeavoring to sell them to wealthy Seattleites. I remember one woman whose husband was the manager of I. Magnin who came to look at the paintings wearing a Chanel suit, who said, "They're beautiful. I wish I could afford them." She could have bought one for four hundred dollars, less than the price of her suit. Those paintings are now in the Museum of Modern Art, the Phillips collection and in every European museum of note.

BT: The portrait of your father by Tobey is extraordinary.

KIZER: I remember reading aloud to them the letters of Lady Mary Wortley Montagu as Daddy posed. Daddy, in a characteristic way, has one hand supporting his chin. Mark was delighted. "That gets rid of the terrible problem of modern portraits: the collar and tie!" There is a timelessness about it. Once, someone inquired, "Is that an ancestor?" And my husband, poker-faced, said yes. I will always miss Mark dreadfully, but I have his wonderful work to look at, every day.

BT: Let's talk about process, how a poem grows. I've seen different versions of some poems, like "Twelve O'Clock," over a period of five or six years.

KIZER: I have one poem, "Halation," which took approximately nine years! But "Twelve O'Clock" started with a photograph from the newspaper of Mrs. E.O. Lawrence —a beautiful old woman who was trying to get her husband's name taken off the Lawrence Livermore Lab because it was producing horrible atomic devices of one kind or another, and she said her husband would hate it. I knew I wanted to write about physicists and physics but I didn't know anything about it because all I'd had was general science in high school, nothing since then. So I began reading books on physics for about two years. More or less popular books, but I was pleased that the little gray cells in the unused portion of my brain were still active enough to take this in.

BT: So the poem began with an idea?

KIZER: No, it began with Mrs. Lawrence because she became my muse, because of the statement she made and, of course, because she was beautiful. I think muses have to be beautiful. And then in the conception of the poem, as I worked on it—a lot of it, of course, in my head—was the dialectic between my mother's and Einstein's sense that the universe was orderly, and Heisenberg's and my sense that it was chaos. There were two other things that I wanted to do in the poem. One was to get Einstein's idea of the simultaneity of time. I wanted everything in the poem to seem to be happening at once. In organizing the poem I would cut the stanzas up and put them on the floor and walk around in my bare feet rearranging them.

BT: So it wasn't that the poem came into your mind as a logical argument, but rather as if it were chunks of mosaic or themes in music, to be arranged so that they interact with each other?

KIZER: Poems, to me, do not come from ideas, they come from a series of images that you tuck away in the back of your brain. Little photographic snapshots. Then you get the major vision of the poem, which is like a giant magnet to which all these disparate little impressions fly and adhere, and there is the poem!

It resembles the sequences of memory. One thing I should make clear is that although I have a very spotty memory in many respects, I have a nearly perfect memory for dialogue, for conversations. The funny thing is that I believe in invention and I believe in lies, but in this poem the dialogue is an absolute recapitulation of everything I've heard. So that when I was four years old, Mother said, "Listen, darling and remember always; / It's Dr. Einstein broadcasting from Switzerland"—that's exactly what she said, and my response, "So what?" is just what I responded. I get indignant when people ask, "Did you really say that? Did these people really say that?"

BT: But why do you think you so perfectly remember such a thing, a little girl not at that time the least concerned with politics or physics? What seals the memory?

KIZER: The pressure of my mother's speech in iambic pentameter of course, "Listen, darling and remember always; / It's Dr. Einstein broadcasting from Switzerland." When someone speaks in that impassioned way, when they speak in perfect iambic pentameter, as most people do under pressure, it's something you remember.

BT: So meter is more than a convention or a straitjacket imposed on the spontaneous freedom of our words, but something towards which passion automatically tends. An internal force.

KIZER: And it is as natural to me as breathing.

BT: The urgency in this poem was . . .

KIZER: The imperative in this particular poem is to tell the truth. I think underlying everything I've written is the great saying of the Society of Friends: "Speak truth to power." That is central to my work going way back to my early poem about the suicide of the Canadian diplomat Herbert Norman, who was accused of being Communist. When I say, "A poet, to whom no one cruel and imposing listens, / Disdained by senates, whispers to your dust," I am doing my best to speak truth to power.

BT: Could we talk about the line breaks in "Twelve O'Clock"?

KIZER: Shall I go into my whole riff about line breaks and about how angry I get with young poets who break lines like sawing kindling, so that it looks nice on the page and violates the integrity of phrase? Line breaks are one of our major forms of punctuation— compared to music, for example, which has infinite numbers of ways of telling you how fast, how slow, when to breathe, when to stop, when to pause; we've got the standard punctuation marks and we've got the line break, and you've got to use the line break to work for you. Also, the line break can provide a kind of emphasis, to indicate shock, taking a deep breath, crisis. In the middle of the poem, "Hiroshima. Heisenberg at first refused / To believe it, till the evening news confirmed / That their work had led Hiroshima's 100,000 dead." Now when you refuse to believe something you take a deep breath before it really hits you. In "the evening news confirmed," again, there is this moment of shock, disbelief, that the line break emphasizes.

I've learned from Robert Creeley about line breaks, too, which in Bob's case are always very, very considered. He's a poet as different from me as anyone could be: a poet who characteristically works in short lines where I tend to work in long ones. But Bob makes full use of the break between one line and the next to make you think, to make you pause, to make you reflect and, most important, to hear Bob thinking, halting, reflecting. So that you get three times the charge out of a few lines of his than you get out of an enormous range of words by other people who don't have this kind of understanding of what a line break means.

You can also use line breaks as a means of reinforcing irony. Near the end of the poem, for example, when I run into Dr. Lawrence on the train, and he tells us not to worry about the atom because it's nothing to concern us, and I say, "So, reassured we said goodbyes, / And spoke of him in coming years, that lovely man." I'm always interested in the fact that audiences get that. In fact they get even more out of it than I've put into it, in a curious way. They get the ambiguity of this very nice person who created this horrible monster that created our overwhelming dread of the future.

BT: Judith Johnson said once that you're really an Augustan poet disguised as a sort of post-Romantic.

KIZER: I think Hayden Carruth said something too that was very close to that. I think I am, actually. I remember after a reading somebody came up to me and said, "I love that political poem of yours," and my husband, who was standing next to me, said "Which one? They're all political," and I was pleased by that. I would feel the same if she had said, "I love that feminist poem of yours." It's a point of view, it's a stance, it's an attitude towards life that affects, and afflicts, everything I do. But one thing that I want to emphasize about my feminism, something that's only become a canon of official feminism in fairly recent times, is this concern with ecology, with saving what's left of the world. My father was an early city planner and a historic preservationist. The thing that underpins "A Muse of Water" is my incorporation of my father's concern with the environment long before the word *ecology* became fashionable. And I've assimilated man's degradation of the environment as a basic feminist concern. Rape is rape, whether it is a human being or a landscape.

BT: How did you come to write "A Muse of Water"?

KIZER: The genesis of that is very simple: Robert Lowell, in Stanley Kunitz's house, saying that women ought not to try to be artists, they should stick to the kitchen. It was right after he'd made a pass at me. He'd been drinking, naturally. It must have been about 1957, he was married to Elizabeth Hardwick, the brightest woman in America. I was so outraged that I went home and wrote "A Muse of Water." It began as a letter to Lowell actually, and then when I'd written a draft of it, I thought, "He doesn't deserve it!" So I took out all the references to Cal, except for a mention of the Charles River in the fourth stanza, which remains like a vermiform appendix.

BT: How about "Semele Recycled"—another feminist poem?

KIZER: That was a freebie. One of the things that happens if you revise interminably, as I do, is that occasionally the Muse says to you, "Well, you've been a good girl, have one on the house." I was driving back from Charlotte, North Carolina, to Chapel Hill, having had minor female surgery—very minor, but still I reflected on the fact that as women go through life they keep losing portions of themselves. Bit by bit they're being taken away, and it occurred to me at that very moment, that the story of Dionysus had to be about a *woman*, not a man at all. The whole dismemberment number is obviously a female myth that got distorted and transformed in the course of the ages. Then I woke up the next morning and wrote the poem. It's the least revised of any poem I ever wrote and perhaps the best.

BT: It seems to me it's also about another kind of fragmentation, the way in which we're real to others only in one aspect, most of the time. A teacher at one time for one bunch of people, a daughter or lover or . . .

KIZER: You could make even more of a synecdoche than that. To your lover you're a vagina, to your baby you're a nipple and so on. But, of course, the other thing is that this is a love poem. I'd had the breakup of probably the great love of my life not too long before; I hadn't seen him for two years. The reconciliation in the poem was just wishful thinking on my part, but it works in the poem.

BT: You can read that reconciliation as fate's magnanimity, but it has also been read as a succumbing to an endless cycle of betrayals! Either way, irony!

KIZER: The irony is certainly there. Irony is my big number. You know I used to get so many letters from students about the ending of "Pro Femina," when I speak of "the luck of our husbands and lovers, who keep free women." So I had a stamp made that said "irony, irony, irony," to put on a postcard and mail it back.

BT: Speaking of "Pro Femina," what about the long sections of that poem that are, however wittily, highly critical of women?

KIZER: I'm addressing women, saying we've got to pull up our socks and do better. I'm dealing with our frailties and our flaws, which men have encouraged. If you read the biographies of women poets of the twenties you discover that they were manipulated into writing poems about loss and love. A coerced sentimentality. You see how they were taken up by second-rate men, second-rate critics, second-rate English professors, and often those were the kinds of men that they married. I was interested in exploring the induced vulnerabilities of women.

BT: Your feminism seems very much of a piece with the rest of you.

KIZER: I think I've really thoroughly internalized my feminism, partly because I got it from my mother and my father; it's something that occurs on a certain level of my work all the time. My mother was a very curious combination—not uncommon in women of her generation—of someone who believed implicitly in feminist principles, who was enormously gifted, who married for the first time at forty, after putting all her little brothers through college and having the great luck to meet my father, but who then never worked again in her life. Never had a job again. She worked very hard at keeping the home, and focused on me to an unhealthy degree. She was offered a job by Eleanor Roosevelt to be on some labor commission, a very hotshot thing, and I remember her saying to me, "But who would get your father's breakfast?" and I was shocked to the soles of my feet! I had been radicalized, and she had done it—that was why that question was so shocking. When my mother died in 1955, my father got his own breakfast for nearly thirty years. He would have been perfectly willing to do it. He felt that my mother was so gifted, and so neurotic, that she needed work. I once remarked jokingly that all my role models were women much younger than I, which is true.

BT: What about the current state of feminist writing? Are there things women still don't say? Matters still suppressed?

KIZER: No, I think the problem is that people are saying things that I wish they weren't saying. I'm not interested in poems about soiled menstrual pads, et cetera. But there are many aspects of women's lives that have been dealt with inadequately: maternity, for one thing. Giving birth. Of course we block a lot of it out, but what we don't remember we can invent. The mother-daughter subject, from both directions, as the mother and as the daughter, how little that's been dealt with.

BT: Before we end, what is your overview? You're in your seventies, you've won the Pulitzer, you've been a chancellor of the Academy; you've had a rich life as an artist, as well as the secular life of family, a long late marriage. How does the poet's life look, from here?

KIZER: Well, in many ways it began as a kind of accident. It could have gone so many ways—either music or theater or, I suppose, if I'd been twenty years younger, film, film scripts. And I sometimes feel nostalgic about that because I think I would have enjoyed it. But I guess it was inevitable that I would settle for poetry. My joke always was that when I was at Sarah Lawrence my music teacher told me that if I wanted to keep at the same level of skill at playing the piano I'd have to practice four or five hours a day just to stay where I was. And that did not appeal. And also I thought it would be easier to go through life with a pencil rather than a Steinway. It is very good for a peripatetic person like me, who writes poetry wherever I am. I guess the thing that really clinched it for me was the notion that I wanted to stay as far away from capitalism—buying and selling, the material world—as I possibly could, and poetry was clearly the solution to that!

I've been enormously fortunate. People say, "How do you feel about your reputation?" My real belief is that I have exactly the reputation I deserve. It's not fame, so fortunately I will probably be able to avoid the kind of biographies that have been written about my friends, which are exploitative and unnecessarily detailed about aspects of their life which I don't think are anybody's business. And as far as honors are concerned, I didn't really receive any until I was sixty and I was over the age of having to worry about whether I would be spoiled. So on the whole I feel comfortable with myself. You know I've always loved that line from Chaucer's *Criseyde*, "I am meyne own woman wel at ease." That's the way I feel. Of course, there are always disasters looming, both cosmic and domestic. But even if it should all end tomorrow I would just hope I've burned enough bad drafts and old love letters!

Carolyn Kizer: A Bibliography

POETRY

The Ungrateful Garden. Bloomington, IN: Indiana University Press, 1961.

Knock Upon Silence. Garden City, NY: Doubleday & Company, 1965.

Midnight Was My Cry. Garden City, NY: Doubleday & Company, 1971.

Yin: New Poems. Brockport, NY: BOA Editions, 1984. (Pulitzer Prize, 1985)

Mermaids in the Basement. Port Townsend, WA: Copper Canyon Press, 1984.

The Nearness of You. Port Townsend, WA: Copper Canyon Press, 1986. (Roethke Prize, 1987)

Harping On: Poems 1985–1995. Port Townsend, WA: Copper Canyon Press, 1995.

The Ungrateful Garden. Reissue. Pittsburgh, PA: Carnegie Mellon Press, 1999.

Cool, Calm, & Collected: Poems 1960–2000. Port Townsend, WA: Copper Canyon Press, 2001.

TRANSLATION

Carrying Over: Poems from the Chinese, Urdu, Macedonian, Yiddish, and French African. Port Townsend, WA: Copper Canyon Press, 1988.

A Splintered Mirror: Chinese Poetry from the Democracy Movement (with Donald Finkel). San Francisco, CA: North Point, 1991.

Euripides' 4, Iphigenia in Taurus. Philadelphia, PA: University of Pennsylvania Press, 1999.

EDITING

The Essential Clare. Hopewell, NJ: Ecco Press, 1992.

100 Great Poems by Women. Hopewell, NJ: Ecco Press, 1992.

CHAPBOOK

Pro Femina. (1964, 1984, 1999). Kansas City, MO: BkMk Press, University
    of Missouri Kansas City, 2000.

PROSE

Proses: Essays on Poets and Poetry. Port Townsend, WA: Copper Canyon
    Press, 1993.

*Picking & Choosing: Essays on Feminism, Japanese Literature and Theodore
    Roethke as Teacher.* Cheney, WA: Eastern Washington Press, 1995.

Contributors' Notes

AGHA SHAHID ALI is on the poetry faculty at the University of Utah and is the author of seven collections of poetry including *The Half-Inch Himalayas; A Nostalgist's Map of America* (Norton); and *The Country Without a Post Office* (Norton). His translation of the work of Faid Ahmed Faiz was published as *The Rebel's Silhouette* and he has edited an anthology of ghazals, *Radical Disunities* (Wesleyan). He has received several fellowships including an Ingram Merrill grant and a Guggenheim.

MICHELLE BOISSEAU has published two books of poems, *Understory*, winner of the Morse Prize (Northeastern University Press, 1996) and *No Private Life* (Vanderbilt, 1990). Her poems have appeared in *The Gettysburg Review, The Southern Review, Ploughshares, Agni, The Ohio Review, The Georgia Review, Poetry*, and elsewhere. With the late Robert Wallace she is the author of *Writing Poems*. Her work has received a National Endowment for the Arts poetry fellowship and two Poetry Society of America awards. She is currently an associate professor of English at the University of Missouri-Kansas City.

In addition to the National Book Award, HAYDEN CARRUTH has been awarded a National Book Critics Circle Award, a 1995 Lannan Literary Award, the Shelley Memorial Award, and fellowships from the Guggenheim Foundation and the NEA, among many other honors. The author of dozens of books of poetry and prose, he is a former editor of *Poetry* and former poetry editor for *Harper's*. He lives in Munnsville, New York.

FRED CHAPPELL, while teaching at the University of North Carolina, Greensboro, for 36 years, has published two dozen books of poetry, fiction, and criticism. His latest novel is *Look Back All the Green Valley* (Picador USA), his latest poetry, *Family Gathering* (Louisiana State University Press).

KELLY CHERRY, Eminent Scholar at the Humanities Center of the University of Alabama in Huntsville, is also Eudora Welty Professor Emerita of English and Evjue-Bascom Professor Emerita in the Humanities at the University of Wisconsin-Madison. She is the author of over twenty books, including *The Society of Friends*, stories; *Death and Transfiguration*, poems; *God's Loud Hand*, poems; *The Exiled Heart*, an autobiography;

and a translation of Sophocles's *Antigone*. Her awards include the Hanes Prize, given by the Fellowship of Southern Writers for a distinguished body of work in poetry (1989).

DOMINIC CHEUNG is currently Professor of Comparative Literature and Chair of the Department of East Asian Languages and Cultures at the University of Southern California. A prominent Chinese poet by the pseudonym of Chang Ts'o, he has 14 volumes of poetry in Chinese. His English collection of poetry, *Drifting*, has recently been published (Green Integer: Copenhagen & Los Angeles, 2000).

LUCILLE CLIFTON was born in Depew, New York, in 1936, and educated at the State University of New York at Fredonia and at Howard University. Her awards include the Juniper Prize for Poetry, two nominations for the Pulitzer Prize in poetry, an Emmy Award from the American Academy of Television Arts and Sciences, and two fellowships from the National Endowment for the Arts. She has taught at the University of California at Santa Cruz and American Unviersity in Washington, D.C. and is Distinguished Professor of Humanities at St. Mary's College of Maryland.

ALFRED CORN's seventh book of poems, *Present*, appeared in 1997, along with a novel, *Part of His Story*, and a study of prosody, *The Poem's Heartbeat*. He has also published a collection of critical essays entitled *The Metamorphoses of Metaphor*. His translation of Aristophane's *Frogs* appeared in the Penn Press Greed Drama series in 1999, along with *Stake: Selected Poems 1972–1992*. He has taught at the City University of New York, Yale, the University of Cincinnati, UCLA, Ohio State University and the University of Tulsa, and currently teaches in the Graduate Writing Program at Columbia. A frequent contributor to *The New York Times Book Review* and *The Nation*, he also writes art criticism for *Art in America* and *ARTnews* magazines. He lives in New York City.

ROBERT CREELEY (b. 1926) is a New Englander by birth and disposition although he has spent most of his life in other parts of the world including Guatemala, British Columbia, France, and Spain. In the 1950s he taught at Black Mountain College and also edited *The Black Mountain Review*, a crucial gathering place for alternative senses of writing at that time. Charles Olson, Robert Duncan, and Edward Dorn are among the company he met there. Subsequently he taught at the University of New Mexico and in 1966 went to the State University of New York at Buffalo, where he still teaches. Although most identified as a poet (*For Love*,

Pieces, Windows and *Selected Poems* are examples of his many collections), he has written a significant body of prose including a novel, *The Island*, and a collection of stories, *The Gold Diggers,* and is also known for the diversity of his collaborations with artists outside his own authority.

TERRY EHRET is the author of *Lost Body* (Copper Canyon Press, 1993), selected by Carolyn Kizer for the National Poetry Series. Other honors include two Pushcart Prize nominations, California Commonwealth Club's Book Award for Poetry, and the Nimrod/Hardman Pablo Neruda Prize. A new collection, *Translations from The Human Language*, will be published by Sixteen Rivers Press in 2001. She teaches writing in Sonoma County where she lives with her husband and three daughters.

Poet/critic JACK FOLEY's most recent books are the essay collections, *O Powerful Western Star* and *Foley's Books*: *California Rebels, Beats, and Radicals* (Pantograph Press). Among his poetry books are *Gershwin, Adrift,* and *Exiles*. Foley's radio show, Cover to Cover" is heard weekly on Berkeley station KPFA; his column "Foley's Books," appears weekly in the online magazine, *The Alsop Review* (http://www.alsopreview.com).

JUDITH JOHNSON, poet, fiction-writer, and performance artist, is the author of two books of short fiction and eight books of poetry, the most recent of which is *The Ice Lizard* (Sheep Meadow Press, 1992) and the first of which was *Uranium Poems* (Yale Series of Younger Poets, 1969). Her inter-media installation/performance piece, "Friedrich Liebermann, American Artist," has been widely exhibited and is now being developed as a multimedia CD-ROM novel. She is editor of the feminist literary periodical *13th Moon* and publishes *The Little Magazine*, now an electronic journal. She is Professor of English and Women's Studies at the State University of New York at Albany, where she has chaired both departments.

MAXINE KUMIN is the author of twelve books of poetry, most recently *Selected Poems 1960–1990, Looking for Luck,* and *Connecting the Dots*. Her memoir of a nearly fatal carriage-driving accident, *Inside the Halo and Beyond*, was just published by Norton and a collection of her essays, *Always Beginning: On a Life in Poetry,* is just out from Copper Canyon Press. Winner of the Pulitzer, Ruth Lilly and Aiken/Taylor prizes, Kumin lives with her husband on a farm in New Hampshire.

CAROL MUSKE (in fiction, CAROL MUSKE DUKES) is the author of six books of poems, two novels and a collection of critical essays. Her third novel,

Life After Death, is forthcoming from Random House in 2001. Her second collection of critical essays, *Married to the Icepick Killer: A Poet in Hollywood* is also due out from Random House in 2002. Her most recent book of poems was *An Octave Above Thunder, New & Selected Poems*. She is Professor of English and Creative Writing at the University of Southern California, where she directs the PhD Program in Literature and Creative Writing. She is the recipient of many awards, including a Guggenheim, NEA, the Witter Bynner Fellowship from the Library of Congress, the di Castagnola Award, the Dylan Thomas Prize, and many others. She lives in Los Angeles.

ROBERT PHILLIPS is the author of six books of poetry, including *Spinach Days* (Johns Hopkins University Press, 2000). He is poetry editor of the *Texas Review* and a councilor of the Texas Institute of Letters. He teaches at the University of Houston, where he was director of the Creative Writing Program and is now a John and Rebecca Moores Scholar. His prizes include awards in literature from the American Academy of Arts and Letters and he is the literary executor for the estates of Delmore Schwartz and Karl Shapiro.

MARIE PONSOT is the author of four books of poems: *True Minds* (1957), *Admit Impediment* (1981), *The Green Dark* (1988), as well as *The Bird Catcher* (Knopf, 1998), which won the National Book Award. She has also written classic textbooks on teaching writing including *Beat Not the Poor Desk*. Among her awards are an NEA Creative Writing Grant and the Shaughnessy Medal of the Modern Language Association.

As an undergraduate, MARGARET RABB studied with Carolyn Kizer, then writer-in-residence at the University of North Carolina. Rabb graduated in 1974 and has continued to live in the country near Chapel Hill. She is now the director of communications and development for an international development program at the University, where she's also taught in the Creative Writing Program. Her new book, *Granite Dives* (New Issues Press, 2000), was written after she turned 40, and every word is indebted to Carolyn Kizer.

C.L. RAWLINS took part in Carolyn Kizer's workshop at Stanford University, where he was a Stegner Fellow in Poetry, 1985–86. He was born in Wyoming and has worked there as a forest ranger, hydrologist, and teacher of both natural science and writing. His fourth book, *In Gravity National Park,* won the Mountain and Plains Booksellers Award for Poetry in 1999.

RUTH SALVAGGIO is the author of several works of literary criticism and theory, including *Enlightened Absence: Neoclassical Configurations of the*

Feminine (Illinois, 1985) and *The Sounds of Feminist Theory* (SUNY, 1999). She teaches at the University of New Mexico, where she is Professor of American Studies.

TERRY STOKES was born in Flushing, New York, in 1943. He wanted to become a rock 'n roll star; he couldn't sing, or dance. He decided to try poetry. He is still trying. He teaches at the University of Cincinnati.

HENRY TAYLOR teaches literature and creative writing at American University in Washington, DC. He has published five collections of poems; his third, *The Flying Change*, received the 1986 Pulitzer Prize in Poetry. His latest book is *Brief Candles: 101 Clerihews*. His essays on recent American poets have appeared regularly since 1968, and seventeen of them were collected in *Compulsory Figures* (1992). His translations from classical drama include Sophocles's *Electra*, 1998.

BARBARA THOMPSON writes short fiction which has appeared in two Pushcart Prize Anthologies and *The Best of Shenandoah*, among other places. In addition to this interview with Carolyn Kizer, her interviews with Katherine Anne Porter and Peter Taylor have been published by *The Paris Review* in their "Writers at Work" series. She is the Trustee of the literary estate of Katherine Anne Porter.

KIM VAETH's *Her Yes* was published by Zoland Books in 1994. Her work has received grants from the Massachusetts Artists Fellowship and the St. Botolph foundation and has appeared in *Ploughshares*, *Grand Street*, and *The Kenyon Review*. In 1998, she completed *Elegies*, the poetic text for an orchestral work by Richard Danielpour commissioned by the Jacksonville Symphony, which was premiered by Frederica von Stade and Thomas Hampson at Carnegie Hall. It was later recorded by the London Philharmonic for release on Sony Classical. She is working on a new poetry manuscript as well as the text for a second orchestral work commissioned by the Pacific Symphony in Los Angeles.

JACKSON WHEELER was born in the Southern Appalachian town of Andrews, NC. He attended UNC-Chapel Hill on scholarship. He has spent the last 26 years of his life as a social worker among mentally retarded people. He is the author of *Swimming Past Iceland* (1994) and *A Near Country: Poems of Loss* (1999). His work has appeared in numerous journals and anthologies. He met Carolyn Kizer in 1972 and her friendship has profoundly changed his life.

About the Editors

ANNIE FINCH's books of poetry include *Eve* (1997) and the epic poem *Marie Moving*, forthcoming in 2002. Anthologies she has edited include *A Formal Feeling Comes*, now in its sixth printing, and with Kathrine Varnes, *An Exaltation of Forms: Contemporary Poets Celebrate the Diversity of Their Art* (Michigan, 2001). Her book on poetics, *The Ghost of Meter* (1993), has just been reissued in paperback. She is currently an Associate Professor at Miami University.

JOHANNA KELLER is the author of *The Skull: North Carolina, 1961*, a long poem published in 1998 by The Press at Colorado College in a limited edition with photographs by the author. She has been the recipient of poetry fellowship grants from the New York Foundation for the Arts and the Ludwig Vogelstein Foundation. In 2000, she received an ASCAP-Deems Taylor Award for excellence in arts journalism for her essays in *The New York Times*.

CANDACE McCLELLAND teaches literature and writing at the Cincinnati Country Day School. She is a graduate of the University of Cincinnati and of Miami University, where she taught Composition and served as poetry editor of *Oxford Magazine*. She is currently at work on *The Steep and Thorny Way to Heaven*, an anthology of trail poems.

Index

A

Academy of American Poets
  Kizer's resignation from, 3–4,
      26–27, 29–30, 195
  programs run by, 186
Achievement in American Poetry
      (Bogan), 75
Adams, Leonie, 199
adjectives, in poetry, 74
Ahmed, Ajaz, 2
Ali, Agha Shahid, 160–161, 215
Alighieri, Dante. *See* Dante Alighieri
Allen, Paula Gunn, 56
alliteration, 103
American Academy and Institute of
      Arts and Letters, 36–37
American Literary Anthology, 185–186
Asian-inspired themes
  in *Chinese Imitations* (section from
      Knock Upon Silence), 14–17,
      78–79, 133–141
  influence on Kizer, 103–104
  in "A Month in Summer," 15–17,
      105–106
  in "Singing Aloud," 104
Auden, Wystan Hugh, 100, 101
Audience, 2
Auerhahn Press, 188
Austen, Jane, 79

B

Bachmann, Ingeborg, 177, 203
Bashō. *See* Matsuo Bashō
"Battle Hymn of the Republic"
      (Howe), 92
"Because You Are Always There"
      (Stokes), 155
Bernstein, Leonard, 183
Berryman, John, 9

Bishop, Elizabeth, 86, 176
Bogan, Louise, 75, 89, 101, 199
Boisseau, Michelle, 169–179, 215
The Book of Songs (Waley), 134
Boyd, Mark Alexander, 79
Bradstreet, Anne, 91
British Arts Council, 183
Broumas, Olga, 128
Brown Paper Review, 185
Brown, Steven Ford, 75
"Bub and Sis" (Creeley), 149
Bullitt, Ashley and Jill, (Kizer's
      daughters), 14, 33, 106
Bullitt, Scott, (Kizer's son), 195
Bullitt, Stimson (Kizer's first husband),
      195

C

Campbell, Joseph, 76, 80, 198
"The Canonization" (Donne), 107
"A Carol for Carolyn" (Finch), 163
Carruth, Hayden, 143–144, 208, 215
Castellanos, Rosario, 56
Catullus, Gaius Valerius, 61
"A Caveat to the Fair Sex" (Montagu), 81
Center for Inter-American Relations,
      187
Centrum, 128
Chametzky, Jules, 183
Chapel Hill, NC, 71–72, 77
Chappell, Fred, 77, 93–95, 215
Chaucer, Geoffrey, 212
Cherry, Kelly, 151, 215–216
Cheung, Dominic, 133–141, 216
child's voice
  in "Gerda," 4, 31–33
  in "The Intruder," 23–25
  in "Pearl," 4
  in "Pro Femina," 25–26

Chinese poetic models. *See* Asian-
    inspired themes
Chinese translations, 177, 204
Cleghorn, Sarah, 92
Clifton, Lucille, 3, 153, 216
Clough, Arthur Hugh, 172, 199
Columbia University, 73, 198
consonance, 103
Coordinating Council of Literary
    Magazines, 183–184
Corn, Alfred, 29–39, 216
Creeley, Robert
    biographical note about, 216–217
    poem dedicated to, 14, 33
    poem for Kizer written by, 149
    use of line breaks by, 208
Criseyde (Chaucer), 212
Cummington Press, 188

D
dactylic hexameter, 10
dance companies, 174–175
Dante Alighieri, 4, 49–50
di Prima, Diane, 188
Dickey, James, 200
Dickinson, Emily, 29, 128
Donne, John, 107, 139
double Sapphics, 177
"Drifting in Montana" (Rawlins), 157
Dukes, Carol Muske. *See* Muske, Carol
The Dunciad (Pope), 59, 112

E
Ecco Press, 4, 8, 49
ecology, 170, 208–209
editing, 92
Ehrenpries, Irving, 72
Ehret, Terry, 41–48, 217
Einstein, Albert, 53, 82, 206
Eisler, Riane, 45, 46
Eliot, T.S., 50, 75
Elizabeth Press, 188
Engle, Paul, 183
Essay on Criticism (Pope), 59

Eyrie, June, 174

F
Federal Arts Agency, 190
Federico, Salvatore, 169
feminist themes
    in "Bitch," 88
    in "Dream of a Large Lady," 56–57,
        59, 89
    ecological concerns and, 208–209
    in "Fanny," 66–68, 89
    in "from 'Pro Femina'," 10–11
    in "Hera, Hung from the Sky," 78,
        89
    in Kizer's poetry, 106
    in *Knock Upon Silence*, 9–11
    in modern poetry, 210–211
    in "Mud Soup," 9
    in "A Muse of Water," 69, 78,
        91–92, 108–111
    in "Persephone Pauses," 78
    political concerns and, 55
    in "Pro Femina," 33, 64–65, 66,
        87–88, 98, 210
    in "Promising Author," 59–60
    in "Semele Recycled," 47–48,
        80–81, 89, 118–119, 209
Field, Edward, 188
Finch, Anne (Countess of Winchilsea),
    92
Finch, Annie, 85–92, 163, 221
Finkel, Donald, 178
Fitzgerald, Robert, 199
Flaubert, Gustave, 31, 197
Foley, Jack, 49–53, 217
freedom themes, 37–39
friendship themes
    in "An American Beauty," 33,
        177–178
    in "Fanny," 20–21
    in "For Jan as the End Draws Near,"
        19–20, 33
    in "For Jan, in Bar Maria," 19, 33
    in "Gerda," 8

in "Poem for Your Birthday," 22,
177–178
in "Twelve O'Clock," 8
Furies, 16

G
gerunds, in poetry, 72–73
Gilbert, Jack, 199
Glück, Louise, 201
Graves, Morris, 204, 205
Graves, Robert, 76–77
Greek mythology
in Bogan's poems, 75
in "Fearful Women," 81–82
in "Hera, Hung from the Sky," 11,
34, 78
influence on Kizer, 76–78
in "A Muse of Water," 78
in "Persephone Pauses," 34, 78
in "Semele Recycled," 34, 43,
80–81, 125
in "The Ungrateful Garden," 77–78,
100–101
in "Voyager," 80
The Greek Myths (Graves), 76

H
Hacker, Marilyn, 175
haibun, 79
haiku, 15–17, 105
Halprin, Lawrence, 183
Hardwick, Elizabeth, 209
Haselwood, Dave, 188
Hawkes, John, 188
Hawthorne, Harry, 198
Heine, Heinrich, 79–80
Heisenberg, Werner, 4, 35, 198, 206
Hemans, Felicia, 92
hexameter, 10, 24, 172–173, 199
Hitchcock, George, 188
Holland, William, 181–193
Hollow Orange, 185
Homer, 59
Hopkins, Gerard Manley, 197

Howard, Richard, 79
Howe, Julia Ward, 92
Hugo, Richard, 199
humor. *See also* irony; satire
in "A Month in Summer," 15–16
in "Mud Soup," 8, 9
in "Semele Recycled," 43–44
Humphries, Rolfe, 199

I
"I Dream It Is Afternoon When I
Return to Delhi" (Agha Shahid
Ali), 160–161
iambic pentameter, 25, 207
iambic trimeter, 12
The Inferno (Dante), 4, 49
International Congress of P.E.N., 187
"Inviting Carolyn Kizer" (Ponsot), 147
irony
Kizer's sense of, 38, 170–171, 210
in "Pro Femina," 170–171, 210

J
Jackson, Helen Hunt, 89
James, Henry, 198
Japanese poetic models. See Asian-
inspired themes
Jargon Books, 188
Jarrell, Randall, 93
Jeffers, Robinson, 196
Joan of Arc, 79
Johnson, Judith Emlyn, 57, 97–120,
208, 217
Johnson, Samuel, 199
Juvenal, 61, 65, 111, 112

K
Kaufmann, Shirley, 42
Kayak Press, 188
Keats, John, 197
Keeley, Edmund, 71
Keene, Donald, 16
Keller, Johanna, xi, 221
Kenyon College, 201

Kim, Che Ha, 176
Kinnell, Galway, 188
Kizer, Benjamin (Kizer's father), 21,
        32, 52, 55, 80, 82, 171, 196,
        205, 209, 210–211
Kizer, Carolyn, works by,
    "Afternoon Happiness," 21, 173
    "Afterthoughts of Donna Elvira," 90
    "An American Beauty"
        friendship theme in, 33, 177–178
        subject of, 21–22, 33
    "Amusing Our Daughters," 14
    "Anniversaries: Claremont Avenue,
        from 1945," 51–52
    "Bitch," 88, 90, 178–179
    "The Blessing," 33, 82
    Carrying Over, 195
    "Children," 90
    Chinese Imitations (section from
        Knock Upon Silence)
        source of material for, 133–134
        version of "People Hide Their
            Love" in, 137
        version of "Tzu-yeh Songs" in,
            134–137, 138–139
        "Winter Song" poem in, 140–141
    "Columns and Caryatids," 106
    *Cool, Calm, & Collected: Poems
        1960–2000*, xi, 37, 125
    "The Copulating Gods"
        author's view taken in, 31
        characters in, 79, 106–107,
            110–111
        first appearance of, 18
        play on "dying" in, 115
    "Cupid and Venus," 79
    "The Death of the Public Servant,"
        31, 62–63
    "Dialogues on the Art of Poetry," 186
    "Dream of a Large Lady," 56–57,
        59, 89
    "The Dying Goddess," 18, 79, 106
    "Eleutheria," 37–39
    "The Erotic Philosophers," 34

"Exodus," 34
"Fanny"
    added to "Pro Femina," 20, 34
    feminist themes in, 66–68
    friendship theme in, 20–21
    merging of political and personal
        in, 64
    natural female power theme in, 89
    satire in, 112–113
    subject of, 20–21
"Fearful Women," 81–82
"Fin-de-Siècle Blues," 8–9, 174
Five Poets of the Pacific Northwest
    (contributor), 200
"Food of Love," 114–116, 118
"For Jan as the End Draws Near,"
    19–20, 33
"For Jan, in Bar Maria," 19, 33
"For My Daughter," 33
"Gerda"
    child's voice in, 4
    friendship theme in, 8
    subject of, 31–33, 171
"The Great Blue Heron," 12–14, 33
Harping On: Poems 1985–1995, 195
    cover of, 169
    German translations in, 177
    poem about Spanish Civil War in,
        51, 169–170
    poems in, 7–9, 51, 169–170
    title of, 81, 169
"In Hell with Virg and Dan"
    critique of, 49–51
    reaction to, 8
    satire in, 4
"Hera, Hung from the Sky"
    critique of, 11
    feminist themes in, 78
    Greek myth in, 11, 34, 78
    natural female power theme in, 89
"Hiding Our Love," 137
"In the First Stanza," 90–91, 204
"Index, a Mountain," 171
"The Intruder," 23–25

Knock Upon Silence
  Asian-inspired poems in, 14–17,
    78–79
  feminist themes in, 9–11
"Lines to Accompany Flowers for
    Eve," 63
"Medicine," 172–173
Mermaids in the Basement, 18–21,
    33–34
Midnight Was My Cry, 17–18, 79
"A Month in Summer," 15–17,
    105–106
"Mud Soup," 8, 9, 90
"A Muse," 21, 106
"A Muse of Water"
  ecological themes in, 209
  feminist themes
    message to women in, 69
    search for self in, 106, 108–111
    suffering by women in, 78
    warning to women in, 91–92
  Greek myth in, 78
  inspiration for, 209
  political themes in, 209
"My Good Father," 80
The Nearness of You, 12, 31, 33
"October, 1973," 64
"The Old Gods," 79–80
100 Great Poems by Women, 92
"Parents' Pantoum," 3
"Pearl," 4, 171
"Persephone Pauses," 34, 78
"Poem for Your Birthday," 22,
    177–178
"Poem, Small and Delible," 58
"A Present for Tu Fu from Li Po," 177
"Pro Femina"
  anti-sentimentist themes in,
    87–88
  child's view in, 25–26
  criticism of, 199
  "Fanny" added to, 20, 34
  feminist themes
    affirmation of women in, 33

  anti-sentimentist message in,
    87–88
  condition of women in, 98
  in end of poem, 66
  message to women in, 64–65,
    210
  historical voice in, 34
  impact of, 4
  irony in, 170–171, 210
  meter in, 10–11, 172, 199
  political themes in, 64–65
  satire in, 98, 111–112
  sensibility in, 25–26
"Promising Author"
  critique of, 34–37
  feminist themes in, 59–60
Proses, 30, 195
"Race Relations," 58
"Running Away from Home," 50,
    113–114
"Semele Recycled"
  critique of, 42–48, 116–119
  feminist themes
    female psyche in, 80–81
    sacred images suggested in,
      47–48, 118–119
  Greek myth in, 34, 43, 80–81, 125
  humor in, 43–44
  inspiration for, 209
  natural female power theme in, 89
"Singing Aloud," 68–69, 104, 117,
    133
"A Slight Mechanical Failure" (short
    story), 31
"So Big: An Essay on Size," 76
"A Song for Muriel," 52, 175–176
"Streets of Pearl and Gold"
  critique of, 17–18
  satire in, 104–105
  subject of, 101–102
"The Suburbans," 78
"Summer near the River"
  compared to "Tzu-yeh Songs,"
    134–137, 138–139

Kizer, Carolyn, works by,
  "Summer near the River" (*continued*)
    critique of, 137–140
    symbolism in, 137–138, 139–140
  "Suppressing the Evidence," 8
  "Threatening Letter," 90
  "To a Visiting Poet in a College
      Dormitory," 34
  "To an Unknown Poet," 36–37
  "Twelve O'Clock"
    friendship theme in, 8
    inspiration for, 206
    line breaks in, 207–208
    political theme in, 4
    principle behind, 4, 35, 198
  "Tying One On in Vienna," 61–62, 64
  "The Ungrateful Garden"
    critique of, 102–103
    Greek myth in, 77–78, 100–101
    meter in, 100–101, 103
  The Ungrateful Garden, 11–14, 195
  "The Valley of the Fallen," 8, 171
  "Voyager," 80
  "Winter Song," 140–141
  Yin: New Poems, 18, 66, 80, 195
Kizer, Mabel Ashley (Kizer's mother),
      12, 21, 24, 32, 33, 53, 55, 80,
      106, 171, 196, 197, 205, 206,
      207, 210, 211
Kumin, Maxine, 1–4, 164–165, 169,
      173, 217
Kunitz, Stanley, 73, 171, 195, 199, 200

L
Lawrence, Mrs. E.O., 206
Lazarus, Emma, 92
Lee, Harper, 183
L'Heureux, John, 2, 82
The Life of Poetry (Rukeyser), 124
Lindsay, Vachel, 30
Literary Programs of the NEA
  grants program at, 181–182
  Kizer's leadership of, 2, 55, 97, 143,
      174–175

  projects sponsored by, 181–193
  public awareness of, 181
Loewenberg, Bert, 198
London, Ann, 21, 82, 178
long lines, 15
Lorde, Audre, 56
Lowell, Robert, 200, 209
lyric form, 10, 30

M
Macauley, Robie, 183
Macbeth (Shakespeare), 24, 25
Mack, Maynard, 202
Marvell, Andrew, 101
The Masks of God (Campbell), 76
Matsuo Bashō, 16–17
Matthews, William, 200
Matthiessen, F.O., 75
McClelland, Candace, xi, 221
Merrill, James, 175
meter
  dactylic hexameter, 10
  in "from 'Pro Femina'," 10
  in "The Great Blue Heron," 13
  hexameter, 24, 172–173, 199
  iambic pentameter, 25, 207
  iambic trimeter, 12
  in "The Intruder," 24
  Kizer's instinct for, 197, 207
  in "Medicine," 172–173
  in "Mud Soup," 9
  pentameter, 51
  in "Pro Femina," 10, 172–173, 199
  sapphic, 24, 111, 177–178
  in "Singing Aloud," 104
  trimeter, 11
  trochaic tetrameter, 9
  in "The Ungrateful Garden,"
      100–101, 103
Millay, Edna St. Vincent, 87, 90
"Mo-ch'ou Songs" (Waley), 134
Modernist movement, 101, 123
Montagu, Mary Wortley, 81, 205
Moore, Thomas, 86

Moraga, Cherri, 56
Morgan, Julia, 129
Morgan, Robin, 82
Moss, Howard, 31
Muske, Carol, 23–27, 159, 217–218

N
narrative form, 30
National Council of the Arts, 183
National Endowment for the Arts
  budget of, 189–190
  criticisms of, 191–192
  funding for, 55
  grants program at, 181–182
  Kizer's work for, 97, 143, 174–175
  legislation for, 182–183
  programs at, 181–193
  public awareness of, 181
  staffing at, 181
National Endowment for the
  Humanities, 182–183
National Institute of Public Affairs,
  183
nature themes
  exaggeration of, 89
  Kizer's lessons in writing about, 73
  in poem about Midas, 100–103
  in "Singing Aloud," 68–69
Neruda, Pablo, 187
"The New Colossus" (Lazarus), 92
New Formalist movement, 175
The New Orleans Poetry Journal, 2
New York City, 191–192
The New York Times Book Review, 23
Norman, Herbert, 207

O
O'Hehir, Diana, 42
Ortega, Rosario, 66
Ozick, Cynthia, 60

P
panegyric, 62
pantoum, 73

"Pantoum, with Swan" (Kumin),
  164–165
The Paris Review, 31, 35, 195
passive construction, 73
Paz, Octavio, 29
Peck, Gregory, 183
P.E.N. (Poets, Playwrights, Essayists
  and Novelists), 187
pentameter, 25, 51, 207
"People Hide Their Love" (Wu-ti), 137
Phillips, Robert, 75–82, 218
Phillips, William, 183
Pitter, Ruth, 199
Plath, Sylvia, 9, 50, 82, 86, 200
Plimpton, George, 185
Po-Chü-I, 14, 19, 141
Poetry in the Schools program, 175
Poetry Northwest, 2, 27, 97, 143, 195
Poets Press, 188
The Poet's Story (Moss), 31
political themes
  connection with feminism, 55
  in "Death of a Public Servant," 62–63
  in "Dream of a Large Lady," 56–57,
    59
  in "Lines to Accompany Flowers for
    Eve," 63
  in "A Muse of Water," 209
  in "October, 1973," 64
  in "Poem, Small and Delible," 58
  in poem about Spanish Civil War,
    169–170
  in "Pro Femina," 64–65
  in "Race Relations," 58
  in "Twelve O'Clock," 4
  in "Tying One On in Vienna,"
    61–62
Ponsot, Marie, 147, 218
Pope, Alexander
  criticism and condemnation by,
    59–60, 65
  political agenda of, 61
  reference to, in *Harping On*, 52
  satires of, 98

Pope, Alexander (*continued*)
  use of epithets by, 112, 124
  on value of revision, 202
Port Townsend, WA, 128
Pound, Ezra, 50
Prague, 26
Prairie Press, 188
Price, Reynolds, 72
pronouns, use of in poems, 74, 128
publishers, 188
Pulitzer Prize
  awarded to Glück, 201
  awarded to Kizer, 18, 80
  awarded to Roethke, 201

R
Rabb, Margaret, 71–74, 218
Rawlins, C. L., 157, 218
revision, value of, 74, 178, 202
rhymes. *See also* meter
  children's sense of, 23
  slant, 19, 173–174
Rich, Adrienne, 56, 100
Rigsbee, David, xii, 75
Ritso, Yannis, 74
Robert Frost Medal, 77
Robinson, Lillian, 57, 58, 66–67
Roethke, Theodore, 9, 195
  autobiographical focus, 30
  book dedicated to, 200
  ill health of, 201–202
  influence on Chinese translations, 204
  praise from, 11–12
  Pulitzer awarded to, 201
  teaching by, 173, 198–199, 202
Root, William Pitt, 128
Rossetti, Christina, 89
Roth, William, 183
Rukeyser, Muriel, 56, 120, 124, 175–176

S
Sacred Pleasures (Eisler), 45, 46

Salmagundi, 185
Salvaggio, Ruth, 55–69, 218–219
Sand, George, 197
Sapphic lyric, 24, 111, 177–178
Sappho, 59, 111
Sarah Lawrence College, 76, 198
satire
  in "Children," 90
  in "Fanny," 112–113
  in "Food of Love," 114–116
  in "In Hell with Virg and Dan," 4
  in "Mud Soup," 90
  in "Pro Femina," 10, 98, 111–112
  in "Running Away from Home," 113–114
  in "Streets of Pearl and Gold," 104–105
sentimentists, 86–92
sestina, 73
Sexton, Anne, 9, 50, 86
Shakespeare, William, 177
Shenandoah, 37
Sigourney, Lydia, 89, 90
Silone, Ignazio, 187
"Sisters" (Clifton), 153
slant rhymes, 19, 173–174
Snyder, Gary, 128
"On Some Qualities in Her Self and Poetry" (Cherry), 151
"Song of Myself" (Whitman), 36
Sonnenberg, Ben, 79
sonnet, 73
Spokane, WA, 114, 197
spondees, 73
St. Augustine, 46
Stafford, William, 94, 200
"Stately Homes of England" (Hemans), 92
Stein, Gertrude, 23
Steinbeck, John, 183
Stevens, Roger, 182, 190
Stevens, Wallace, 41
Stevenson, Fanny Osbourne, 20, 34, 64, 66–68, 78, 112–113

Stevenson, Robert Louis, 20, 67, 78, 112
Stokes, Terry, 155, 219
Stonewall Press, 188
Stover, Carl, 183
Summer Seminars Program, 26
Swallow, Alan, 188
Swift, Jonathan, 46, 53
Swinburne, Algernon, 199

T
Talisman Press, 188
Tang dynasty, 177
Taylor, Henry, 7–22, 219
Teasdale, Sara, 87, 90–91
"The Testament" (Tu Fu), 204
tetrameter, trochaic, 9
Thomas, Dylan, 197
Thompson, Barbara, 195–212, 219
Thompson, Jan, 19, 33
Tobey, Mark, 204–205
Todd, Ruthven, 33
Torre Bueno, J.R. de la, 183
Toscanini, Arturo, 198
"Trail All Your Pikes" (Anne Finch, Countess of Winchilsea), 92
translations
    of Chinese poems, 133–142, 177, 204
    of German poems, 177, 203
    of *The Inferno*, 4, 49
    value of, 73, 203
trimeter, 11, 12
Trinkhaus, Charles, 198
trochaic tetrameter, 9
Tu Fu, 204
"Tzu-yeh Songs" (Waley), 134–137, 138–139

U
University of New Orleans, 26
University of Washington, 198
The Unreal Dwelling (Bashō), 16–17

"Upon Appleton House" (Marvell), 101

V
Vaeth, Kim, 127–131, 219
"A Valediction: Forbidding Mourning" (Donne), 139
Vaughan, Henry, 73
"Venus and Cupid" (Boyd), 79
verse essay, 10
verse memoirs, 31
verse narratives, 30
villanelle, 73
Voltaire, François-Marie, 52

W
Wagoner, David, 199, 202
Waley, Arthur
    Chinese translations by, 14, 133–137, 140–141
    Kizer's introduction to poems of, 196
Washington, DC, 191
"The Waste Land" (Eliot), 75
Weil, James, 188
Weiss, Daniel, 201–202
Wheeler, Jackson, 71–74, 219
White, Nancy, 183
The White Goddess (Graves), 76–77
Whitman, Walt, 197
Whittemore, Reed, 183
Wilbur, Richard, 175
Williams, Jonathan, 188
Wilson, Edmund, 199
"Women" (Ritso), 74
Wong, Nellie, 56
Woodbridge, John (Kizer's husband), 26, 128, 174, 196
Woodrow Wilson National Fellowship Foundation, 189
The World Between the Eyes (Chappell), 95
Wright, James
    on Kenyon College atmosphere, 201

Wright, James (*continued*)
  poem written about, 33, 37–39
  recollections about Roethke, 12
  Roethke class taken by, 199
Wu-ti, 137

Y
The Year of My Life (Issa), 15
Yeats, William Butler, 46, 53, 73, 104
Your Native Land, Your Life (Rich), 56
Yuasa, Nobuyuki, 15